the **condor** and the co

books by christopher isherwood

novels

all the conspirators
down there on a visit
goodbye to berlin
the last of mr. norris
   (english title: *mr. norris changes trains*)
a meeting by the river
the memorial
prater violet
a single man
the world in the evening

autobiography

christopher and his kind
kathleen and frank
lions and shadows
my guru and his disciple

biography

ramakrishna and his disciples

plays (with w. h. auden)

the ascent of f6
the dog beneath the skin
on the frontier

travel

the condor and the cows
journey to a war (with w. h. auden)

collections

exhumations
where joy resides: a christopher isherwood reader

translations

the intimate journals of charles baudelaire
the yogi aphorisms of patanjali
   (with swami prabhavananda)
shankara's crest-jewel of discrimination
   (with swami prabhavananda)
the bhagavad-gita (with swami prabhavananda)

the **condor** and the **cows**

a south american travel diary

christopher isherwood

photographs by **william caskey**

foreword by **jeffrey meyers**

university of minnesota press
minneapolis · london

Frontispiece: The plaza from the tower of San Francisco, Quito.

Copyright 1948, 1949; renewed 1977 by Christopher Isherwood

Foreword copyright 2003 by the Regents of the University of Minnesota

Originally published in hardcover by Random House, Inc., 1949

First University of Minnesota Press edition, 2003

Published by the University of Minnesota Press
111 Third Avenue South, Suite 290
Minneapolis, MN 55401-2520
http://www.upress.umn.edu

Library of Congress Cataloging-in-Publication Data

Isherwood, Christopher, 1904–1986
    The condor and the cows : a South American travel diary / Christopher Isherwood ;
  photographs by William Caskey ; foreword by Jeffrey Meyers.— 1st University of
  Minnesota Press ed.
        p.   cm.
    Includes bibliographical references.
    ISBN 0-8166-3982-5 (PB : alk. paper)
    1. South America—Description and travel.   2. Isherwood, Christopher, 1904–1986.
  Travel.   I. Title.
    F2223.I8 2003
    980.03'3—dc22

                                                                                    2003020078

Printed in the United States of America on acid-free paper

The University of Minnesota is an equal-opportunity educator and employer.

12 11 10 09 08 07 06 05 04 03   10 9 8 7 6 5 4 3 2 1

to **catherine hogarty caskey**

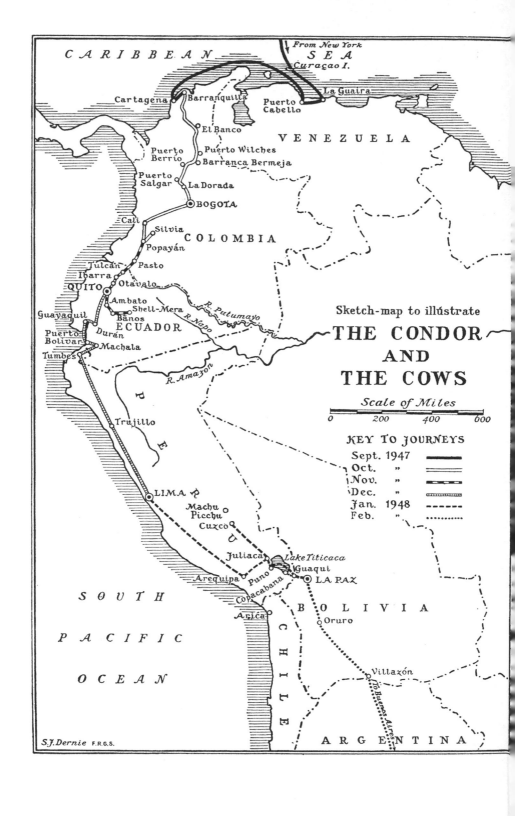

CARIBBEAN SEA

From New York
Curaçao I.

La Guaira

Cartagena   Barranquilla   Puerto Cabello

VENEZUELA

El Banco

Puerto Berrio   Puerto Wilches
Barranca Bermeja

Puerto Salgar   La Dorada

BOGOTA

Cali

Silvia   COLOMBIA

Popayán

Tulcán   Pasto
Ibarra
QUITO   Otavalo

Ambato
Shell-Mera   R. Putumayo
Baños   R. Napo
Guayaquil   Durán   ECUADOR
Puerto Bolivar
Machala
Tumbes

R. Amazon

P   E

Trujillo

R   U

LIMA

Machu Picchu
Cuzco

Juliaca   Lake Titicaca
Arequipa   Puno   Guaqui
Copacabana   LA PAZ

Arica   BOLIVIA
Oruro

SOUTH

PACIFIC

OCEAN

C   H   I   L   E

Villazón
(To Buenos Aires)

ARGENTINA

Sketch-map to illústrate

THE CONDOR
AND
THE COWS

Scale of Miles

0   200   400   600

KEY TO JOURNEYS
Sept. 1947
Oct.   ″
Nov.   ″
Dec.   ″
Jan. 1948
Feb.   ″

S.J.Dernie F.R.G.S.

contents

illustrations

foreword

Jeffrey Meyers

CHRISTOPHER ISHERWOOD followed D. H. Lawrence's innovative travel writing by shifting the center of interest from the external world to the self and by emphasizing the spontaneous revelation of his personal feelings and thoughts. Isherwood combined description and interpretation with social criticism and political commentary, and was more interested in people and landscape than in history and art. He preferred a rough to a comfortable journey, popular to high culture, colloquial to mandarin style. He was engagingly frank about the backward and brutal people, the boring voyages and self-created torments. Like Lawrence, he was forced to admit: "Travel seems to me a splendid lesson in disillusion—chiefly that."[1] On setting out for Australia, Lawrence noted the masochistic aspect of travel: "one suffers getting adjusted—but that is part of the adventure. . . . I love trying things and discovering how I hate them."[2] Isherwood also felt the excitement of the new more than made up for the hazards of the journey. He willingly endured the "incidental beastliness of travel" and knew the worst trips made the best reading. Like Lawrence, he honestly portrayed his discomfort, disenchantment, and despair.

The short, ruddy, and vivacious Isherwood was born in Cheshire in 1904, the son of an army officer killed in action in 1915. He met two lifelong writer-friends at school: W. H. Auden at St. Edmund's and Edward Upward at Repton. Isherwood went up to Corpus Christi College, Cambridge, but left without taking a degree, and had a brief career as a medical student. He published his first two novels, *All the Conspirators* (1928) and *The Memorial* (1932), in his twenties. He taught English in Berlin during the last four years of the culturally lively but decadent Weimar Republic, which was extinguished by the Nazi takeover in 1933. His experience in Germany inspired his next two novels, *Mr. Norris Changes Trains* (1935) and *Goodbye to Berlin* (1939), with its famous line (influenced by Katherine Mansfield's aesthetics): "I am a camera with its shutter open, quite passive, recording, not thinking." The "Sally Bowles" chapters were dramatized by John Van Druten as *I Am a Camera* (1951), and turned into the tremendously successful stage musical and film *Cabaret*.

Isherwood collaborated on three plays with Auden in the 1930s, and published his autobiography *Lions and Shadows* in 1938. He and Auden traveled to China (then at war with Japan) and coauthored a travel book, *Journey to a War* (1939). That year both writers emigrated to America, where Isherwood became a pacifist and a Vedantist. During the war he worked, rather incongruously, as a screenwriter for MGM and Warner Bros. in Hollywood, and for the Quakers in Pennsylvania. His novel *Prater Violet* was published in 1945, and he became an American citizen the following year.

In 1947 he was commissioned by his publishers Random House and Methuen to write a travel book on South America. In September 1947, long before mass tourism and with no knowledge of Spanish, he set out for a six-month tour of Colombia, Ecuador, Peru, and Bolivia on the west coast, and of Argentina on the east coast. "The Voyage Out," the title of his first chapter, echoes the title of the first novel by his friend and mentor, Virginia Woolf, published in 1915.

Isherwood traveled with the twenty-six-year-old photographer Bill Caskey (he was the camera), who took the brooding black-and-white photographs. Capturing the sharp contrasts of light and shadow, humanity and cruelty, he portrayed the colonial architecture, squalid tenements, bullfighters, horsemen, Indians, painters, prisoners, llamas, lakes, landscapes, volcanoes, ruins, riverboats, and religious ceremonies. A lapsed Catholic, Caskey was born and raised in Kentucky, where his father bred horses. He had been briefly in the navy, but was discharged after a homosexual scandal. Caskey and Isherwood became lovers in 1945 and split up six years later. Seventeen years younger than Isherwood and more energetic in the debilitating Andean altitudes, Caskey was bored by intellectual discussions and discreetly slipped away to take his photographs.

Caskey was a heavy drinker with a violent temper. Even when sober, his face was "flushed, swollen, furious." Though Isherwood is necessarily discreet about their homosexuality, he reveals the tension between them when he writes that Caskey, drunk on Pisco Sours, "leaned over and smacked my face—neither of us can now remember why," which suggests that they both were drunk. He also doesn't mention that Berthold Szczesny, their generous host who was about to marry a rich Argentinean girl, had been the first of his many German lovers in Berlin. He later frankly portrayed Berthold as "Bubi" in *Christopher and His Kind* (1976).

The Condor and the Cows (1949) is one of the very few classic travel books on South America. It was preceded by W. H. Hudson's *The Purple Land* (1885) on Argentina; A. F. Tschiffely's *Tschiffely's Ride* (1933), an account of ten thousand miles on horseback through North and South America; Peter Fleming's *Brazilian Adventure* (1933); and Evelyn Waugh's *Ninety-two Days* (1934) on a journey in Guiana and Brazil. It was followed by Bruce Chatwin's *In Patagonia* (1977) and Paul Theroux's *The Old Patagonian Express: By Train through the Americas* (1979), which roughly followed Tschiffely's route and (like Isherwood's book) covered several countries.

Often bored in South America, Isherwood wondered what he was doing there, and worried about how to gather the necessary facts and about how he'd manage to finish the book. On September 19, 1947, just before sailing from New York, he expressed Lawrencean doubts about the beginning of the journey: "Usual jitters and misery. Why do I do these things? . . . [I'm] tired of roving." He never, as one critic pointed out, "had the unflagging enthusiasm of the real traveler and travel writer, nor did he enjoy the almost masochistic discomforts."[3] As his biographer noted, he "admitted the book fails to satisfy what he considers to be the fundamental criterion of any travel book, the need for a goal, for a reason for having gone any-where in the first place. 'The ideal travel book,' he has said, 'should be perhaps a little like a crime story in which you're in search of something and then either find it or find that it doesn't exist in the end.'"[4] Unlike Lawrence's travel books and his own *Journey to a War*, which featured Auden in the leading role and briefly portrayed the war as they watched a spectacular air raid from the lawn of the British Consulate in Hankow, the South American book has no real goal beyond Buenos Aires and the end of the voyage.

On December 27, 1948, nine months after leaving Argentina and while writing the book, Isherwood said he felt constrained by inherent good manners: "I should really have approached it in the spirit of *The Air-Conditioned Nightmare* [Henry Miller's 1945 satire on America], but my fatal politeness gripped my pen, and anyhow one cannot insult all kinds of people who sincerely tried to please us and probably thought us as dreary as we thought them."[5] The previous month he'd scrupulously examined his feelings ("bored . . . ashamed . . . bored . . . ashamed") and complained about the difficulty of writing in a letter to his friend John Lehmann: "I am churning out a travel-book, which is going to be my longest and worst work, I fear. I just can't do straight journalism, and the truth is that South America *bored* me, and I am ashamed that it bored me, and I hate it for making me feel ashamed. However, I am determined to go through with it and then get on with the novel, which at least will be an *honourable* failure." Later on, Lehmann recorded that "Christopher revised his opinion of the book, and even came to regard it as one of his best."[6]

Isherwood acknowledged the influence of Joseph Conrad's savage portrayal of "Costaguana," a backward South American state, in *Nostromo* (1904). In that complex and ambitious novel, Conrad describes the country's greed and exploitation, poverty and oppression, barbarism and cruelty, rapacity and misrule; its corrupt politics and futile revolutions, moral darkness and disintegration of humane values:

> [There were endless] stories of political outrage; friends, relatives, ruined, imprisoned, killed in the battles of senseless civil wars, barbarously executed in ferocious proscriptions, as though the government of the country had been a struggle of lust between bands of absurd devils let loose upon the land with sabres and uniforms and grandiloquent phrases. . . . [It was a] nightmarish parody of administration without law, without security, and without justice.

Conrad also quotes Simón Bolívar's despairing remark: "America is ungovernable. Those who worked for her independence have ploughed the sea."[7] Writing to the novelist James Stern from Quito on November 20, 1947, Isherwood echoed Conrad's dark view and blamed the Catholic Church for the desperate conditions on the continent: "There is a dreadful squalor, a kind of evil laziness and despair, beneath everything. The Church seems almost wholly evil, like a great black toad on the Indian's back. The Indians are incredibly energetic, lively and often gay, but they are worked like beasts, and their masters look on with their weary old syphilitic eyes of imperial Spain. . . . The whole place is rotten with guilt."[8]

Explaining the title of the book, Isherwood writes that "the

Condor is the emblem of the Andes and their mountain republics, while the Cows represent the great cattle-bearing plains, and, more specifically, Argentina." Later in the book these apparently benign symbols become savagely Darwinian and symbolize the internecine warfare of the continent: "Condors will peck out the eyes of cows and then drive them with their wings off the edge of a cliff; the cows get killed and the condors eat them." A more effective and enticing title, using Isherwood's descriptions of places he had seen, would have been *Stone and Sky* (earth and spirit) or *Mountains without Name*.

This travel book, like *Journey to a War*, is based on Isherwood's diary. A dutiful but not passionate traveler, he fears he can't—or won't—respond to South America and his book will have to be "very, very short." His persona, a striking contrast to the grim experiences he describes, is "bohemian, lively, happy-go-lucky"; he dreams of voluntary exile in the tropical paradise of Curaçao; he dines out on stories of Nazis in Berlin, missionaries in China, and movie stars in Hollywood. He was, as Stephen Spender observed, "attractively disgusted and amiably bitter." His finely crafted style is spontaneous, breathless, sketchy; and the book is loosely structured by the vagaries of his voyage.

Isherwood illuminates his narrative with Proustian aesthetic analogies. A holiday should be as "self-sufficient, deep, brilliant and compact as a Vermeer." The portraits sculpted on Incan drinking vessels, "startlingly expressive, verging on caricature," remind him of Thomas Rowlandson. He recognizes the "dusty blots of bluish green" sea from Winslow Homer's paintings of the Gulf. The paradoxical Conradian jungle, "so green, so dense, so crowded, so oppressively alive, so empty and yet so obviously inhabited," naturally recalls "a Rousseau painting framed in great green leaves." The Ecuadorian social protest murals, derived from José Clemente Orozco and Diego Rivera, provide "an aesthetic medium for those who can no longer find inspiration in the idiom of Roman Christianity. The agony of the masses is substituted for the agony of Christ. The peasant mother takes the place of the Virgin and Child. God the Father . . . has given up his central station to the figure of Karl Marx."

Isherwood sometimes fails to respond to what should have been the most dramatic and promising experiences of the journey: the bullfight in Bogotá (where the bulls must have been led out of the ring by steers, not cows); the Spanish colonial city of Cuzco, filthy and ridden with smallpox and typhus, which he calls "one of the most beautiful monuments to bigotry and sheer stupid brutality in the whole world"; and the towering ruins of Machu Picchu, "a landscape built by titans in a fit of sheer megalomania."

But his style is triumphantly precise, witty, and brilliant. Edmund Wilson described it as "accurate, lucid and cool . . . a perfect medium for his purpose. . . . You seem to look right through Isherwood and see what he sees."[9] He says that Argentineans, who consume an enormous quantity of beef, "have a placid, somewhat bovine expression." Alligators keep "their mouths slightly open with an air of contented depravity." A volcano blew the top off what used to be the highest mountain in the world and reduced it to a mere nineteen thousand feet. Flashes of lightning, "illuminating vast rugged tracts of cloudscape in silent electric spasms," make him (in a military metaphor) "feel like a stone-deaf man watching an artillery bombardment, for there is seldom any thunder." And in an intensely visualized set-piece he describes the afterglow of a chromatic sunset, "with clouds flashing like splinters of crystal, against glimpses of sky which were very old bright innocent blue, such as you see in the paintings of the primitive Italian masters" (the "innocent blue" is a fine touch).

Isherwood recreates the unnerving atmosphere by conjuring up a series of grotesque details in short, cinematic images. A monastic library owned a copy of *Mein Kampf*. An elaborately dressed child on the ship "looked more like a grown-up midget. She was quite startlingly cross-eyed." On the train, locusts "flew in through the window and jumped around the compartment like violent clockwork toys." A drowned shapeless animal floated down the river "with two or three buzzards perched on it, pecking at the flesh." The sun transformed a slaughtered steer into "a silver mountainside trickling with streams of dark golden blood." Two young men, arrested for attempting suicide at a waterfall, struggle violently while handcuffed to a policeman and try to drag him into the water. Fake shrunken heads, imitating the trophies of the Jivaro Indians, are specially "prepared by medical students from cadavers in the dissecting room." During electroshock treatments in the Quito *Manicomio* (madhouse), the patient's "arms stiffen and shoot out, the body writhes, the pointing fingers move slowly through an arc, the eyes bulge and stare."

The book describes travel as torture. Tourists as well as Isherwood— a sacrificial figure who suffers in our stead—slog down the coast and across the mountains on their *via dolorosa*, "gasping in high altitudes, vomiting and terrified in planes, rattled like dice in buses, dragged out before dawn to race along precipice roads, poisoned with strange foods, tricked by shopkeepers, appalled by toilets." In a Lawrencean passage, Isherwood declares that intense disillusionment, provoked by the contrast between ideal expectations and grim reality, is "the irony of travel. You spend your boyhood dreaming of a magic, impossibly distant day when you will cross the Equator, when your eyes will behold Quito. And then, in the slow prosaic process of life, that day undramatically dawns—and finds you sleepy, hungry and dull. The Equator is just another valley; you aren't sure which and you don't much care." No wonder that he believes Brazil "must be the most interesting and exciting country in South America": he never saw it and never had the chance to become disenchanted.

In *The Condor and the Cows*, a diapason of disappointment, Isherwood (like Lawrence) discovered how much he hated things. La Guaira is a "dirty, shabby little place." Barranquilla is "not particularly interesting." Bogotá, "depressingly undistinguished," makes him "tense, restless, uneasy . . . lazy, exhausted and sad." Tulcán is "dreary, dirty and icy cold." Cangaime, in the Ecuadorean jungle, is "oppressive and sinister." Lima makes him feel idle and weak. His description of the demonic and menacing Andes above Lake Titicaca echoes Lawrence's phrase about "the eternal, negative radiance of the snows"[10] in *Twilight in Italy*: "The snow-mountains were pink where they faced the sunrise, the great lake was icy black, the pure thin air was bitingly cold. When you breathe it in deeply it seems to possess you." La Paz, the highest capital, leaves him gasping and "painfully out of breath." In Copacabana, Bolivia, he picks his way through "piles of drying excrement." "We had grown weary," he confesses, "of those inhumanly gigantic mountains, that somber plateau haunted by its Incaic ghosts, the weird rarefied manic-depressive atmosphere."

Isherwood looked forward to moving from the condors to the cows, from the mountains to sea level at Buenos Aires, from an Indian to a European culture (the Indians had been exterminated in Argentina). But he deplores the Argentinean hypocrisy and insulting attitude toward women, and concludes that he's been "traveling through an empire in the final stage of its dissolution." He is, however, perceptive about political conditions. Twelve years before Adolf Eichmann was captured by Israeli agents, Isherwood mentions rumors that Nazi leaders were hiding in Argentina. And thirty-four years before the Falklands War of 1982, he warns that the British occupation of the islands is a century-old "Argentinean grudge." He's ambivalent about the dictator Juan Perón: "some find him cultured and intelligent, others pompous and stupid." But he chivalrously defends Evita Perón, who was often attacked for her humble origins and shady sexual past: she is "the First Lady, the dazzling representative of their Party's wealth and power, the shining exemplar of what any of them might become, the projection of their dearest dreams."

Isherwood's account of his meeting with the scholarly, not-yet-blind Jorge Luis Borges—who seemed more than five years older than his youthful visitor and, like Isherwood, died in 1986—is disappointingly confined to one sentence. (In *The Old Patagonian Express*, Paul Theroux includes a long, illuminating interview with the elusive Borges, whose reputation continued to rise in English-speaking countries.) But Isherwood spent a lot of time with Victoria Ocampo, the wealthy, well-born woman (the opposite of Evita Perón) who owned and edited *Sur*, the leading literary magazine in South America. He describes her, with some uneasiness about her imperious manner, as "an aristocrat—fearless, generous, commanding, demanding. . . . She is a big strong woman, with decisive gestures. . . . She has a way of holding your arm, to steer you in the required direction, which makes you feel like a murderer under police escort." The simile is revealing, for he resented her unremitting domination and wrote in his diary: "She is described fairly, I think, though a bit too politely. What a bullying old cunt!"[11]

Ocampo and Isherwood shared a passionate interest in T. E. Lawrence. Her brief but perceptive book (using Lawrence's serial number in the RAF) *338171 T. E. Lawrence of Arabia* (1947) was translated from French by David Garnett, introduced by T.E.'s brother A. W. Lawrence, and published in English in 1963. During the thirties Auden and Isherwood had idolized the heroic Lawrence, who inspired the mountaineer Ransom in their play *The Ascent of F6*. A repressed homosexual, Lawrence had been tortured and raped by a Turk during the Arab Revolt, and later hired someone to whip him for experiencing masochistic pleasure during that episode. He died in a motorcycle crash in 1935. Reviewing Liddell Hart's book on Lawrence, Auden also spoke for Isherwood when he wrote that Lawrence came nearest to exemplifying "most completely what is best and significant in our time, our nearest approach to a synthesis

of feeling and reason, act and thought, the most potent agent of freedom . . . the most relevant accusation and hope."[12]

In his review of *T. E. Lawrence by His Friends* (1937), the timid
Isherwood, who shrank from hardships, admired "the tough faithful
body which, already, he had punished so cruelly for its obstinate will
to remain alive. . . . Like Shelley and like Baudelaire . . . he suffered,
in his own person, the neurotic ills of an entire generation."[13] In *The
Condor and the Cows*, after describing Ocampo's very different kind
of admiration for Lawrence, he strongly identifies with the flawed and
wounded hero: "I am much closer to him, in a sense, than she could
ever be. He is part of the mess I am in. What bind me to him are
his faults—his instability, his masochism, his insane inverted pride."
He then thriftily repeats the Shelley–Baudelaire sentence from his
review (substituting "epoch" for "generation") and concludes: "I belonged to that epoch. I can never escape him now."

Isherwood, whose suffering is put into perspective by T. E.
Lawrence's, does not merely give a negative account of the five
countries he visited. He also provides elegant and convincing geographical, historical, and political explanations for these disastrous
conditions. The violent, blood-soaked land, so different from the
green and pleasant England, engenders violence: "Thunder and
avalanches in the mountains, huge floods and storms on the plains.
Volcanoes exploding. The earth shaking and splitting. The woods
full of savage beasts and poisonous insects and deadly snakes. Knives
are whipped out at a word. Whole families are murdered without
any reason. Riots are sudden and bloody and often meaningless." In
a humane passage, he observes that the historical disasters began in
the sixteenth century with the Spanish invaders, whose elemental
sins afflicted, in a deadly and unending cycle, all subsequent generations: "I suppose one must ultimately blame the Conquistadores;
their original crime haunts this unfortunate land like a curse. Oppression degraded the oppressed, as it always does, and their cynical
self-contempt was bequeathed, as it always must be, to the heirs of
the oppressors. The Spaniards brought Christianity, which might
have been a great cohesive force—but the Catholic Church was
hopelessly compromised by the policy of imperial Spain."

Isherwood doesn't blame the conquistadors for all the problems.
The equally bloodthirsty and imperialistic Incas, who went in for
human sacrifice and fill him with horror, also bear part of the burden. He describes their absolutist society as "a culture of mass, of

authority, of order. . . . Much ritual, little spirituality. Much gold, little elegance. Much feasting, little fun." The fourth part of the equation is the Church, which he had already condemned in his letters. He agrees with the Protestant missionary who maintains that "nearly all Catholic priests in South America are greedy, lazy and corrupt. Most of them are the fathers of children, and they squeeze exorbitant offerings from their congregations in order to support their mistresses. . . . It can't be denied that the Church in South America is a disgrace to Catholicism."

Isherwood expresses a Conradian view of contemporary politics in these countries, which oppress their own people and seem to hate and fear all their neighbors. In a generic sentence that seems to come right out of *Nostromo*, and that applies to all governments since Bolívar "ploughed the sea" and liberated these countries from Spain, Isherwood states: "Bustamente has filled up the cabinet posts with Army men, who used to be ministers under General Benavides, the last dictator." These dictators, of course, come from and are supported by the army, whose generals are completely malign: "They make and unmake presidents, crush popular demonstrations, split into factions and fight each other like feudal barons."

The Condor and the Cows, with its Lawrencean technique and Conradian ideas, was enthusiastically reviewed by many leading critics. In the *New York Times* of October 2, 1949, the Spanish and Portuguese translator Samuel Putnam praised the liveliness and powerful effect of the book: "For the sensitive nonspecialized reader it will make the big, sad, mist-shrouded, sun-parched continent to the south of us come alive with an emotional impact, a vividness and sense of tangible reality that no scholarly treatment can hope to give." Morton Dauwen Zabel, a professor at the University of Chicago writing in the *Nation* of October 29, admired Isherwood's perception and vivid style: "His eye and wit are as lively as ever—the same quick sympathies, the squirrelish scrutiny, the open nerves and senses. . . . His gift and eye are a poet's, and these permit his final pages to rise to an eloquence and vision of their own." In the *New Statesman and Nation* of November 19, V. S. Pritchett, who would bring out his own travel book, *The Spanish Temper*, in 1954, explained how Isherwood had, with cinematic sketches, overcome the limitations of an uneventful journey and unexciting characters:

Isherwood has conveyed the crowded effervescence of being there, he has persuaded one, that on such a trip, this is exactly what the normal, nonplussed traveler would have seen and heard on a journey that was undramatic and unromantic, but was heady, busy, disturbing. . . . *The Condor and the Cows* is not the Isherwood we have known, it is a larger, cinematic version, but the smaller, agile, eel-quick figure is there inside, and the two have made between them an irresistible feature.

In *Journey to a War* Auden and Isherwood described their encounter with the flamboyant Peter Fleming, adventurous brother of the creator of James Bond and author of *News from Tartary* (1936), an account of his journey from Peking to Kashmir. He was married to the actress Celia Johnson, sported (like Isherwood) a Gentleman's Tropical Exploration Kit, and seemed a living parody of the pukka sahib. Reviewing Isherwood's second travel book in the *Spectator* of December 9, Fleming compared his charming persona to a fictional creation and admired his ability to create characters: "Detached, self-effacing, too humble to be called urbane, Mr. Isherwood suggests the hero of a novel by Mr. Evelyn Waugh . . . an intelligent, negative, stoical figure who accepts, without reacting to them, the strange experiences that come his way. . . . There are throughout the book flashes of brilliant perception and interpretation; and the descriptions of people are often (though of places less often) extraordinarily good."

Edmund Wilson, the leading American critic, had in 1939 praised the style of *Goodbye to Berlin*. Defining the virtues of *The Condor and the Cows* in the *New Yorker* of January 14, 1950, he observed that Isherwood had transcended the usual travel diary and assumed the sacrificial role to save readers from following his perilous path:

> It makes a very entertaining narrative, distinguished by the same cool observation as his stories about Germany between the two wars. . . . [It is] the personal account of wanderings in unfamiliar countries that sticks close to the incidents of travel yet aims to convey some accurate ideas about the peoples and localities visited. . . .
>
> One is immensely grateful to the writer for having suffered the discomforts of . . . dreary journeys by train, dangerous drives along precipices, and repellent accommodations, in order to

tell us, in pleasantly assimilable prose, what is to be found in those inaccessible places.[14]

Notes

1. D. H. Lawrence, *Letters. Volume IV, 1921–1924*, ed. Warren Roberts, James Boulton, and Elizabeth Mansfield (Cambridge: Cambridge University Press, 1987), 286.

2. Ibid., 234, 239.

3. Jonathan Fryer, *Isherwood* (Garden City, N.Y.: Doubleday, 1978), 225, 226.

4. Brian Finney, *Christopher Isherwood: A Critical Biography* (London: Faber and Faber, 1979), 201.

5. Ibid.

6. John Lehmann, *Christopher Isherwood: A Personal Memoir* (New York: Henry Holt, 1987), 77–78.

7. Joseph Conrad, *Nostromo* (1904; New York: Signet, 1960), 83, 156.

8. Finney, *Isherwood*, 197–98.

9. Edmund Wilson, Review of *Goodbye to Berlin*, *New Republic*, May 17, 1939, in *From the Uncollected Edmund Wilson*, selected and introduced by Janet Groth and David Castronovo (Athens: Ohio University Press, 1995), 205–6.

10. D. H. Lawrence, *Twilight in Italy* (1916; London: Penguin, 1962), 12.

11. Christopher Isherwood, *Lost Years: A Memoir, 1945–1951*, edited and introduced by Katherine Bucknell (New York: HarperCollins, 2000), 136.

12. W. H. Auden, Review of *T. E. Lawrence* by B. H. Liddell Hart, *Now and Then*, Spring 1934, in *The English Auden: Prose, Essays, and Dramatic Writings, 1927–1939*, ed. Edward Mendelson (New York: Random House, 1977), 321.

13. Christopher Isherwood, Review of *T. E. Lawrence by His Friends*, edited by A. W. Lawrence (1937), in *Exhumations: Stories, Articles, Verses* (New York: Simon and Schuster, 1966), 24.

14. Wilson, *Uncollected Edmund Wilson*, 326–27.

the **condor** and the **cows**

to the reader

THIS BOOK is based on a diary which I kept from day to day during our trip. In rewriting it, I have altered three or four names and concealed the sources of much information, in order not to embarrass individuals who were generous enough to talk to us frankly, sometimes indiscreetly. Because I do not wish to take advantage of hindsight, I have let my remarks about Dr. Jorge Eliécer Gaitán stand exactly as I first set them down. I hope they will not seem tasteless or offensive in view of his tragic murder on April 9th last year in Bogotá and the terrible acts of violence which followed it. Much else has happened since we left South America —Rómulo Gallegos has been elected President of Venezuela and later expelled by a military junta; President Bustamante has outlawed the Apra Party and himself been exiled to Argentina, while Haya de la Torre has taken sanctuary in Lima's Colombian embassy; there has been another attempt to overthrow the Bolivian Government; in Argentina, a plot to assassinate the Peróns has allegedly been discovered, Miguel Miranda has fallen from power, and my friend Rolf Katz, whose pen remains as sharply pointed as ever, has nearly had to fight a duel with the head of the Buenos Aires stock exchange. I have no doubt that many other equally sensational events will have taken place by the time this book is published.

The meaning of its title should be evident, but perhaps I had better explain that the Condor is the emblem of the Andes and their mountain republics, while the Cows represent the great cattle-bearing plains, and, more specifically, Argentina—no offense intended.

I shall not try to forestall criticism by apologizing for the many absurdities, inaccuracies and errors of judgment which will probably be found in my work. A diarist ought to make a fool of himself, sometimes. He aims at being impressionistic and spontaneous, rather than authoritative. That is why I have done no systematic reading on this subject. Increased knowledge could only have induced humility and an inferiority complex. Most likely, it would have stopped me writing, altogether.

However, a certain number of books came into my hands, more or less by accident, as we traveled, and I have gratefully taken something from all of them. Here is a list:

New World Guides to the Latin American Republics. Edited by Earl Parker Hanson. 3 vols., Duell, Sloan and Pearce, New York.

We used Volume Two, which covers all the states of the West Coast including Bolivia, and I have quoted from it very extensively. I cannot imagine a better guidebook.

The South American Handbook, 1946. Trade and Travel Publications, London.

This useful yearbook covers the whole of Central and South America, so its information is necessarily rather compressed. Curiously enough, its mileages and altitudes often differ greatly from those given in the *New World Guides*. I have followed the latter, because it is more detailed.

Colombia: Gateway to South America. Kathleen Romoli, Doubleday and Company, Garden City, New York.

This is the most popular book on Colombia in English. The authoress is sometimes a little too enthusiastic, but she is very readable and she really makes you want to visit the country—even after you have been there.

. . . and Points South. Oden and Olivia Meeker, Random House, New York.

This takes you down through Central America and right around the continent—very fast. It is dazzlingly, and sometimes desperately, bright, in the *New Yorker* manner. But it is a little museum of amusing and accurately described details and contains a lot of good advice. No politics. Few generalizations of any kind. Excellent on food.

Call For Forty Thousand. John J. Considine, Longmans, Green, New York.

A study of the condition of the Catholic Church in South

America and its shortage of priests, written after a tour of inspection of the Maryknoll missions. This is the sort of book non-Catholics seldom read, which is a pity. It would give them a broader view of the religious problems involved.

The Highland Tribes of Southern Colombia. Gregorio Hernández de Alba, Smithsonian Institution, Washington.

Inca Culture at the Time of the Spanish Conquest. John Howland Rowe, Smithsonian Institution, Washington.

The Distribution of Indians and Indian Languages in Peru. John Howland Rowe, American Geographical Society, New York.

The first two of these monographs are parts of a large volume, the *Handbook of South American Indians.* They are, of course, absolutely authoritative. Both authors avoid obscure technical terms.

Lost City of the Incas. Hiram Bingham, Duell, Sloan and Pearce, New York.

Rather too journalistic in style, and perhaps too speculative. But the first-hand account of the explorations is very vivid, and the photographs of Machu Picchu are magnificent.

Bolívar and the Independence of Spanish America. J. B. Trend, Hodder and Stoughton, London.

I am ashamed to say that I had never read a life of Bolívar before. This, for a short one, couldn't be better. It is unsentimental, sharp and exciting. Like a good novel.

And, speaking of novels, Joseph Conrad's *Nostromo* is still, after forty-five years, a wonderfully life-like picture of a backward South American state—never mind which.

Saying thank you is a business which is apt to bore the reader, but I must do it. Everybody we met was kind to us. Any mention of a name, however casual, should, therefore, be taken with a bouquet. Here are some people to whom we are equally grateful—for hospitality, information and advice—and whom I have only omitted from the text for lack of space.

In Bogotá: Srs. Gustavo Restrepo and Fabio Gómez, and their families; Ambassador and Mrs. Beaulac, and Messrs. Canter, Vebber and Wieland, of the U.S. Embassy; Messrs. Millman and Tett, of the British Cultural Institute; Dr. Neil Mackay, of the British Council; Srta. Sylvia Lopez.

In Quito: Mr. and Mrs. Le Lièvre; Dr. Luis G. Camacho.

In Lima: Dr. Bruno Vargas Buenaño; Mr. and Mrs. Folger Athearn; Mr. Delgado Arias, of the U.S. Embassy; Mr. and Mrs. Ralph Emery; Mr. Harry Tomlinson, of the Grace Line; Miss Mackay.

In La Paz: Mr. Ifor Rees, British Minister to Bolivia; Mr. Peter Jones, of the Institute of Inter-American Affairs; Messrs. Ashton and Murdoch, of the British Legation; Mr. William Dodge.

In Buenos Aires: M. René Berger; Sr. Pancho Moraturi; Mr. William Harris; Mr. Ralph Siegmann; Herr and Frau Josef Gielen; Mr. Lawrence Smith; Mr. Mickle; Sr. Luis Saslavsky; Sra. Delia Garcés; Sr. Alberto de Zavalia; Ambassador Bruce, Miss Gill and Messrs. Conklin and Oakley, of the U.S. Embassy; Sr. Luis Baudizzone; Dr. Enrique Gil; Sr. Guillermo Guevara; Mr. William Johnson and Sr. Roberto Payro, of the *Time-Life-Fortune* office; Mr. Bernard Redmont, of the *U.S. News-World Report*; Herr Thorlichen.

Outside of this list, I must specially mention three people: Sr. Jorge de Castro, who, with René Berger, made our few hours in Rio unforgettable. My cousin Barbara and her husband Rudolph von Strachwitz; our meeting in Buenos Aires was, for me, the happiest accident of the entire journey.

As for the usual acknowledgments—portions of this material in the form of magazine articles, with or without Caskey's photographs, have already appeared in the following British and American publications: *The Geographical Magazine, Holiday, Horizon, Illustrated, Penguin New Writing, Vogue, Zero.*

C. I., April, 1949.

the voyage out

September 20, 1947.

FIRST MORNING AT SEA, somewhere off the coast of New Jersey. First morning of unsticky sunshine, sootless air, after the weary Manhattan summer. The clean cool cabin, the berth so comfortable, the easy powerful motions of the ship, the laxative plumbing and the liberal shower. Breakfast ready in the dining room, beautiful with cereals and coffee, eggs, toast, fruit and cream. Then the swimming pool and the sun deck till lunch. And South America still five days away.

It is time to wake Bill Caskey. He is asleep in the upper berth, his head burrowing into the pillow, his lips emitting short angry-sounding snores. Caskey wallows in sleep, as if in a hot bath, and wakes slowly, his face flushed, swollen, furious.

He is twenty-six years old, Kentucky-Irish. I suppose Dr. Sheldon would classify him as a small viscerotonic mesomorph. His friends often compare him, not unkindly, to a pig. I needn't add any epithets of my own. He will probably describe himself, by degrees, as the account of our journey continues. He is a photographer by profession, and is coming along with me to take pictures for this book. He speaks as little Spanish as I do, and has only been abroad once before, on a short trip to Mexico City.

We share a table with a married couple from New York. They are cruise passengers, booked for the round-trip—Curaçao, La Guaira, Puerto Cabello, Cartagena and home. He is a lawyer and an amateur footballer, in his early thirties; a husky good-looking Jewish ex-college boy who is growing fat somewhat apologetically. She is Spanish-Irish, and still very attractive.

They have been married about ten years, have children, seem happy. This is their first long trip alone together since the honey-

7

moon. It was, almost certainly, her idea. He's a little unwilling. He can't quite relax. For him, as for so many Americans of his kind, a pleasure journey is just another sort of investment—a sound one, most likely, but he has got to watch it. With his puzzled collegiate frown, he is perpetually trying to assess the whole undertaking in terms of value and service. He isn't in the least stingy—all his instincts are generous—but he is determined not to be gypped. He inspects the ship, the cabin, the food, the stewards, the dance band, the amusements,—and asks himself: "Are these the best return we can reasonably expect for our money?" I think he's fairly well satisfied, so far.

She is equally determined—to enjoy herself and to make him enjoy himself too. The energy which she brings to this task is really beautiful and touching. Again and again—while they are in the swimming pool, or drinking a glass of wine, or dancing together—her smiles and her gestures appeal to him to come back with her through the years, to help her recapture the mood of their courtship. And, for the moment, he responds. He is shy and pleased. Suddenly, they both look very young. Then that worried frown returns, and he is caught in another calculation.

Perhaps even she isn't quite consciously aware of the significance of their trip. A holiday of this kind is the test, and may be the vindication, of an entire relationship. After years of accepted routine—office work, raising children, shopping, cooking—you take your marriage out of its little suburban frame and set it against a tremendous classic background of ocean, mountains and stars. How does it stand up? Is it self-sufficient, deep, brilliant and compact as a Vermeer? Or a messy amateur sketch which doesn't compose?

What can we do to help them? We have our place, of course, in the scheme of travel values. We belong to that necessary class of Some Interesting People We Met on the Boat. We are like The Ruins and The Little Restaurant with Atmosphere. No journey is complete without us. We shall be discussed and described to relatives and friends at home.

Our duty, therefore, is to be strange. Not alarmingly odd; that would scare them. Not enviably independent; that might make them feel somehow dissatisfied with the limitations of their own lives. I must tell stories about China, England, Germany, Hollywood; about Nazis, missionaries and movie stars. I must appear bohemian, lively, happy-go-lucky. But I must also drop reassuring hints of wander-weariness, of a longing to settle down in a home of my own. . . . And I must make it very clear, especially to him, that I really earn and respect money.

Meanwhile, the waitress watches us. She looks tired and has a gentle indulgent smile. She is quietly firm about punctuality at meals. Like all women who work on passenger liners, she resembles a hospital nurse. At present we are merely under observation; later, some of us may become seriously ill. On the last homebound trip, they ran into the outskirts of a hurricane and most of the crockery in the dining room was smashed.

But now the weather is perfect. The ship swings eagerly forward through the newness of each brilliant morning; and the Atlantic, more sparklingly alive than any landscape, already has those dusky blots of bluish green which you recognize from Winslow Homer's paintings of the Gulf. The swimming pool is a yelling fish pond of children. The grown-ups, with or without figures, display themselves in gaudy beach clothes and daring swim suits. All have books, but few read for more than a minute at a time, since concentration relaxes too easily into the pleasure of animal sensation. Soothed and excited, we are swept along, our wills all pointed toward our destination, comfortably surrendered to the energy of the engines. On the shore, the circumstances of our lives await us; neatly stored in cellars or scattered here and there in the houses of our friends. We shall have to resume them in due course. But, for the moment, we have all died —tidily or untidily, according to our natures—and rest between death and rebirth in this low kind of heaven. We chatter and behave without responsibility, like immortals.

After the mid-day heat, lunch and a siesta, the late afternoon is majestic and calm. Cumulus clouds are grouped along the sealine like crumbling Greek monuments. The ocean seems immemorially old—as, indeed, it is. This is the hour for meditation, philosophy and emotionally significant platitudes. The mind, which has idled all day long, begins to bestir itself. You feel almost disembodied—surveying the past without regret and the future without fear or desire. It would not be hard, now, to renounce everything earthly—except, perhaps, the cocktail you are sipping.

Many of the passengers dress for dinner and the dancing which follows. The Latin American girls, particularly, achieve an effect of the most expensive elegance. They wear more makeup and jewelry than would be usual in New York. By half-past nine, the lounge looks like a night club. But luxury has no glamor on a one-class ship. For dramatic contrast, the First Class needs a Second and a Third. When Auden and I were crossing the Indian Ocean, nine years ago, we could wander at will through all the levels of French colonial society. On the main deck was a Parisian ballroom, where silver-sheathed women floated in the arms of bankers and rubber magnates; below this was the comfortable second-class world of the solid bourgeois—mothers knitting and chatting, family-fathers playing cards in their shirtsleeves; below this again was the Third-Class dining room which a detachment of marines had transformed into a Toulon dive—caps stuck on the backs of their heads, cigarettes in the corners of their mouths, they danced to the wheezing of a concertina, lewdly grinning. And out on the fore-deck under the stars, some elderly turbaned Asiatics had spread their rugs and were sitting cross-legged, puffing at water-pipes, while a flute played and a little Negro boy wriggled his belly and his hips. . . . That ship was like a whole city. Ours is only a wealthy suburb.

September 23.

Curaçao: The long barren island, shaped like a ship hit broadside by a gale—it seems to be listing. On the west, the land slopes up gently to a central range of sharp-peaked hills; on the east, it falls steeply away to the shore. Almost no vegetation and hardly any houses, until you round the cape and see Willemstad. The toylike prettiness of the town makes you gasp. It is absurdly gay; orange, crimson, scarlet, parrot-green and canary-yellow. I don't know if this architecture is typical of the Caribbean, but it is extremely individual: ridiculous little classical porches, window-frames decorated with bold slapdash festoons of color, an air of mock grandeur, of Negro high spirits, and something of the décor of the Russian ballet.

On the waterfront are an old Dutch fort and a row of tall seventeenth-century houses which might have been lifted bodily from a canal-side in Amsterdam. They have the same narrow gables and bas-relief figures, the same hooks for hauling furniture and goods to the windows of the upper stories. The harbor is within and behind the town, a large lagoon called the Schottegat. To enter it, you pass down a long channel which is like a main street. Your arrival has an atmosphere of welcome and triumph. Ships' sirens hoot their greetings. The ancient pontoon-bridge, the "Queen Emma," swings back like a gate to let you through. Everybody waves—Dutch and Chinese schoolboys, Negro women with baskets on their heads, Venezuelan girls on the vegetable-boats from La Guaira, American sailors washing their dungarees. The ship seems to have grown suddenly enormous; from the boat-deck you can look out over the rooftops.

Around the Schottegat are the plants and storage-tanks of the oil-refineries. The place reeks sourly of oil. The water of the lagoon is covered with a thin rainbow film and its shores are funereally edged by yards of shining jet-black scum. You might as well be in Wilmington, California. This is the main source of Willemstad's wealth, a grimy utilitarian backyard behind a pretty showcase of imported goods. Since the town is practically a free port, prices are much lower than in the States, not to mention super-expensive Venezuela. A shopping mania attacks our fellow-passengers. Wherever we walk, we meet groups of them burdened with bags full of Chinese curios, silks, linens, perfumes and bottles of Curaçao. (For some top-secret reason, the peel of the island's oranges is considered superior to any other as an ingredient in the making of this liqueur.)

But it is much pleasanter just to sit drinking beer on the upper balcony of the Hotel Americano. From here, looking across the harbor entrance to the Governor's old yellow mansion with its heavy white plaster moldings, you can see everything that happens in the center of town. The narrow streets and the waterfront square are thronged with jingling bicycles. Straw-haired Dutch policemen direct the traffic. Dutch officers walk briskly past in tropical uniforms, their stern young faces burned brick-red. Negro women saunter easily along, in clean white dresses which deepen the midnight blackness of their skin. A nun with flapping garments is driven by the breeze like a little ship. The population seems to spend its time crossing and recross-ing the channel—over the Queen Emma, or by ferry when the bridge is open. Vessels enter the harbor continually, or depart and are quickly lost to view in the blinding glitter of the sea. All this color and movement, all this going and coming, are a natural part of the surrounding atmosphere, the immensity of sunlit water and blue windy sky. Laughter and light, the sea breeze and the human gestures, the sparkle of waves and eyes, seem to blend into each other and create the very element of happiness. The tourist on the balcony, with his passport and his money in his pocket, readily accepts Willemstad as a paradise and slips into daydreams of a voluntary exile. "I could live here," he thinks, "for the rest of my life. I could buy that red house on the hill. I should have everything I want. I should make friends. I should meet extraordinary characters. There would always be new faces, new people passing through. I'd entertain them all. I'd become a famous figure. In Europe and the States, travelers would say to each other: 'So you're putting in at Willemstad? Oh, there's a man there you mustn't miss on any account. Known all over the Caribbean. They call him Curaçao Chris. . . .' "

The single brutal word SHELL, painted black on silver storage tanks in the harbor, should be enough to recall the tourist from his daydreams. For, alas, Willemstad is among the least secure of tropical-island retreats. It depends on Venezuela for its crude oil and its food, and on the world's shipping lines for its trade. It is at the mercy of every economic crisis, not to mention local political disturbances and global wars. It has little agriculture and hardly any rainfall. If its life-lines are ever cut, or interrupted even for a comparatively short period, most of its inhabitants will have to quit or starve. This is no place for beachcombers. The romantic tourist had better leave it to its extremely businesslike trades-people, pay for his beer and get back on board his ship.

September 24.

Most of the passengers were disembarking at La Guaira, Venezuela, so last night we had a "get-together" dinner, followed by an improvised floor show. The getting-together, as always, meant paper caps, which we wore with the dessert, and toy trumpets, which emitted loud farting sounds. Personally, I hate caps but like trumpets—which may merely mean that I hate uniforms but like speaking in public. Our table-companions both put on their caps without hesitation. She adjusted hers at a becoming angle; he clapped his on his head with the assurance of a man who has attended many a business convention. They were both rather scared of the trumpets, however, and only joined in after Caskey had produced some extraordinarily obscene noises. Meanwhile, in the center of the room, three small Ecuadorean children were sabotaging the self-conscious gaiety of the grown-ups by a ruthless orgy of stamping and screaming. The little boy, who is fat and squat with an archaic Inca face, has advertised his presence consistently throughout the voyage. He has two pleasures: gorging food and bullying his sisters. He pinches them, kicks them, chases them around the decks, or pushes them into the swimming pool, hurling himself on top of them. Caskey and I have long since voted him Most Loathsome Child on Board. (Other awards still to be made are: Greatest Drip, Biggest Slob, Hottest Pants, Most Embarrassing Newlyweds, Cutest Cup of Tea, All-American Ghoul and Least Likely to Return.)

The floor show produced a surprise—at least, to us. It seems that one of our fellow-passengers was a famous Venezuelan radio and cabaret star, on her way home from an engagement in New York. A tall, thin, vivacious lady with an upswept coiffure, she wore her long black lace gown with an air of consciously comic elegance. Gracious and perfectly assured, eyebrows passionately arched, eyes and teeth flashing temperament, she advanced sinuously to the microphone and began, in a tiny voice, with slight gestures of her jeweled fingers, to indicate the effect of a song. It was a beautifully impressionistic performance, and she was loudly applauded.

Nearly all of the passengers who weren't disembarking had planned a trip to Caracas, the capital city, which is only about twenty miles inland from La Guaira, up in the mountains. Those who knew Caracas already were enthusiastic in its praises: even its high prices—the result of the oil boom—were quoted somewhat admiringly. "Oh, it's so *modern!*" Caskey mimicked them, in mincing tones: "It's so *clean!* It's so *American!* And a Martini costs a dollar seventy-five! They must taste simply *delicious!*" Perversely, we decided to spend the day in La Guaira, which everybody describes as "a dump."

This morning, very early, I went up on deck—and there was South America. Its mountains rose up sheer and solemn out of the flat sea, thrown into massive relief by tremendous oblique shafts of light from the rising sun. The gorges were deep in crimson shadow, the ridges were outlined in dazzling gold. The town of La Guaira lay scattered over the slopes and along the shore. It was very still. You could hear a church bell, and the chugging of a customs launch starting forth to meet the ship. And, already, you could smell the land. A harsh disturbing smell, after the cleanness of the sea. A smell which presaged the long journey ahead of us, with all its excitements and fatigues. The smell of an alien civilization, a foreign language, other faces and different food. A smell which made my dim mental pictures of the expected continent suddenly sharp and three-dimensional and real. A smell which somehow conveyed to the mind, more instantly and powerfully than any word or image, the obvious but staggering fact that South America actually exists—that it is down here, all the time, every day of our lives. . . . Caskey, who by now had joined me at the rail, said without hesitation that it was garlic.

An hour later, this overpowering spectacle of the landfall was nearly forgotten. The sun had risen high into the sky, the air had grown heavy and humid, and the ship had tied up alongside a big modern dock. All was noise, detail and distraction. Porters—some of them wearing the crumpled paper caps of last night's party—brought baggage from the cabins, jostling the departing passengers on the stairs. Big Negroes, seated on upturned packing-cases, were unloading light cargo from the hold with a minimum of effort; they merely gave each crate a push to propel it along the runway, to a point from which a standing chain of men—all noticeably smaller—had to pass it from hand to hand into the warehouse. A little nineteenth-century Belgian locomotive with an immense smokestack puffed back and forth, whistling and scattering the crowd. A customs official sat at a table on the dock, bewildering his victims with green and white questionnaires. Soldiers and police simply watched. Taxi-drivers, guides and all manner of waterside touts darted this way and that, twisting, waving their arms, standing on tiptoe, shouting and grimacing to attract the attention of their prospective customers, lined along the rail of the main deck, high above. "Hi, Johnny! Señor! Mister! Psst, psst! Taxi? Caracas? Thirty dollars? Twenty-five?" The tourists, when picked out individually, at first coyly averted their eyes from their wooers, exchanged unnecessary conversation with their neighbors, blushed and smiled. Nevertheless, they were seduced, one by one. A girl would laugh and shake her head firmly, but not look away—contact had been established.

"Only twenty-five, Señora!"

"No, no. Too much. *Es mucho.*"

"No, Señora! No much! I show you everythings. Casa Bolívar. Government Palace. Cathedral. Avila Hotel. Very good!"

"No, no. *Mucho. Mucho.*"

A few more exchanges, head-shakings, consultations between the girl and her husband—and the unequal struggle would be over. They wavered, they gave in, they descended from the ship, they were whirled away. At sailing-time that evening, I told Caskey, they would return, having spent far more money than they intended and therefore determined to convince themselves and all the world that the excursion had been worthwhile, that Caracas was the most delightful city on the continent. Conscious of our superior discrimination, we started out on foot to discover La Guaira.

It is, to be frank, a dirty, shabby little place; as different from Curaçao as one could imagine possible. But it has its own charm: the steep streets losing themselves in stony trails up the fertile sides of the mountain, the colored houses faded to such delicate tints of lilac, rose and orange that their neglect seems to display a sort of passive genius for leaving well enough alone. Outside the dock gates there is a small park with a statue, palm trees and flower beds full of a tropical plant which has dark bronze leaves veined in gold. We sat there for some time, trying to absorb Venezuela through our eyes, ears and noses. There seemed to be an extraordinarily large number of people about: by constantly passing and repassing, the inhabitants create the effect of a population three times its actual size—like the single camel in an oriental play which creates the illusion of a caravan. And what a variety of race mixtures! Negroid Chinese, Negroid Indian, Indian Spanish, Spanish German, Irish Spanish; red hair with Mongolian cheekbones, black woolly hair with light-blue eyes, thick lips with a thin aquiline nose. Caskey exhausted much patience vainly trying to photograph a very old Negress who was studying the lottery numbers in a newspaper. She never looked at him once or showed awareness of his presence, but every time he had her in focus she turned her head or moved away.

On the walls around the square were placards of a circus act, "Miss Aida, The Sister of the Devil," and presidential election posters with portraits of Rómulo Gallegos, the handsome candidate of the Acción Democrática Party, who is also a famous novelist. I wish all presidential candidates would write novels: one could learn so much about them in advance by reading their books.

Wherever you look, there is a profusion of American goods: jeeps, trucks and passenger cars on the streets; ice-boxes, cash-registers, typewriters, radios and chemical products in the shops. They catch the eye, amidst the shabbiness and disrepair of their surroundings, with the shiny newness of toys which will soon be damaged or broken. Yet perhaps the Latin American attitude toward these appliances is saner than ours. Things are made to be used, and even misused, for material purposes; in the States they are too often exalted into symbols of social position and power. No doubt a Venezuelan is proud for a while of his new car, but I don't imagine him much dismayed by a scratch on the paintwork, a smashed headlamp, or a buckled fender. These things are bound to happen sooner or later—probably sooner, considering the way he drives.

We took a bus out to Macuto, which is a fashionable winter resort. There are a lot of grand villas along the seashore and a big hotel, but the season hasn't started yet and the place is still half empty. The afternoon was steamy and hot. Clouds kept forming and dissolving over the mountains; now and then there were a few drops of rain. High overhead the buzzards circled, their pale wing-tip feathers outspread like fingers. I have decided to describe them as "condors" in my letters home. We sat in a café drinking excellent beer from Caracas and watching dark-skinned boys swimming in the bright rough water. Country people went by in large straw hats. A waiter with a broom swept up the fine aromatic dust which fell continually out of the air; and a brown baby wandered about stark naked except for a pair of black patent-leather boots. An enormous laziness stole over us; we seemed to inhale it with the perfume of the dust and the flowers. It was altogether too much trouble to think what I was feeling about Venezuela. Maybe at that moment I wasn't feeling anything; we were simply there. Suddenly I became alarmed. Maybe, I thought, I'm not going to feel anything about South America, anywhere, ever. . . . . "You know," I told Caskey, "I believe this travel book is going to be very, very short." "All the better," said Caskey, grinning. "There'll be more room for my pictures."

Walking through La Guaira on our way back to the ship, we were stopped by the sentry in front of the barracks. With great politeness, much Spanish and many gestures, he explained that pedestrians are not allowed to use the stretch of sidewalk which passes the barracks gate; they must circle out into the roadway. We obeyed, greatly mystified. No doubt there is a simple and sensible reason for this regulation. But it is just the kind of thing which makes a sensational journalist decide that the government fears a revolutionary putsch.

September 25.

Today we put in for several hours at Puerto Cabello, "Port Hair"—so called, it is said, because you could make a boat fast by a single hair in the calm sheltered lagoon. Seen from the water, the place looks wildly romantic: an empty golden sweep of bay, the lighthouse and the white buildings against a dark secret wall of tropical forest, mountains far in the background gloomy beneath a load of thunderclouds. Scene for the opening chapter of a boys' adventure story. A young man goes ashore here on his first voyage out from England. He is to visit some old friends of his father—a family of local aristocrats who live impoverished on a great half-ruined hacienda, a few miles from the city. (Already he has fallen in love with a miniature of their beautiful daughter, Dolores.) At an inn on the waterfront he asks where he can hire a horse. The proprietor, a one-eyed Chinese, learning his destination, immediately becomes evasive and drops mysterious hints. The price of the horse is doubled. But our hero insists. When he reaches the hacienda it is already dark. The gates are standing open. He rides up to the house, dismounts and enters. Lamps are burning in all the rooms. There is no one about. In the marble and brocade *sala*, with its gilt mirrors and faded ancestral portraits, he finds a parrot which has escaped from its cage and perched on the outstretched hand of a statuette. "Ask Mr. Lancaster," it says, and laughs shrilly. There are stains on the marble. By Jove—they look like blood. . . . The young man turns abruptly and sees a little one-armed Portuguese watching him from the doorway with a sneering smile. "You are looking for Don Francisco, Señor? He and his family left here many days ago—on a very long journey. . . ."

Actually, Puerto Cabello—or as much as we saw of it—seemed a sleepier but cleaner version of La Guaira. There is the same polychromatic shabbiness, the same wealth of imported U.S. goods. In the dockyard were thousands of old-fashioned toilet bowls which had never been uncrated; enough for an entire city. An exquisite flamingo-pink oil tank is recommended to connoisseurs of industrial architecture.

We spent most of our time ashore drinking in a Moorish-style café near the harbor. Some sailors off an American ship were sitting at a near-by table, loudly discussing a friend who had married a rich Venezuelan girl. "Hell," said one of them (the least attractive): "I like money—but not that much." Their envious bitchiness so much disgusted Caskey that he began, equally loudly, to describe male gold-diggers—the frustrated type especially—whom he had met while in the Navy at Miami. "They're far more conceited than women. And the older and uglier they get, the worse they are. They think they've only got to——" (here he became unprintable) ". . . to have the daughter of a millionaire throw her pants at them." The sailors were listening by this time, and I feared there would be trouble. Luckily, however, a diversion was created by the entry of three Venezuelans—a child of about four years old and her two parents. The parents were dressed quietly and poorly but the little girl was decked out in the strangest, most bizarre finery. With her frilled skirts, her necklace, her earrings, her powdered cheeks and her painted lips, she looked more like a grown-up midget. She was quite startlingly cross-eyed.

The sailors were playing the juke box, and at once she began to dance, posing and pirouetting around the room. These were no mere childish antics; what made them so extraordinary was their quality of professionalism. This was a performance. Obviously she had been taught, she had practiced—and apparently she had been brought here to go through her act. But why? There were barely a dozen people in the café, not nearly enough to form a worthwhile audience. There was no hint of a desire to collect money. The father and mother glanced at us from time to time, but only as if to appeal to us to share in their admiration, which was simple, unconditional and touching.

Now and then, the little girl paused to demand beer, which her parents were drinking. They allowed her several sips and then tried to refuse, but she screamed so savagely that they had to yield. Wildly excited, she had passed altogether beyond their control. She hopped, she twirled, she waved her arms, she collided with tables and chairs. The Bacchanal might well have lasted for hours —perhaps it did. For now another little girl appeared; she was a hunchback. Immediately, the two of them started dancing together. . . . "Let's go," I said hastily to Caskey. "This is turning into a story by Truman Capote."

September 28.

Here we are. The voyage is all over. We have been in Cartagena since yesterday morning.

We have arrived—but the traveling, the act of penetration, has not yet begun. So far, we have made no personal contact with Colombia. We are still tourists. I'm afraid we shall see nothing in this city except the sights.

"It's a nice clean little town," one of the ship's officers told us, as we approached down the long pale-blue waterway and turned the point into the Boca Chica—the harbor entrance. The surface of the channel was littered with floating vegetable wreaths, some variety of water-hyacinth. When the rainy season begins, they are swept out of the stagnant shallows of the rivers where they grow and away downstream into the ocean. You sometimes find live snakes still coiled around their roots. They give the place an air of melancholy. It is as though a mass funeral ceremony had just been performed for all the soldiers and pirates whose bones lie unburied in the bay.

Meanwhile the cruise passengers—not having to worry about packing or baggage declarations—were snapping their cameras at the old yellow walls and the Colonial forts, throwing coins to boy divers from rowboats, or reading aloud to each other what the guidebook says about Henry Morgan and Sir Francis Drake. This was to be their big day; their one authentic glimpse of the Spanish Main. English-speaking guides and sightseeing cars waited on the dock to receive them, to rush them around the churches and the fortifications, to bewilder them with dates, statistics, historical misinformation and mispronounced words, to revive them with lunch at the El Caribe, to deliver them safe back to the ship which was sailing again at four. By dinnertime they would be far out on the cool sea.

All morning long I envied them, as we sat sweating in the customs warehouse. It was stupefyingly hot; everybody, including the local inhabitants, seemed half-dazed. I saw two boys greet each other and remain holding hands for several minutes, as if simply too lazy to let go. The examiners sat in a bower of baggage within a wire cage. Three were more or less active, the rest were spectators. Hour after hour, as the weary farce of inspection proceeded, they languidly fingered sport jackets, stockings and shoes, yawned, fiddled with their pens, asked questions without paying the slightest attention to the answers. Now and then they left the cage in a body and were gone for long periods. At last our names were called —our first names only, since the others were apparently too difficult to pronounce—and we fought our way through an obstinate cluster of loungers into the examiners' presence. By this time we had waited five hours, and my earlier mood of homicidal fury had dissolved into humble and perspiring patience. I was polite and almost cheerful. Christopher, I told my examiner, was English for Cristóbal. This pleased him greatly. 'Cristóbal Colón . . . Cristóbal Colón . . .' he kept repeating—at least a dozen times— while he briefly poked into our suitcases.

The Hotel El Caribe stands on an elbow of the beach, about two miles outside Cartagena. It is a tall bare building with big rooms and windows through which the sea breeze blows; you feel much cooler here than in the city. The guests are mostly rich cosmopolitan families or U.S. businessmen who have to stay at "the best hotel in town" in order to uphold the dignity of the firm they represent. Caskey, alone in the lobby soon after our arrival, found himself being eyed speculatively by a well-dressed, very attractive girl who was sitting with a much older man. Presently the older man left, and the girl came over to him. "Excuse me," she said in a low voice, speaking excellent English, "do you want to sell any dollars?" Caskey said that he thought he might—we are both still a bit cautious about "free-market" operations—and they agreed to meet later. However, since then, we have only seen the girl together with the older man, and she makes no sign of knowing us.

After dinner we went into Cartagena. It seems that the town

only comes to life at night; everybody was out of doors, strolling through the park or talking in excited groups around benches. In their thin white clothes, under the brilliant street lamps, they appear as animated and unsubstantial as moths. Creature of a different zone, I felt sticky and all too solid. I suppose it is really no hotter or more humid here than in New York during August; but here you are among people who inhabit the climate like an element. They don't fight it with appliances, they adapt themselves to it, physically and psychologically. It has become a part of their nature.

This morning, somewhat doggedly, we went sightseeing. In blazing sunshine, we trudged up the La Popa hill. (Caskey has boycotted all "unnecessary" taxi-riding since yesterday, when we were charged ten dollars for getting ourselves and our bags from the ship to the hotel.) There is a ruined convent on the top, and, thank God, a café where you can buy Coca-Cola. In early Colonial times, a priest found some Indians up there worshipping a goat, and promptly drove the goat over the precipice—one of those silly displays of bad temper which are so often rather approvingly described as "stern fanaticism;" probably he was just hot and irritable after the climb, as we were ourselves.

We also visited the city walls and some of the churches. Our appearance attracted a small swarm of schoolboys, anxious to air their English and perhaps earn something as amateur guides. They became a great nuisance. Finally in San Pedro Claver we tried to get rid of them by kneeling down to pray. Not in the least abashed, one of the boys immediately knelt beside me, crossed himself, and started chattering into my ear. Another mounted the steps of the high altar and pointed to the gilded chest which holds the tiny body of the saint. "Psst! Psst!" he called. "Look, Mister! Come here! Look! Psst!" I tried to think about San Pedro Claver, who used to beg from door to door for money to give to the Negroes who were brought here in the slave-ships—the Slave of the Slaves, they called him—but it was impossible. We had to leave. When we got back to the hotel we found that Caskey's swimming trunks, which he had left to dry on the balcony outside our room, had been stolen.

I keep looking out of our window across the sunlit plain toward the stormy mountains, which rumble with thunder all through the afternoon. For me they represent "The Interior"—that somber anatomical phrase which suggests mysterious darkness, winding secret paths and ominous sounds. It is there that we have to go.

Between the coastal plain and the high plateau there is no reliable road and no railway connection whatsoever. But the average guest at the El Caribe makes nothing of the journey; the air line will fly him to Bogotá in less than three hours. Colombia has jumped straight from the Horse to the Air Age. There are planes going daily in every direction—across the jungle, over the mountains, into places which can otherwise only be reached by a mule-trail.

However, we have other plans. On the ship we talked to a Colombian who advised us to travel inland up the Magdalena River to a point from which we can take a train to Bogotá. That way, we shall see more of the country. The river steamers start from Barranquilla. We are going there by road later this afternoon.

up the river

September 29.

THE SUN SET soon after we left Cartagena, so most of our 86-mile drive was in the dark. My impressions were chiefly of traffic hazards: piles of building materials in the urban districts, wandering herds of cattle in the country. As soon as we entered one of the little towns our driver would begin to toot monotonously on his horn, for the entire population was out of doors, blocking the street. They gave way to our passage slowly, without haste or alarm, peering into the car and shouting remarks which made everybody laugh goodhumoredly. When stared at, it is really much more friendly to stare back; turning your eyes away—as nearly all of us instinctively do—implies lack of interest, superiority.

After fifty miles of jarring bumps, abrupt twists and flooded hollows, our driver turned and told us: "Here the good road ends." We laughed, but he was right. What followed was much worse. It began to rain, hard—not for long, fortunately, or I think we should have stuck. Just outside Barranquilla, we stopped at a customs shed. The driver jumped out and chatted amiably with the officials. Returning to the car, he told us that he had bribed them not to search our baggage by promising to bring them a bottle of rum on his way back to Cartagena. We, of course, were to pay for the rum.

A racket? Naturally. The Government is being cheated. What do we care? We are being blackmailed. What does the Government care? Suppose we refused the rum? They would discover something dutiable, ten times its value, in our baggage. But the question is merely academic. No tourist will ever refuse. Why, at least, couldn't our driver have told us before we started: "The trip will cost you so and so much, plus a bottle of rum?" Because, I

23

suppose, he enjoys acting out this little comedy: to give away the plot in advance would spoil his fun.

It sounds priggish and naïve to attach any importance to this incident at all. Isn't it exactly what every traveler tells you to expect? Isn't it simply a specimen of that delightful picturesque South American dishonesty? Isn't it part of the national charm? Isn't it a huge joke? Perhaps, in a few weeks, I shall think so, or be forced to pretend to myself that I think so: the alternative is trouble. Certainly, I've laughed off dozens of similar situations in different parts of Europe, not to mention China. No doubt it's because I haven't traveled for so long that I see things as a newcomer, through Caskey's indignant eyes. But meanwhile I protest. I don't like it. I am not amused.

The Hotel Del Prado is larger, grander but less comfortable than the El Caribe. There is no hot water in our room. However, the bar is fairly cheerful and there is a big swimming pool, surrounded by palm trees and flowers. The first person we met on arrival was Emilio, our Colombian friend from the ship. He greeted us like a host; here, on his native soil, he seems much livelier and more expansive. He is about thirty, neatly dressed, with bright alert eyes and a tidy little mustache, very correct and polite. He has studied farming in the States and now owns a dairy farm up on the plateau outside Bogotá. He will fly there in a few days. His mother, whose heart is weak, can't stand such a sudden change of altitude; she'll make the journey by river boat and train, like ourselves.

Emilio sat with us while we ate a late dinner. At a near-by table was Dr. Jorge Eliécer Gaitán, one of Colombia's most prominent political leaders. He used to be a criminal lawyer. Emilio regards him as a dangerous demagogue. He has split the Liberal Party, turning his half of it into a "popular movement" which is supported to some extent by the Communists. He has a great following among the workers; in his speeches, he always refers to his Indian blood and poses as one of themselves. He is square, smallish, very dark, shrewdly attentive, gracious, quite cold. Capable, when the occasion demands, of battle cries and passionate gestures. In repose, as impassive as a crocodile. Not a man to be friends with, but one you might temporarily rely on to get you out of some nasty emergency, such as a rape charge. He ran once for president, unsuccessfully. Next time, Emilio thinks, he will be elected.

Emilio says that he himself belongs to no party, although, like everybody in Colombia, he is deeply interested in politics. He found people in the States politically apathetic, which amazed him. "Politics are the most important thing in life." What he thinks of the U.S. economic policy in Colombia, we couldn't discover. No doubt he is careful not to hurt our feelings. He lost no opportunity of praising American techniques and machines, but the word "Oil" was never mentioned.

He is very patriotic, likes Venezuela, hates Peru. The Peruvians, he says, are militaristic land-grabbers; they have taken a big chunk of Ecuador, pushing right through to the bank of the Rio Putumayo. Colombia, on the other hand, actually gave some border territory back to Ecuador today. Emilio's patriotism is also local. His family comes from Medellin, capital of the Department of Antioquia, and he is extremely proud of being an Antioqueño. Antioqueños, according to Emilio, are of pure Basque and Spanish descent, unmixed with Indian; the elite of the entire population. Wherever you go in Colombia you will find them in the leading executive and commercial positions—such is their energy and initiative. "You know," he added smiling, "they call us the Jews of Colombia. In fact, they say that the Jews are just Antioqueños degenerated!" As for Medellin itself, it is the most progressive city in the country, a model industrial community. We don't even have to take Emilio's word for this. An American business man at the El Caribe described it to me yesterday as "a perfect little Chicago." The South American Handbook is more cautious, as befits a British publication: "The city has been called the 'Manchester of Colombia,' but the public services are reported to be bad." (Remembering the public services in Manchester, England, I find the "but" somewhat enigmatic.) In any case, we have quite decided that we don't want to go to Medellin.

Most of Emilio's friends in Bogotá are Antioqueños, and he describes their achievements with possessive pride. One of them manages the best newspaper. Another has invented a soft drink which is so popular that even Coca-Cola can't compete with it. This drink was evolved by democratic methods. The inventor brought flavors from the States and invited the neighbors to try them in various mixtures until one was voted the most satisfactory.

This morning, we went into town early to see the agent of the company which operates the Magdalena River boats. He has a bust of Verdi on his desk, and on the wall a colored print of Jesus with the Sacred Heart, illuminated by red and blue electric lights. There was much handshaking and bowing and we all sat down in an atmosphere of extreme leisure, as if settling ourselves to wait for the Last Judgment. It grew hotter and hotter. Flies buzzed. Passers-by paused to stare in from the street through the doorways and windows. Others actually wandered right into the office and out again, like sleepwalkers: a man languidly offering to sell a bottle of whisky in a crumpled paper bag; a little girl with lottery tickets. There are lottery ticket-sellers' unions, whose members in their turn farm out the tickets to children and old women, getting a percentage on the sales. Emilio says that the lotteries used to be a racket but have now been cleaned up. Most of the money goes to the hospitals.

I looked through a weekly picture magazine largely devoted to the alleged crimes of Dr. Matallana, a Bogotá lawyer who is accused of having murdered ten people. His technique, it seems, was to find clients who were in danger of scandal or arrest, get a power of attorney to administer their property, and advise them to leave the country. At this point they would disappear. If their friends asked questions, he would explain that they were hiding abroad under assumed names and had better not be communicated with. Matallana denies all this but the press takes it for granted that he is guilty. He has become a national figure, known almost affectionately as "Dr. Mata"—a pun on *matar*, to kill.

At length, after telephoning the docks, the agent told us that the boat won't be ready to sail till tomorrow night at the earliest; something is wrong with the engines. We walked about the town. Caskey bought some lighter-fluid which burns with a thick smoky flame, filling the bedroom with smuts. At the post office they had no air-mail stamps of high denominations. So many small ones were necessary that we couldn't get them all on to our postcards.

After lunch, we visited a soap factory owned by one of Emilio's best friends, a very pleasant young man named Jorge. They were students together at an agricultural college in California. Jorge calls Emilio "Profi" or "Professor." They started talking politics at once, goodhumoredly arguing, for Jorge is a strong Conservative and a great admirer of Laureano Gómez, his party leader. He even has a portrait of Gómez over his office desk. Emilio attacked Gómez, who has been supporting Gaitán simply in order to split and ruin the Liberal Party. According to Emilio, the Conservatives are so rigid in their mental processes that they can imagine no enemy other than the traditional Liberals; they can't see where their real danger lies. It is the old, old story.

In the soap factory there was the usual nauseating stench of decaying animal fat. A long shabby row of buzzards waited, perched on the roof; occasionally one of them would swoop down to grab a morsel. They are almost as tame, here, as barnyard fowls. You see them walking and pecking around in the dirtier streets. This part of town is called "The Black District"; it is a slum area, with water from the river seeping up through cracks in the roadway. Soon it is to be torn down, drained and rebuilt. Most of Barranquilla is modern, fairly clean but not particularly interesting. In the Prado section, where our hotel is, are more or less luxurious villas—some Mauresque, some semi-classical—of an arresting ugliness.

We all drove out in Jorge's car to see the city water-works. The population of Barranquilla has increased so enormously during the past ten years (it is now around 200,000) that these are becoming inadequate. The buildings are charming, spotless as well-kept bathrooms, and surrounded by lawns and gardens. The water is pumped up out of the Magdalena River—a dirty brown soup which is then treated with alum, allowed to precipitate, filtered and chlorinated. This process was explained to us enthusiastically by the head chemist, who showed us around. I'm afraid I didn't listen very carefully; but I enjoyed simply being near him. He had the aura of a man whose occupation is absolutely honest, beneficial and non-violent. I began to feel very happy and peaceful. It was almost as good as visiting a monastery.

On the way back, Emilio remarked how different the Costeños —the people of the coast—are from the people of the mountain areas. They talk very fast, slurring their words and never pronouncing the final s. Curiously enough, this is also a characteristic of other Costeños, in Venezuela and Cuba. The Cuban Costeño accent is almost indistinguishable from the Colombian. Many South American countries are divided in this way, by altitude; you get two different races, the Ups and the Downs.

Jorge took us to his club for a drink. The bar was air-conditioned; our sweat-soaked shirts dried on our backs and we awoke, for half an hour, from the tropical heat-daze. Jorge talked about the local gipsies; there are several thousand of them in Barran-quilla. He knows many of them well and is sometimes invited to their feasts. They live in squalor, but some are quite rich. One came to him to borrow twenty cents, and, a few minutes later, apparently having forgotten the loan, pulled a wad of bills out of his pocket and started to count them. Another consulted Jorge about government securities; he had ten thousand dollars to in-vest. They make their money by trading and bargaining, and hardly ever settle down to a fixed job. If they give you a present they are apt to show up later and ask you, quite unabashed, to pay for it. Just the same, Jorge admires them. They have their own kind of dignity. Once, he met a gipsy leader who had been in prison for theft and asked him jokingly if he didn't feel ashamed of himself. "Why should I be ashamed?" the gipsy answered. "Prisons were made for men."

September 30.

Our sailing has been postponed till 3 P.M. tomorrow. I hope we shall really leave then. This hotel depresses me. There are many American women who have been staying here for months on end. They are the grasswidows of employees of the Tropical Oil Com-pany, which has camps and fields along the Magdalena River. They are waiting to move into apartments or houses, which are ex-pensive here and hard to find. Wearily yawning, bored to death, they sit around in the garden. The energy of their children keeps them in a perpetual state of irritation. Occasionally, if an attractive man passes, their eyes may show an idle flicker of interest. I sup-pose they have their dreams and their secrets. But they fill the place with an atmosphere of sulky sadness; Somerset Maugham characters who will never be used.

We spent most of the day in the pool. Although it is so hot, the sun seldom shines for long. The sky is full of dark steamy clouds.

In the hotel lobby you can actually buy today's issue of the *Miami Herald*, which is flown in regularly from Florida. This after-noon, in desperation, we did.

October 1.

Emilio's mother is traveling with a friend, and several other ladies were coming down to the dock to see them off, so we decided to split into two parties. Caskey went on ahead with all the baggage in one car; the rest of us followed in another. We stopped at a friend's house to chat and drink coconut juice. It was one of those pauses which the Latins know so well how to create; pauses that seem to the tense Anglo-Saxon like mere dawdling. Actually they have great psychological value, for they break the strain of departure and explode the myth of hurry. This was like the end of a journey, not the beginning. We had endless ages at our disposal. . . . In point of fact, we stayed only about twenty minutes and should have reached the River Terminal in plenty of time even if the steamer had been punctual, which it wasn't.

There sat Caskey on the baggage, a small, grimly stoical figure, all chin and shoulders, like a statue of the Last Pioneer—his horse dead, his ammunition gone. Let the Redskins come. He wasn't going to budge. He had been talking to a tall tight-lipped weather-beaten oil-driller from Oklahoma, who is traveling a hundred miles up the river to a town called Plato, near which there is a camp. He was very friendly and bought us two Cokes, but was pessimistic about the prospects of our trip. "Your partner here says you didn't bring any food along? That's too bad. The stuff they give you on the boat is awful—nothing but rice. You can't eat it. How do you like hot weather? It's going to be hotter than hell. And the boat's sure to get stuck some place; they always do. Probably take you two weeks to make it. Well, you can get a plane on from Barranca. You'll have had plenty by then."

He himself usually travels back and forth by the weekly hydro-plane, known as "the puddle-jumper." I asked him about mosqui-toes. Yes, there were plenty. What did he do about them? "Noth-ing. Just let 'em chew." He has had malaria badly several times, but now he doesn't get it any more.

Our boat, the *David Arango*, arrived about an hour later. These Magdalena boats look like Mississippi River steamers in the days of Mark Twain: lofty and topheavy, with curtained decks, tall twin smokestacks and a big paddle-wheel at the stern, they have the air of disreputable old hotels. Ahead of them, they push long iron barges which carry their cargo: flour, soap, oil, furniture, livestock, assorted hardware and two or three automobiles.

On board there are three classes: Luxury, First and Steerage. Our Luxury tickets to Puerto Salgar (the maximum distance) cost thirty-five dollars each. A Steerage ticket costs only seven dollars, but doesn't entitle you to a bunk; you must bring your own hammock and sling it wherever you can find space on the bottom deck, between the paddle and the engines. Already the Steerage is so crowded that you can't believe there will be room for another human being; hammocks are criss-crossed over and under each other in every direction. The heat down there, so close to the furnaces, must be nearly unbearable, and yet there are many women and small children among the passengers.

Up here on the third deck, we are in comparative comfort. The Luxury cabins are advertised as air-conditioned, which they certainly are not; a draft of ordinary air is simply fanned in through a ventilator. There is barely room to turn around. The bunks are very hard. There are no portholes or windows; only movable louvre-shutters without any kind of netting to keep out the insects. Nevertheless there is a toilet, a washbowl and a shower for which the river-water has been more or less successfully filtered; at any rate it is no longer dark brown. Also, the whole place seems very clean.

The girl who asked Caskey to sell her some dollars in the El Caribe is on board. Her name is Carmen. The elderly man we saw with her is her father. He's here too, along with her mother and her brother. They are Antioqueños, and they are going to a river port called Puerto Berrío from which they can take the train to Medellin. Their reason for making this journey rather than flying is that they want to keep an eye on their brand-new Buick which has just been delivered from the States. Colombian dock-workers are apt to be casual, and even maliciously careless, in handling freight. The Buick is on the barge which we are pushing, so Carmen's family can watch over it from morning till night.

As for the mystery about the dollars, it seems that Carmen buys them whenever she can for her mother, and she didn't want her father to know this. Probably the two women have been running up dressmakers' bills in New York.

October 2.

The food on this boat isn't so bad, after all. Lots of rice, as the Oklahoman predicted, but also quite a variety of dishes, including goodish meat, eggs, slices of banana (fried to an extraordinary hardness), papaya and an unidentified vegetable which looks and tastes like soft white wood. To follow, there is an assortment of little fruit-pastes and preserves and some exceedingly bitter black coffee. In the bar you can get excellent Barranquilla beer, several sorts of hard liquor—the local rum is the cheapest—and U.S. cigarettes. The water must be drinkable, for everybody drinks it.

The stewards are all very friendly. One of them is a mute—we can't be sure if he is also deaf. Anyhow he seems to understand everything. He has a beautiful sardonic Indian face. He communicates with the others by a system of graphic but highly impressionistic signs.

We talked to a young Canadian named Doug, also an oil-man and also disembarking at Plato; he was going to a camp close to the Oklahoman's. He would be there, probably, for a six-month stretch, but the prospect didn't seem to worry him. He was a keen naturalist. "When you live in the back country you've got to specialize. People who generalize are bored people." He had already specialized in trees and flowers. This time, he was going to study birds—shooting them, stuffing them and sending them back to a museum in Winnepeg. This was the only way you could get them through the customs. When he returned home, the museum would let him have half of his specimens; he would send everything in pairs. In his district, he told us, there were poisonous snakes that dropped on you from trees; the birds had to build next to bees' nests to protect themselves from the monkeys; when you went into an Indian hut you could hear the termites chewing inside the bamboo walls.

I should have extracted a lot more information from Doug if he hadn't been busy specializing in another direction; during most of the time he was on board he talked to Carmen, or rather, flirted—with that peculiar bright-eyed innocent-cynical hygienic ruthlessness which is so typical of North American young men. I think he hoped to get invited to her home in Medellin, next time he had leave. No one could blame him. She is lusciously pretty, in her little white shorts, striped shirt and tennis cap, with her red-gold hair and big dark eyes. She looks like a Californian campus belle. Also, I think, she is good-natured and no fool.

Her brother is even more Americanized than she is. He has been educated in the States, sprinkles his conversation with "Jeez!" and "Jeepers!", and wears a watch-chain which jingles with fraternity keys. He likes to be called Stevie; it was his name in college. He tells us that he and his mother are on a diet for ulcers. "The captain of this boat has orders to give us anything we want. The president of the company wrote him a special letter about us." He speaks highly of a hotel in Medellin where the service is so good that "You never touch a doorknob or light a cigarette." And yet, despite this silliness, I must say that neither Stevie nor any of our other fellow-passengers—nearly all wealthy people accustomed to luxury—have uttered one word of complaint about the discomforts of this journey. They are neither peevish nor aggressive, and they go out of their way to be courteous to Caskey and myself, although some of them speak hardly any English.

Meanwhile the boat pushes smoothly forward, its paddlewheel beating the brown water with a sound which is like a succession of short sharp snores, turning this way and that to follow the invisible channels of the stream. The Magdalena is wide but shallow, and very hard to navigate; we are carrying six pilots who relieve each other continuously in pairs. The surface is full of eddies and little whirlpools around sunken rocks. Water-plants come floating down to meet us, and broken rafts, and sometimes a drowned shapeless animal with two or three buzzards perched on it, pecking at the flesh. I suppose they go on eating till it sinks. In the far distance, this morning, you could see the snow peaks of the Santa Marta range, strung along the sky, their lower slopes invisible, as if suspended above the moist green landscape. Doug said they were nearly nineteen thousand feet high.

We took part in the horse races, betting as a firm of four with Carmen and Doug, and won a little money which we spent on Cuba Libres in the bar, while the ship's band played; two small drums, a banjo, gourd-rattles and a boy beating time with a pair of beer bottles. About three o'clock this afternoon we reached Plato. It is a tiny place. Doug and the Oklahoman disembarked. Although we knew them so slightly, their departure had a certain air of drama. They seemed to be vanishing into the wilderness forever.

Heat lightning this evening, all along the horizon. But the night is clear.

October 3.

Caskey woke up in the middle of last night while we were landing at a village. He went out on deck to watch. The inhabitants were all on the shore, holding lighted candles.

The vegetation has become much thicker and wilder. Often, though the stream may be half a mile wide, the steamer is obliged to hug the bank so closely that the branches scrape our sides and we look right into the jungle, as if through the windows of a hot-house. The effect is oddly artificial. The vines appear to have been deliberately festooned around the trees, like Christmas decorations. It is all so green, so dense, so crowded, so oppressively alive, so empty and yet so obviously inhabited. We have seen no wild animals so far. But now and then a great white heron beats slowly over the river or settles peacefully into a bed of orange blossoms, as if the whole tree were its nest.

Actually, all of this country is populated, but unobtrusively, furtively almost. Amidst the tangle of the woods you notice banana trees planted in rows, or there is corn in clumps amongst the undergrowth. There will be a fenced enclosure with some cows, apparently abandoned here in the wilds. And then, quite unexpectedly, we pass a hut or an entire village. Indian families stand at their doors to watch the steamer and wave their hands. Man, woman and child; a Rousseau painting framed in great green leaves. Their huts are almost a part of the surrounding jungle, bamboo walls and a palm thatch. Such a life, such poverty, are beyond the grasp of one's imagination. Perhaps it is better than living in a city slum, perhaps it is worse. Nobody can tell. There are no standards of comparison.

We stop frequently. Sometimes at clearings, where firewood for the furnaces has been cut and stacked; sometimes at villages, to take on passengers. The steamer simply pushes the bows of the barge up against the bank, a plank is thrown across and a cable made fast to a tree. This morning, as we were passing a village, a dugout canoe shot out from the shore to meet us and a young man jumped daringly aboard in mid-stream, while the entire population watched, with shouts of encouragement and good-byes.

The barge is used as a promenade deck by the Steerage passengers. They sit on the crates, smoking and chatting or making love. They wash their clothes in the river water and even scoop it up and drink it out of bowls. The Indian girls wear their hair in long braids; if they have some gold-filled teeth, this is considered an extra attraction. Stevie told me this. He takes an anxious interest in the Steerage passengers because he is always afraid they will scratch their initials on the sides of the Buick; they are apt to do so, especially when a car is new. Today he went out on the barge and personally supervised the readjustment of the tarpaulins; but they aren't quite big enough and, however you fix them, part of the paintwork is exposed.

The great social event of our day is the horse racing. Everybody takes part in this, with passionate enthusiasm, waving their five-cent betting tickets as if thousands were at stake, and yelling for their favorites. "La Chanaca! La Chanaca! Azucita! Azucita! Cinco! Dos! Seis!" (Azucita means Little Sugar. La Chanaca seems to be a sort of generic pet name for any horse, like Gee-Gee.) Carmen's father nearly always wins; like many rich men, he is a fantastically lucky gambler. There is a little crippled boy from downstairs who comes up for the races and begs money from us to buy tickets. He has blond hair and the face of a charming monkey. While the race is on, he gets absolutely beside himself with excitement and hops around on his crutch, screaming his number. When it is his turn to throw the dice he does his best to cheat, and sometimes succeeds. There is no particular reason why we shouldn't play all day; later on, perhaps we shall. When the steward finally rolls up the racetrack and carries off the wooden horses, we break up slowly and unwillingly into small groups. Some go to their cabins to sleep. Some read or play cards. There are frequent discussions of how long the trip will take. The river is very low, and several steamers are said to be aground already, higher upstream.

One of the ladies has a pekingese dog and spends much of the day combing or washing it. She is a very sympathetic character. She told Carmen how much she liked being in Paris before the war, because, when she felt lonely, she had only to call an agency to get a male escort to come out with her to supper and dance all evening. "Such good-looking young men, too. Evidently, I am not a young woman, and even as a girl I was not attractive; but they were so charming to me, so kind. They tried to make me believe that they were really enjoying themselves."

We stopped at El Banco just after dark. This is much the largest place we have seen on the river, so far; an old town, dirty and beautiful, the scene of one of Bolívar's bloodless victories in his first campaign of liberation. Along the river front there are massive stone water-stairs, on which a wild scramble took place for no apparent reason whatsoever except a blind urge on the part of everybody concerned either to leave or board the boat as quickly as possible. On the narrow gangplank the two streams of human beings collided, surged and mingled; a yelling mob of white-cotton clothes and dark bodies—yellow, red, velvet black and plum purple, with an occasional, strangely arresting blond head. Above the confusion the ship's band played its lively clattering music, and through the open doors of the church on the hill there was a glimpse of a priest at the altar, a remote quiet candle-lit figure, saying vespers.

October 4.

After yesterday's great heat it is cloudy and much cooler. It seems as if we had been on this boat for weeks already and yet neither Caskey nor I are bored; we are never tired of watching the gradual unwinding of the river and the shores. In the distance, now, you can see the Andes; a blue range on either side of the valley. There are parklike clearings with vivid green patches of swamp and slim trees with smooth white trunks like flagpoles, perhaps two hundred feet high, standing out majestically against the blackness of the inner forest. We see a lot of pink herons and splendid blue macaws with streaming tail feathers and orange breasts. The water is broken by long sand-islands, littered with driftwood which looks like sun-bleached bones. Once, we nearly stuck and had to back downsteam to try another channel.

This morning, we stopped at a large village. The palms along the shore were full of buzzards. A crowd of children came on board with bowls of bananas and melons for sale. When it was time to leave they waited till the very last moment and then raced back along the barge and jumped frantically for the receding bank, some clinging to tree roots, some slithering in the mud, some falling into the water.

A conversation with Carmen about the racial question. It began when Caskey mentioned the Antioqueños and Carmen startled us by saying, "We are the Jews of Colombia"—an echo of Emilio's words. Since that evening at the Del Prado we have often discussed what he really meant by them. Did they prove that Antioqueños have no anti-Semitic prejudice; that they admire Jews and are proud of resembling them? Or, alternatively, that the Antioqueños themselves are of Jewish origin, but are unwilling to admit it; that they are afraid people will take them for Jews and therefore hasten to forestall identification by hiding behind a comparison? I couldn't very well ask Carmen this right out, but I did ask her how Jews were thought of in Medellin. She said without hesitation that they were unpopular; if they patronized a night club, Antioqueños would avoid it. Negroes and Indians are also socially barred, but as they hardly ever become rich the problem scarcely arises. Carmen is now feeling personally insulted because, last night at the bar downstairs, "a great big Nigger" dared to put his arm around her waist and ask her to dance. And yet today, just before lunch when the ship's band was playing, she climbed onto the piano and sat there singing and flashing the most provocative smiles and glances around, like the star of an operetta. She is neither stupid nor innocent enough to do this kind of thing unconsciously. She must know perfectly well the effect she produces. Maybe it's part of her act as the American college girl, but if she goes on trying it in this country she will get into trouble—and then, I suppose, she will be outraged and amazed. Just the same, you can't condemn her, despite her prejudices. She is frank and cheerful and very friendly. I always enjoy being with her.

One of the attractions of the bar is a deck-hand who is the best imitator I have ever heard. He can imitate all kinds of animals, an American radio program (in fake-English), a train, an airplane dropping bombs, a violin, a banjo being tuned, etc, etc. His barking drives the pekingese nearly frantic, especially when he does a whole dog-fight, with dogs of various sizes.

This afternoon we put in at a little natural meadow amidst the jungle and several men went ashore with machetes, big sword-like knives, to cut grass for the two cows we carry. They are kept in a wooden hut in the bow of the barge. At another village, a padre came on board and said vespers. I talked to an elderly man from the Ministry of Education in Bogotá. He is going to Medellin to inspect schools. He said that many of the larger villages in the Magdalena Valley have primary schools, but that they don't do much good because there are no books. Pupils who have learned to read forget again through lack of practice, and all their "education" consists in being able to sign their names to legal documents on the few necessary occasions of their lives. He was bitter against the Catholic Church, which has plenty of money and maintains excellent schools, but only in the wealthy districts of the larger cities. It leaves the Government to educate the peasants.

"Is it true," he asked, "that *Treasure Island* is the most famous American novel?" He is a great admirer of English poetry, especially Shakespeare, Wordsworth and Longfellow. He recited "The Village Blacksmith" and "The Seven Ages of Man." I could scarcely hear a word, for the ship's boiler had started to emit ear-splitting blasts of steam and the noise around us was terrific. Then, since neither could understand the other, we began to recite different poems simultaneously. ". . . to a summer's . . ." ". . . make our lives . . ." ". . . temperate . . ." ". . . departing . . ." ". . . winds . . ." ". . . footprints in . . ." ". . . too hot . . ." etc, etc. When we finally said good night, he yelled into my ear that it was a rare pleasure to meet an educated man and have a good talk about literature.

October 5.

Sometime during the night, we ran aground. I kept waking and thinking that we must still be anchored by the village; but this was only because of the wet roosters on the barge, crowing indignantly in the rain. It was still raining and we were still stuck at dawn. There were low clouds over the river. It looked brimming full, but the water around the boat was scarcely two yards deep. A canoe with an outboard engine appeared and carried our steel cable to the shore; the pilots were trying to drag us off the sandbank with the capstans. It was eleven o'clock before they succeeded.

While we were at lunch the dumb steward signed to us to come out on deck and look at the monkeys. He did this by simply nodding toward the woods and scratching his chest comically under the nipple. There they were, two small black ones, sitting motionless on a high branch. Caskey, busy eating, didn't share my excitement. "I refuse to leave my lunch," he said, "for anything less than a tapir."

At five-thirty we reached Puerto Wilches, the terminus of a short local railway. It has none of the charm of El Banco. A few muddy streets of wooden houses roofed with corrugated iron, mere boxes to sleep in, bare with the wretched unhomely bareness of the hot lands; a weak naked light-bulb hanging in the midst of an almost empty room, a cheap radio crackling and shouting, some naked children sitting on a bedstead, on the walls a colored print of the Virgin and a cover girl from a U.S. magazine. The only picturesqueness was provided by an encampment of gipsies who had pitched their big tents near the railroad station. They seemed to have no furniture except for gaudy piles of striped cotton bedding. The women were in costume, with earrings and bracelets. They puffed at their cigarettes with the sophisticated air of lady novelists in the twenties. We watched the porters carrying crates from the barge. They are incredibly strong. Often it takes two men to lift a load onto their backs.

October 6.

Yesterday evening, after we were in bed, there was a fight in the bar. The bartender refused credit to a drunk and the argument ended in bottle-throwing. Both men were badly cut, and the drunk had to be locked in a cabin.

Early this morning they killed one of the cows, for our food. Its hide is stretched out to dry on the side of the ship.

Barranca Bermeja—so called because of the reddish-brown oil-stained cliffs on which it stands. This is one of the headquarters of the Tropical Oil Company. There is a pipeline from here to Cartagena, and a petroleum plant enclosed, among neat silver tanks and dreary model bungalows, within a wire-netted compound which you aren't allowed to visit without a special permit. This style of architecture should be known as Oil Colonial. We saw several posters appealing to the Colombian worker to fight "El Imperialismo Yanqui." Carmen announced that she needed exercise, so she borrowed a bicycle and rode back and forth along the dock among the porters, causing a major erotic sensation.

On beyond Barranca, we saw two alligators—the first, for they are becoming scarce now, because the Indians shoot them for their valuable skins. They squatted half awash on the edge of the water, their mouths slightly open with an air of contented depravity, and then, at our approach, slipped into the river and vanished.

As the breathless sweltering afternoon drew on, thunderheads piled up above the mountains. The atmosphere became charged and tensely expectant. At five-thirty the brief ominous tropical evening begins; at six it is nearly dark. Mosquitoes come swarming up the beam of the ship's searchlight, moths cling in sticky masses around the lamps. We hurry to our cabin to smear our hands, necks and faces with insect-lotion. Lightning starts to flash out along the horizon, illuminating vast rugged tracts of cloudscape in silent electric spasms. You feel like a stone-deaf man watching an artillery bombardment, for there is seldom any thunder. Quite suddenly, without emphasis or warning, it begins to rain as if the heavens had burst open forever.

It is after a rainstorm that you can really smell the river. It is a smell that haunts the imagination until you fancy it everywhere —on your skin, in your hair, on your clothes, in the mattress, in the food. The whole boat seems to stink of it. Sweet, stale and rotten, it fills you with all the weariness of the passive tropics, where only the insect is never idle, and the vegetable is more energetic than man.

There was no moon and the night was very dark, so the Captain decided not to risk another grounding but to tie up beside the bank until morning. Carmen, Caskey and I went fishing from the barge. Carmen lost her hook in some weeds. We caught nothing, perhaps because the current was too strong.

October 7.

This morning we passed several oil-camps, and some of the houseboats on which drillers and geologists travel up and down the river to inspect new sites for wells. Stevie told me that this part of the country used to consist of big cattle ranches, but that now the Tropical Oil Company—usually known as "Troco"—is buying up more and more land. We are now in Antioquia, or rather, skirting its border, and Stevie's departmental patriotism is correspondingly inflamed. Antioqueños, he complained, did all the country's work but most of the money they made went to Bogotá in taxes. According to him, there is a serious movement in Medellin in favor of a federal constitution for Colombia; this would leave Antioquia freer to develop its own resources.

The ladies wanted to play cards in one of the cabins, and needed an extra chair. I had some trouble getting it in through the doorway, but finally succeeded. Emilio's mother, complimenting me, said: "He's a pure Antioqueño!"

Around three o'clock, we reached Puerto Berrío. It seemed almost miraculous, actually to have arrived. The dock was piled high with crates, stacked all anyhow and looking as if a push would tumble them into the river. There was an erratic crane which picked things off our barge, waved them around for a while, bumped them into every near-by object and occasionally dropped them where they started. When this happened, the dock-hands roared with laughter; big half-naked Negroes, they danced and postured to the music of our band.

Most of our fellow-passengers were getting off here. Stevie was last seen fluttering anxiously around the Buick, which had suffered some minor scratches from the ropes of the crane. Carmen vowed she would read this diary when published. If it ever is, and she does, I'm sure she will forgive my more personal remarks. We were both really sorry to see her go.

In the evening, Caskey and I took a walk in the town. There seems to be no central avenue, or any attempt at planning. The unpaved streets are thick with mud. Nevertheless, it is busy, alive and cheerful; you feel something of the notorious Antioqueño energy. Caskey said that the Middle West must have been like this, during the pioneer period. There is a kind of red-light district; little hotels and dance-halls with very young girls sitting in front of them, their legs wide apart and their skirts pushed up almost to their waists to show their thighs.

October 8.

Today, the scenery has been more beautiful than ever: wooded islands in the river, red bluffs hung with vines which trail through the rapid current, tree-orchids in the forest, rolling uplands spreading to the mountains which are close now and visible in all their contours.

This evening, the Captain invited us all to a "special dinner," which merely meant that Caskey and I had to leave our separate table and sit bored and silent while the others talked. Finally, to encourage me, Emilio's mother asked me to count up to a hundred in Spanish. I did.

Later we stopped, in order that the crew could dig clay from the bank to fill a hole in the casing around the boiler. Now we have started again, after some really alarming snorts and steam-bursts which shook the whole ship. I kept expecting a major explosion.

October 9.

As I write this, we are trying to get around a big curve in the river, with high cliffs along its outer shore. It is called the

Vuelta de Pajaral. The current, after all this rain, is so strong that it seems doubtful if we'll make it. We are barely holding our position, although we have edged over into comparatively calm water. We were to have reached our destination, Puerto Salgar, this afternoon; but, as things are, we may have to wait here a day or two, until the flood slackens. The pilots say that they never know how to pass this place. It is a mystery. You just have to go on trying.

Now we're out in the middle again. The paddlewheel groans, the whole ship creaks and strains, jets of steam shoot out with volcanic force. You feel the tremendous and rather frightening power of the water. Some of the ladies have produced their rosaries and started to pray. We are beginning to slip backwards. . . .

Later. Finally, as if in desperation, the pilots swung the boat right over against the cliffs, where the current seemingly was strongest. The barge banged into them so violently that it might well have broken loose or started a landslide, but it didn't, and we inched our way around the bend. After this, there were no more hazards. We arrived at Puerto Salgar just as the sun was setting.

We were met by a young man named Arturo. He is the son of the lady who has been traveling with Emilio's mother: a strikingly handsome boy with a very new mustache, who has studied in Los Angeles and speaks quite fluent English. Like Emilio, he is a farmer. Arturo took efficient charge of our disembarkation. We left most of our baggage at the terminal of the Bogotá railway in Puerto Salgar—there is nothing much else there except a military airfield—and then crossed to La Dorada on the opposite bank of the river in a big canoe with an outboard engine. Now we are installed in the Hotel Departamental, where we have a high room with extremely high windows; comfortable in a bleak tropical fashion but rather like a prison cell.

We have just been out for a walk with Arturo in the town. He talked a lot about his girls, including his present fiancée, who has broken with him because he didn't write her for a week. This didn't seem to worry him much. He sent her a telegram which, he was sure, would fix things up. He is a charming, very sympathetic boy, full of national hospitality toward us two gringos, and anxious to show himself as a blend of tough American businessman and sophisticated Latin lover. We suspect that his family bosses him. Colombian young men, Emilio told us, are apt to be very much under their parents' thumb. He made an important ceremony of buying several bottles of Caldas rum, which is supposed to be superior to any other. La Dorada is in Caldas Department, while Puerto Salgar is in Cundinamarca; so the rum will have to be smuggled across the river tomorrow.

October 10.

We got up and breakfasted early. The river had risen during the night and was swirling past at a great speed. Emilio's mother, rather nervous, spent some time deciding which of the canoes looked safest, but we made the crossing without accident.

Puerto Salgar stands only a few hundred feet above sea level, at the foot of the mountains; Bogotá, on the top, is at 8700. The small powerful locomotive (made in Pennsylvania) begins to climb at once, cracking its train of four or five coaches like a whip around the sharp curves of the narrow single track. At first, it is still very hot. There are densely wooded ravines, with palm trees growing right to the summits, and the coal-black Rio Negro plunging down amidst the rocks below. Then the clouds shut in, rain beats against the windows, the temperature quickly falls. The long-suffering body, which must somehow adapt itself to all its master's whims and wanderings, shivers suddenly and wants a coat. The lungs breathe the thinning air and the nerves send out their first signals of uneasiness. The muscles, so long relaxed in the sweating heat of the plains, begin to tighten and ache. Your insect-bites stop itching.

We climbed through tall wet woods and banks of great dripping ferns. Emilio's mother got off the train at a station called Villeta, with Arturo and her friend. She will stay there for a while, to grow accustomed to the altitude before finishing the journey. Saying good-bye, they all warned us solemnly of the dangers of Bogotá, which they described as a den of thieves and cutthroats. Never venture alone into the back streets at night. Never leave your baggage unwatched for a single instant. We promised to be cautious, and were handed over to the care of the lady with the pekingese dog.

The climb continued. At the little stations where we stopped, muffled women sold cooked chicken wrapped in banana-leaves, and fruit and buns. A peasant boy bought me a banana. Indeed, all the passengers were friendly, and offered us food. The pekingese dog was put into a scarlet woolen jacket.

Above the woods are pale barren upland meadows, sloping steeply from ridges of naked rock. The gorges far below are choked with thick white cloud; now and then you get tremendous glimpses of precipice and valley. The terror of the great mountains stirs in you. Man ought not to live up here. It is far too high. The villages have a strangely mournful atmosphere of squalor, quite different from the squalor of the lowlands. Their huts look cold and wet and sad. Along the river, there was always laughter and shouting and the waving of hands. Here, the dark Indian faces are unsmiling and aloof. Wrapped in their small blanket-capes, people go silently about their business, or crouch in doorways, staring.

But the journey has a final surprise; for suddenly the train is over the top of the pass and making its short descent onto the plateau, the savannah of Bogotá. As the hills open and draw back, you get an extraordinary feeling of release; all sense of the altitude disappears. The sun was shining brightly on the flat green plain. Dotted with white farms, pastures and groves of eucalyptus, it looks like the San Fernando Valley in Southern California. Indeed, it is a complete little country, which might have been transplanted here entire from the temperate zone. If you stayed here for any length of time, the tropical coast of Colombia would probably begin to seem as remote as the North Pole.

Bogotá lies at the far end of the plateau. Because it was built right under the encircling mountains, its climate is gloomier and wetter. It was raining when we got here this afternoon. The railroad station is filthy, and the porters invade the coach in a yelling mob, as if they were about to massacre all its occupants. Our baggage got divided between two of them, one on either side of the train. Wild with alarm, after so many warnings, Caskey and I ran after them, shouting; but they had no dishonest intentions. The lady with the pekingese, most helpful and unexpectedly agile, came to our aid, found us a taxi, and recommended the Hotel Astor. We have just arrived there and eaten a large late tea. I am writing this in our bedroom while Caskey does the unpacking.

in bogotá

October 12.

OBVIOUSLY, the Hotel Astor was once a private house. It is a gloomy rambling old place, built around an interior courtyard which the rain has filled with dismal puddles. Downstairs there is a long dark dining room, decorated and furnished in a style which Caskey describes as Hollywood Baronial; it has a massively carved mantelpiece and several sideboards stacked with heavy silver plate. At teatime this is the rendezvous of Bogotá's upper-class ladies. Mostly in elegant black, with furs and jewels, they form big gaily chattering groups, eat enormously and later retire to play bridge. The food is very good here, but you get far too much of it. The waiters seem quite dismayed because we can't manage five courses.

There is no public lounge, unless you count a large half-lit windowless hallway out of which several bedrooms open, on the upper floor. It has little furniture; one sofa, two or three chairs and a telephone which would appear to have been installed here in order that the maximum number of people can overhear a conversation. We have already noticed that the acoustics in Bogotá are almost painfully good. Perhaps this is because of the altitude. Nothing escapes you—no sound in the next room, no voice in the courtyard, no footstep on the stairs. As for the traffic outside, it seems noisier than Third Avenue; the taxi-horns jab at your nerves like pins. We have to sleep with the windows closed. This doesn't matter much, however, because our room is enormous and anyway very cold.

The Carrera Septima, on which this hotel stands, is one of Bogotá's main business streets. It has no character, beyond a superficial North American showiness. There are neon lights, U.S. advertisements with Spanish captions, movie theaters with Hollywood films (*El Huevo y Yo* is now playing), bars decorated in

44

New York style, department stores full of U.S. gadgets, fashions and drugs.

After supper on the evening of our arrival, Arturo suddenly appeared. He hadn't been able to stand Villeta, he told us. It was raining hard, and the place was dull anyway—not a pretty girl in sight. A family car was available, so he had impulsively jumped into it and come straight on up to Bogotá. Now he was all ready to show us the city.

He drove us out to the residential suburbs, which extend for miles; only then did we begin to realize how big Bogotá is. There are some fine houses, certainly, but the general effect is depressingly undistinguished. Nowhere could we see the least signs of a modern national style, even a bad one. The Spanish houses look more Californian than Spanish. And there are rows of bastard Tudor villas which must be among the ugliest things of their kind in the world. In the midst of this wild, largely undeveloped country the British and American architects and their pupils have managed to create an oasis of respectable boredom, an atmosphere of stodgy security, which is as tame as anything in Greater London.

Arturo, however, is touchingly proud of all this. He kept pointing out to us the homes of what he called "the high people," meaning the leading citizens. Later, he took us up to the top of the Parque Nacional, which is on the slopes of a steep hill above the city. It was a dark foggy night, but the view by day must be magnificent. Arturo added drama to the occasion by telling us that we ran a great risk in coming here at such an hour; many people had been set on recently and murdered by thugs. When we got out of the car to stroll around, he kept glancing significantly over his shoulder into the blackness of the surrounding trees. I don't believe he was really in the least scared, only hospitably anxious to give us an extra thrill. As we drove downhill again on the way home, he added further warnings. We must beware of so-called invitations; it was an old Bogotá custom to let the guest pay the bill. And we must be very careful with the local girls; nearly all of them had syphilis. He then proposed a tour of the night clubs, which we declined. Not having Arturo's inexhaustible energy, we were both very tired.

A walk in the city yesterday morning corrected many of our negative first impressions. Bogotá's dullness is merely suburban; the center of town is full of character and contrasts. In the strolling crowds, business suits mingle with blanket capes. Right around the corner from the U.S. drug stores you see Indian women sitting behind their wares on the sidewalk. If New York seems very near, so do the mountain villages.

Around the Plaza Bolívar are the steep narrow streets and massive mansions of the old colonial quarter, with their brown-tiled roofs, barred windows, carved doorways and deep sheltering eaves. We saw several modern apartment buildings of severe and beautiful design, and went into a church where there were wonderful old walnut altars. The slums are a warren of muddy lanes and wretched crumbling hovels, but some of these will shortly disappear; for Bogotá is frantically busy tearing itself down and building itself up in preparation for the Pan-American Conference, early next year. You see scaffolding and workmen everywhere. One whole street of mud huts was being demolished by hand; Indian women were ripping the filthy thatch from the roofs and carrying it away in baskets. Later there is to be a broad roadway through here to the park. But where will its former occupants live?

Bogotá is a city of conversation. As you walk along, you have to keep skirting couples or small groups, all absorbed in excited talk. Some of them even stand out in the middle of the street, holding up the traffic. We suppose they are mostly discussing politics. The cafés are crammed, too; and everybody has a newspaper, to quote from or simply wave in the air.

I have never seen so many bookshops anywhere. In addition to dozens of Latin American authors I have never heard of, they stock innumerable translations—anything from Plato to Louis Bromfield. Bogotá, of course, is famous for its culture. There is a saying —reported, I believe, by John Gunther—that here even the shoeshine boys quote Proust. It's nice to imagine one of them, brush in hand, pausing to remark: ". . . there is in love a permanent strain of suffering which happiness neutralizes, makes conditional only, procrastinates, but which may at any moment become what it would long since have been had we not obtained what we were seeking, sheer agony . . ."

Caskey pointed to a clothing-store window, in which there was a life-sized cardboard head of the Mona Lisa, wearing a rubber bathing-cap. "You see," he said, "they just can't *live* without Art in this town." Nevertheless, we had to admit that, in the States, the head would probably have been a professional cutie's.

We had barely returned to the hotel when Arturo arrived to take us out again—this time to the Monte Blanco, a big ice-cream and sandwich parlor where the junior smart set of Bogotá meets twice a day, at noon and five o'clock. Arturo seemed to know everybody in the place, including an American girl who sings in the night clubs and on the radio. She was friendly and self-assured, accepting Arturo's extravagant compliments for exactly as much as they were worth. I liked her good-humored toughness. She has been here for some while, and has evidently acquired a wide experience of the Latin American approach to women. It neither annoys nor impresses her.

We then walked over to have lunch with Arturo's sister and brother-in-law. On the way, Arturo met many more friends—at least one on each block. At lunch we were introduced to about a dozen relatives; aunts, uncles and cousins. Everybody was charming—but I couldn't help feeling overwhelmed by a claustrophobic sense of "family." Imagine what it would be like to get engaged to a Colombian girl!

In the evening, we went to a Bob Hope movie—a confession of failure. So far, despite Arturo's kindness, we have failed to make contact with Bogotá. We are homesick and bored. The weather doesn't help. Today, it is raining again and I sit shivering at the table in our huge bedroom, trying to force myself to write an article about the Magdalena River. Caskey, on such occasions, is much more resourceful than I am. Right now, he is cutting his toenails with great care, completely absorbed. Suddenly he looks up and says with his sleepy drawl: "Bogotá—it's gorgeous!" And we both start to laugh.

October 16.

A gap in this record, owing to the sudden expansion of our social lives. We have certainly made contact—with what, exactly, it's too early to say.

On Monday, we called at the U.S. Embassy and the British Cultural Institute. I am already beginning to realize my enormous advantage in being Anglo-American. No American, and few Englishmen, would take me for anything but a Britisher, yet I have lived long enough in the States to have developed a kind of bi-focal vision, and this, it seems, is now starting to operate. Indeed, there is a danger that I shall find the British and North Americans here *too* interesting and not be able to concentrate on the local inhabitants.

The British I see, essentially, as schoolmasters. That is to say, they have a vocation, a mission—to teach. To teach what? I suppose, in the nineteenth century, there were many people who would have answered, quite frankly and unblushingly: "The British Way of Life." All that has changed, now. The British official abroad nowadays is modest, subtle, apologetic, humorously self-critical. His manner is almost Chinese, and you half expect him to greet you with: "My poor country is honored . . ." Nevertheless, the sense of vocation persists—instinctively, subconsciously—and it reveals itself, now and then, in a little sigh and some such wistfully spoken phrase as: "What one *does* rather wish one could get the people here to realize is . . ." "The people here" never *will* realize, of course; he knows that. But he is very patient, and gently amused. Meanwhile he performs his unobtrusive national rituals, welcoming all who care to take part in them; and his presence infiltrates the community, like a tactful reproach.

The North American official is every inch a businessman. He represents his government just as he would represent a private firm. The President's photograph above his desk is simply a picture of the Boss. "What can I do for you?" he asks, and the offer is as genuine as his excellent teeth. He is all ready for business. He has goods to sell—the best goods in the world—and he will give you plenty of whisky while you make up your mind about buying them. The U.S. Constitution, for example—that's a product he can highly recommend. He knows it inside out and will explain to you exactly how it works, with sincere technical enthusiasm, as though it were a refrigerating plant. His frankness is very attractive. It will only become sinister if and when he develops into a conscious technocrat, ruthlessly determined to make the world safe for iceboxes. . . . Meanwhile, he goes cheerfully ahead with his promoting, and secretly rather despises the devious ways of the professional diplomats. Why beat about the bush? Why fuss with a lot of protocol? And why the hell talk French?

The American Cultural Institute here is simply a business college for Colombians who wish to work in the United States.

The British Cultural Institute is a complete little aquarium of British life. Upon entering, you plunge at once into the world of J. B. Priestley, Dylan Thomas, tweeds, terriers, buns and tea.

It was teatime when I arrived, so I met most of the teaching staff. I told them about my visit to England last winter—the blizzard, the Labor Government and the coal crisis, the latest rationing decrees, *The Winslow Boy* and *The White Devil*. It was all very snug and nostalgic and pleasant, and Bogotá faded into a mere backdrop—the view through the window of the Carrera Septima in the rain.

Nevertheless, it was here that I met Mr. Howard Rochester; he is a teacher at the Institute as well as being a lecturer at the University. Rochester is a Jamaican by birth, but he now lives permanently in Bogotá and is married to a Colombian lady. Slender and catlike, with a soft melodious voice and a small black beard, he moves gracefully about the room, dropping into and out of conversations, flashing his brilliant mischievous smiles—now lively and gossipy, now pedantic and earnest. If you mention a book or a writer he doesn't know, he frowns and looks badly worried; but this happens very seldom for he is incredibly well read, in three or four languages.

Everyone agrees that Rochester is the foreigner's ideal guide to Colombian culture. He knows nearly all the painters, writers and composers in town. Also, he is one of those rare people who really try to answer your questions. To hear him conscientiously struggling to evaluate the exact significance of some poet, you would think he was testifying on oath in a murder trial. He frowns painfully, clasping and unclasping his long fingers: "Could one say he is—fantastic? No . . . That's too strong. . . . Eccentric—not exactly eccentric . . . Odd? Quaint? No, no—he's not quaint. . . . Perhaps—yes, I think one could safely call him *capricious*. But please don't misunderstand me . . ."

The first person Rochester introduced us to was Edgardo Salazar Santacoloma, the essayist and political journalist. Salazar—we have already learned to avoid the mistake of using the mother's family name, which comes last—is a youngish man, around thirty, very thin, pale, cadaverous, ascetically good-looking. His body is tense with nervous energy. He wears dark glasses, and laughs in violent spasms. On Tuesday evening, Rochester invited Salazar, Caskey and myself to a bar for a *tertulia*—a real sit-down-and-drag-out discussion; *tertulias* are a great feature of Colombian literary life.

We started off on Shakespeare. How, for example, should Hamlet be presented on the stage? Rochester was all for authenticity: we should show Hamlet exactly as Shakespeare wrote him. The whole problem was to get back to the poet's original intention. I supported an opposite view: Hamlet belongs to everybody, and each of us has the right to interpret him according to our own taste and contemporary conditions, etc, etc. . . . Unfortunately, I lack the intellectual stamina necessary for prolonged argument. I prefer either to lecture or to listen; so the *tertulia*, as such, petered out and soon we were asking each other questions.

I wanted to know about literary movements. Rochester mentioned the *Piedracielistas*, the "Stone and Sky" Group. But he added that this wasn't, strictly speaking, a "movement" at all, and that it wasn't characteristically Colombian. The chief members of the Group—Arturo Camacho Ramirez, Jorge Rojas and Eduardo Carranza—have quite distinct styles and show different influences. As for the name *Piedra y Cielo*, it is taken from a volume by the Spanish poet Juan Ramón Jiménez: "Stone" refers symbolically to the things of earth and matter, "Sky" to the things of the spirit. I suppose the general aim was to employ extremely "concrete" words to describe abstract mental experiences—which is more or less what García Lorca does; but even Rochester seemed a little vague about this. Anyhow, the Piedracielistas are no longer quite modern; they belong to the thirties. The latest generation of writers have reacted in favor of traditionalism.

I asked about Colombian humor. Rochester thought it could be better described as wit or *esprit*. There is a good comic writer named Lukas Calderón, but it would be difficult to translate him because his work is full of topical allusions and puns—perhaps somewhat in the manner of the Viennese.

Salazar began to question me about my own books. When we got to the plays I wrote with Auden, I had to explain that there are mountains in the Himalayas which are known simply by their geographical survey numbers, such as "K.I."—hence our invention of "F.6." Salazar wrote in his notebook: "*Montañas Sin Nombre*," mountains without a name. I think this would make a beautiful title for a novel, if it hasn't been used already.

Rochester has also introduced us to León de Greiff, the poet,

to Otto de Greiff, his brother the musician, and to Eduardo
Zalamea Borda, the novelist. León is large and bearded and bohemian; one imagines him dominating an artists' café in Paris
and reciting his verses in a rich sonorous voice:

> "This woman is an urn
> Full of mystical perfume,
> Like Annabel, like Ulalume . . ."

Otto writes poetry, too. He has made a complete translation of
The Ancient Mariner. Here is the "water, water, everywhere"
stanza:

> Agua, por todas partes agua,
> y chirriaba el calor, en la borda;
> agua, por todas partes agua,
> y, para beber, ni una gota.

Zalamea has written a novel called *4 Años A Bordo De Mi
Mismo—Four Years Abroad Myself*. It is about life among the
Indians of the Guajira Peninsula, in the north of Colombia, and
is said to be extremely coarse in its language. So far, I have only
read the postcript which I will quote because it amuses me—although Zalamea crossed it out with his fountain pen before giving
me the book:

> I started to write this novel on Friday, May 9th, 1930, at 9
> o'clock at night, among noisy loungers, on a "Continental"
> typewriter of which I don't know the number. In the offices of
> La Tarde, 14th Street, Number 89.
> My work on it was interrupted for a long time and it was
> finished today, January 24th, 1932, at 11.30 at night, on an
> "Underwood" machine, number A23679867. 57th Street, num-
> ber 11. A dark night, gray and blue, starless, foggy. Wind SSW,
> low clouds, rejoicing, immense rejoicing! And for what?

I find Zalamea very sympathetic. He is vigorous and lively; not
at all "artistic" or refined. He keeps trying to lure me into making
indiscreet political remarks, but I am careful because I fear he will
print them. Yesterday he took me to the offices of *El Espectador*,
the liberal newspaper he works for, and introduced me to the editor, an elderly man whose name, I believe, is Luis Cano. The editor
made a great impression on me; he is one of those people whose

integrity is so evident that you feel touched and ashamed, and want to protect them. He asked me what my politics were. I answered that I was a Liberal, and immediately felt like a hypocrite—although this is approximately true—because it pleased him so much. "Let us hope that you will *die* a Liberal," he said, patting my shoulder.

These people we have met all seem to agree in regarding William Faulkner and John Dos Passos as the two best modern North American writers. Zalamea finds U.S. literature deeply pessimistic and ascribes this to the depressing effect of capitalism upon art in the States. However, he draws no such conclusions from the work of Sartre and Camus, both of whom are greatly admired here. Quite naturally, French culture is the ultimate criterion by which everything artistic is judged in this country; and I suspect that Colombians follow the French in thinking that the U.S.A. would do better to stick to writing crime stories and making automobiles.

A warning to writers who are planning a trip down here. Before you leave home, pack at least three dozen copies of your books; or, if that is too bulky and expensive, take a poem, a short story, a magazine article—it doesn't much matter what—and have it printed in pamphlet form. Otherwise, you will be as embarrassed as I am. Authors keep presenting me with inscribed volumes, and I have nothing to offer them in return.

The day before yesterday, Arturo and his sister drove us to the Falls of Tequendama. They are about thirteen miles from Bogotá, at the edge of the plateau, where the river drops 450 feet into the gorge below. This must be breathtaking in clear weather. But all we got were glimpses through the fog which kept rolling up the face of the precipice. Tequendama is a favorite spot for suicides—perhaps because there is something hypnotic about that great feather-bed of foam heaving over the rocks. A policeman with a dog is always on duty to prevent them. He sits forlornly beneath a palm-thatch shelter, with a pair of handcuffs dangling from his belt. Arturo asked him if he always knew which of the many visitors were planning to kill themselves. "Almost always," said the policeman. "And when I don't, my dog does." Some of the suicides don't give in without a violent struggle; finding themselves hand-cuffed to the policeman, they are apt to try to drag him with them into the water. It must be one of the world's most unpleasant jobs.

October 19.

In today's edition of *El Tiempo* there is a long account by Salazar of our conversation with Rochester. It says that Caskey, "throughout the entire discussion, listened with an imperturbable patience"—which is tactfully put. Actually, he was sitting there looking like an unplugged lamp. Since then, whenever I have a cultural date, he usually goes off to develop his negatives or wander with his camera around the streets.

This afternoon we went to the bullfights with Oswald Pope, a teacher at the British Institute who is a great *aficionado*. Pope took us to visit Paco Lara, one of the toreros, while he was dressing for the ring in his hotel bedroom. Lara is a Spaniard. Like many others, he fights in Latin America during the winter season. He and Alvarez Pelayo are the two popular stars in Bogotá this year.

Lara is a smallish, solidly built, handsome young man with dark wavy hair and a slight cast in one eye. Pope says that he is always terribly nervous before his fights. If this is so he has great control of himself, for he laughed and chatted gaily, only once showing a little tension when his dresser was too slow. The dresser is a slim dark-skinned youth who works for love, as a sort of acolyte, because he hopes to become a torero himself one day.

The dressing takes a long time and a lot of care. First, Lara puts on his undershirt—a torn one, for luck. Then a pair of skin-tight sky-blue breeches covered with sequins. These have to be tugged at and smoothed until they are perfectly adjusted. Then the pink clocked stockings. Then the artificial hair-piece which has taken the place of the traditional bullfighter's queue. Then the white frilled shirt. (At this point Lara pauses to kiss each of the ten or more holy medals which hang from a silver chain around his neck.) Then the narrow pink tie and the pink sash. Then the vest and the black pumps. Then, last of all, the jacket of heavy blue silk, wonderfully embroidered in silver braid, with a cross of black ribbons on the arm in memory of the torero Joselillo, recently killed in Mexico.

Throughout this process, Pope talked bullfighting shop with Lara, and Caskey took photographs. I merely watched, feeling as uncomfortable as you do in the presence of someone who is about to undergo a dangerous operation, and glad that my lack of Spanish excused me from speaking.

Lara's dressing table is covered with pictures of the Virgin and the saints. He had already lighted two candles in front of them, and now that he was dressed he would want to be left alone to pray. Pope had instructed us, on leaving, to wish him a great triumph. "Just mumble anything—speak English if you like—but say *triunfo* very distinctly."

Unfortunately, Lara didn't triumph today. He was unlucky with his bulls, which were all of poor quality. This made him angry, and so reckless that I hated to watch him. But Pelayo got most of the applause. He is tall and smooth-looking, more like a dance-band leader than a torero, but very skillful and very brave. He was badly gored in Spain this year, and is only just recovering. Pope went into raptures over the elegance of his passes with the cape. Pelayo has the air of literally playing with the bull, half absent-mindedly, as a grown-up plays with a child. One of his bulls was very good. After it was killed, it was dragged around the ring and cheered. The others ran about vaguely and wildly; one had explosive banderillas stuck into its back to pep it up, another wouldn't go through the cape at all and had to be coaxed out of the ring by cows. Pope says that the local bulls are usually of poor quality. He himself would like to start a farm and breed them, somewhere up here on the plateau.

I hope I shan't go to any more bullfights. Not because they are cruel or because they disgust me. Actually, I find them very exciting. But I would die of terror if I had to face a bull myself, and therefore I have no right to demand this spectacle. I despise myself for taking part in it, just as I despise the sadistic coward who yells at a beaten boxer in the ring. None of this applies to Pope, who has fought bulls himself and anyway takes a genuine technical interest in this sport. And it doesn't apply to the great majority of the people in this crowd today. To them, bullfighting comes as naturally as football. Almost any Colombian, if he sees a bull in a field, will strip off his coat and start making passes at it. The students of the Jesuit College hold a bullfight every year, and often someone gets gored. The head boy stands on a table in the middle of the ring, dressed in white. As long as he keeps his nerve and doesn't move a muscle, the bull won't touch him.

October 23.

Now that our stay in Bogotá is almost over, I must sort out some general impressions.

Certainly, we have enjoyed a wonderful amount of hospitality, both foreign and domestic. A dinner at the U.S. Embassy, where we met those two redoubtable professional travelers, Oden and Olivia Meeker; their efficiency makes me realize what a lazy amateur I am when it comes to fact-collecting. A memorable cocktail party in a penthouse, at which Caskey drastically improved U.S.-Colombian relations. And many lunches with all kinds of people, from the Principal of a girls' high school to the ex-Governor of a Department. I have tried to show my gratitude in the only way I can, by playing my part as a minor cultural object. I have been interviewed by three newspapers, spoken on the radio, and addressed a *tertulia* at the British Institute. The *tertulia* opened badly because I was nervous, but ended warmly because there were plenty of cocktails. Zalamea told me that I had "the eyes of absolute truthfulness," and we embraced repeatedly, somewhat to the surprise of Rochester who had apparently decided that I was the frigid British type.

Nevertheless, I feel that I shall remember Bogotá in an atmosphere of sadness. This has nothing to do with our hosts or our experiences. It is largely due to the weather. Everybody tells us that we picked the worst time of year to come here; it has rained, on and off, nearly every day. And the town itself is rather somber; the houses are seldom brightly painted and the inhabitants tend to dress in quiet dark colors. Then there is the altitude, which affects you in various mildly unpleasant ways: gas-pains, known as "Bogotá belly," or a tightness around the heart muscles, or a vague irrational sense of anxiety, as if you had forgotten some important obligation. In the mornings I feel tense, restless and uneasy; in the afternoons lazy, exhausted and sad.

Here are some miscellaneous facts and opinions which I noted down after various meetings and interviews. It is better to report them without mentioning names, in case I am misquoting. I think, on the whole, that the opinions fairly represent group attitudes, not merely the prejudice of individuals. All my informants were, as they say, "responsible" people. None of them, however, were members of Gaitán's party, so the remarks about him are necessarily one-sided.

I asked a Colombian Liberal: "What do you think of Gaitán? I've heard people call him a Communist. Is it true?"

"Certainly not. Gaitán has no clear political line. He's an opportunist. His models are Mussolini and Perón. He wants to create a Workers' Party on the Perón pattern. He'll probably be elected President, but he'll never be able to abolish our other political parties. Colombians wouldn't tolerate that. Colombia is essentially democratic."

"What's his foreign policy?"

"He is opposed to the United States. That shows how unrealistic he is. Colombia can't get along without the States; they are our chief customer—almost our only one. We are a semicolonial economy."

"Are Americans hated here?"

"I wouldn't go so far as that. I think most of us prefer the British, however. We always suspect the Americans of playing politics. Even their cultural attachés seem more interested in politics than in art and literature. They should send us a real writer, a poet. The French understand that. But then, I must admit, the French have practically no trade with Colombia. They can afford to be disinterested. . . . You probably read about the incident here, shortly before you arrived, when Washington protested to our Government against what it called the coffee-shipping monopoly and the U.S. Embassy windows were stoned? The U.S. officials were very sensible. They didn't make any fuss. And our newspapers deplored the whole affair. Just the same, the demonstration represented very real and strong feeling; not only on the part of the students—they are a great political force here—but also of the small business men. There is a special resentment, I think, against the oil companies. It is said that they are taking our oil and hoarding it, in case the United States should get into a war."

"Are the Russians powerful here?"

"No. And they haven't a chance of becoming so. They can't get any trade started here. Washington sees to that. As for our Communist Party, it is split from top to bottom, into two factions. People say Washington is responsible for that, too. American agents infiltrated the labor unions and caused dissension."

Later, I quoted this remark to an American official, who

róared with laughter. "I only wish we were that smart!" he said: "No . . . the Communist Party split, as they often do, on a question of tactics. One side wanted to go all out, as aggressively as possible; the others were for caution and diplomacy. They haven't much direct influence, anyway. But if some agitation gets started they'll run to the head of the procession, make speeches and try to convince everybody that they're leading it. That's what happened the other day, when we got our windows smashed. . . . The way they talk about Washington, you'd think it was some kind of a totalitarian political bureau, owned and operated by Wall Street. And all this stuff about Yankee Imperialism! If Colombians would get together and work out a reasonable economic plan, and extend taxes to finance it, they could have all the foreign capital they wanted. The present income-tax is a farce. And the labor unions aren't properly run. The leaders don't do enough for the men. They have no schools to make them into more efficient workers. There's even a sort of class system: the workers who get paid by the month look down on the day-laborers. . . . Yes, of course, there's some anti-American feeling. Under the circumstances, it's very natural. Colombians see U.S. goods and services and firms everywhere. They benefit from them but they don't like them, because they feel it reflects on their own lack of enterprise; they ought to be running things themselves. Well, one day they will . . ."

I talked to several Colombians about the next American elections. All of them wished that Henry Wallace might become President. He is still immensely popular here. "But we hear," said one of them, "that Eisenhower may be running. Do you think he could win?"

"It's quite possible."

"That would be the worst thing that could happen."

"What makes you think so?"

"He is a general. . . . Of course, that may not mean quite the same thing in the States, I admit. In Latin America, we always distrust the Army. We have good reason to. Colombia is actually much better, in this respect, than most other countries. Here we have such a reverence for law and order that nobody dare go very far beyond it. On one occasion, some Army officers went to the President and ordered him to resign. They had the document ready, but the President, to gain time, pretended he had lost the official seal. The rebels quite agreed that the resignation would not be legal without it, so they all started hunting around the palace, and meanwhile loyal troops arrived and the rebellion failed. . . . Another time, when part of the Army was attempting a *coup d'état*, the rebels wanted to concentrate their men in the Plaza Bolívar. To do this, they needed trucks. The truck-drivers demanded payment in advance, in cash. So an officer went across to the bank with a check. "We're very sorry," the cashier told him, "but we are not allowed to cash any checks because a State of Emergency has been declared." So that rebellion failed too. . . . That's the value of our traditions. Take away our traditions, and we have nothing. We should become another Bolivia."

"What part does the Church play politically?"

"The Church is less important, politically, than it used to be, but it is trying hard to regain its power. The Archbishop and most of the bishops are anti-Franco. The smaller clergy are mostly in favor of him, but that's only due to their ignorance. During the Civil War, the great majority of Colombians supported the Spanish Republican Government. . . . The Church is inclined to disapprove of the United States, because they are thought to set a bad moral example. Your sex life is much freer than ours, and the young people find this attractive. . . . Many of us Liberals would like to see the creation of a national Catholic Church, independent of Vatican politics, but I don't think that's likely to happen at present."

"Do you think there is a possibility of woman's suffrage in Colombia?"

"The Conservatives are in favor of it, because they know that most women would vote for them. We Liberals know this, also. I'm afraid that is the reason why—although we support woman's suffrage in theory—we never do anything about it."

I asked a visiting British educationalist his opinion of Colombian culture. "Of course," he said, "it's pretty much limited to the big cities. Your Colombian intellectual's a great quoter. It's hard for him to think independently. He reads a lot of foreign stuff—particularly French. But when it comes to the literature of the other Latin American countries, he's inclined to be insular. As for the rest of the reading public, literacy's a very new thing for them; their choice of books is indiscriminate. You've noticed all the bookshops? That's because they have no lending libraries here; you've got to buy. The market's flooded with cheap Argentine translations, mostly in very bad Spanish. Comparatively little gets published here; but they do have one very good scientific journal, with excellent printing and color plates. There's a shortage of textbooks. The best ones come from Mexico. . . . Before things get better in the country districts, you've got to find more teachers—at present, they can't be persuaded to leave the towns. And you've got to improve the children's diet. There's a lot of malnutrition. The peasants eat too many starches. If they have milk, they don't give it to their kids, they sell it. When they fall sick, they go to the local medicine man. None of these chaps have licences, of course—there are very few qualified doctors—but some of them are amazingly skillful. They'll always start by examining your urine, no matter what's wrong. They haven't any anesthetics, so they do their surgery without; tell you to watch that bird outside the window, and then take your finger off with a chopper. Luckily, most of their patients have very strong constitutions. . . ."

October 24.

This afternoon, we leave. Two of our Bogotá friends, Pablo Rocha and Steve Jackson, are driving us down to a winter resort called Apulo, at the foot of the mountains. We shall stay there a day or two, and then continue our journey by train. Pablo Rocha is an architect. He went to a British public school—Harrow, I think—and speaks perfect English; since then, he has traveled a great deal. He looks like an aristocratic polo-player, has beautiful manners, and is very hospitable and kind. Steve Jackson is a large good-humored relaxed American boy who has spent some time in this country working as an interior designer. Both of them can be extremely funny and silly on suitable occasions, and I'm sure we shall enjoy making this trip with them.

Salazar has just visited us. He brought with him an ivory paper-knife as a farewell present, and a recording-machine, into which he asked me to read a somewhat embarrassing passage from one of my novels. During this operation Caskey packed our bags, with the expression of one who is forced by circumstances to be present at an abortion but is determined to see, hear and know nothing of what takes place.

the road to ecuador

THE DRIVE DOWN to Apulo began very pleasantly. We were all in good spirits; and even a flat tire, which had to be changed on the road a little below Tequendama, didn't do much to spoil them. After it was fixed, we zig-zagged rapidly around the descending curves of the mountain, through successive zones of agriculture; maize on the higher slopes, coffee beneath, and sugar-cane in the deep valleys. Coming down from the plateau is much more agreeable than going up, because it is a process of physical relaxation. The tropical atmosphere steals soothingly upon your senses. You begin to breathe easily, inhaling warm rich vegetable odors.

It was already night when we reached the side road which leads to Apulo. Most people come down here by train, and this road is no more than a neglected trail, boggy and rough, with a big rocky hump in the middle. After a mile or two of cautious bumping, the battery was abruptly knocked from underneath the car, out went our lights and we stopped. There followed one of those experiences which everybody gallantly conspires to pretend are lots of fun: a long muddy tramp in the dark to the hotel, help to be fetched, bags to be carried, and a late weary bed without supper.

The Hotel Apulo is large, and the Casino opposite has highly chic interior decoration, including a bar made of sea shells; but this grandeur seems vulgar and heartless in contrast to the dirty poverty of the village. The natural surroundings are delightful, however; birds and flowers everywhere, the rapid river winding through the woods, the old stone bridge to the island where the women wash their clothes. We have spent most of our time here lying beside the hotel swimming pool, except when the hot sunshine is interrupted by short violent showers. Pablo Rocha pointed out one of our fellow-guests as "the man who brought the *bidet*

60

to Colombia." Last night, we went to the movies. The screen
was out of doors in a back yard; we watched it from the upper story
of a tumbledown house which formed the auditorium. Clark
Gable barked Spanish at Jean Harlow through the lurid episodes
of *China Seas*.

October 28.

Yesterday morning at half past nine, we said good-bye to
Pablo and Steve and got on board the *autoferro*, for Ibagué. The
autoferro is a diesel-driven coach which runs on the railroad tracks
and is much quicker than the ordinary train. The railroad doesn't
cross the central cordillera; you have to hire a car from Ibagué
to Armenia, where the line begins again. The top of the pass is
11,000 feet; it was foggy up there and very cold. You come down
the other side into the Cauca Valley, which is considered to be
one of the most fertile and beautiful places in Colombia. We
didn't see much of it, unfortunately. By the time we left Armenia,
it was already nearly dark. We got to Cali around nine o'clock at
night.

Pablo Rocha had advised us to stay at the Hotel Alférez Real.
When we arrived, we were disconcerted to find the doors guarded
by police and a big crowd assembled outside. A banquet was being
given in honor of Gaitán, and we had to hurry through our meal,
before this started. Then we went up to a balcony above the dining
room and watched the proceedings. Gaitán, in action, is every
inch the criminal lawyer. When he speaks, you can well imagine
him defending a client; the controlled voice slowly and deliberately gathering volume, the slight economical gestures indicating
a vast reserve of arguments and a polite contempt for the prosecution's case. Again and again, during his speech, some enthusiastic
supporter would shout his name. Gaitán winced at these interrup-
tions, and extended his hand to check them. His pained yet
pleased manner seemed to say: "Thank you, thank you—but this
is really unnecessary. And embarrassing. My opponents will think
you are on my payroll. . . ."

This hotel is almost on the edge of town, in the modern business district. From our window, we look across the river, which
rushes loudly over a weir and big rocks, to a park and a white
apartment building with electric signs advertising Croydon rubber
shoes and Camel cigarettes. Behind are the green hills with a few

residential villas on their lower slopes. Forty years ago, Cali was still the same four-hundred-year-old village which the Conquistadores had founded. Sewage still ran along gutters in the streets, and the population lit their houses with candles.

At breakfast this morning we were greeted by the unexpected appearance of Salazar. He has just flown in from Tumaco, a little island far down the coast near the Ecuadorean frontier, where a fire, a few days ago, almost completely destroyed the town. Salazar and a friend have been interviewing the survivors. Now he wants to talk to Gaitán. In a few weeks he'll be off to New York. He is always hopping around like this, it seems; skimming insecurely in tiny planes over the mountains. Like most Colombians, he is recklessly air-minded.

Today he took us to see the San Francisco church and monastery. The inside of the church is modern and ugly, but it has an old Spanish-Moorish tower, a mudéjar, which is supposed to be the only one in Latin America. In the monastery, they have paintings of former abbots and monks, crude and extraordinarily expressive, with a boldness of characterization which is almost as indiscreet as caricature. There are tame myna birds in the cloisters; one of them can whistle the opening bars of Eine Kleine Nachtmusik. We were taken to visit a monk who is 103 years old. He lay resting on the pallet in his cell, a rosary in his hands. Our guide told us that he had been a businessman, and had only entered the Order when he was forty-five. There he lay, big and heavy, with a pale blotched face and a queer smell, something like an ancient book. He seemed perfectly contented. And he had that air, which is so mysterious and awe-inspiring in the very old, of waiting. "If I will that he tarry till I come. . . ." As we left, he uttered a loud belch.

In the afternoon Salazar drove us, with two girl cousins, to the Country Club. It is an elegant place, in quite good taste (hacienda style) except for a hideous yellow pergola. On the way, we passed a hospital, half-built. A portrait-bust in front of it was already overgrown with weeds. Public works seem to take a long time, here.

At lunch today in one of the city's grandest restaurants, we ate, against our better judgment, some kind of bluish-black meat which reminded me of the "strange flesh" referred to in Antony and Cleopatra, "which some did die to look on." It has already made

Caskey sick—and when Caskey admits he is sick, that really means something. He is one of Nature's Christian Scientists.

October 29.

With Salazar to see Dr. Buenaventura, an old gentleman who has turned his house into a private museum. The most tiresome thing about public museums is their necessary neatness; only a private collector can afford the luxury of utter confusion. In a place like this you are never bored, because you never know what you will find next. A gold Incaic ritual mask lies between an instrument from a wrecked airplane and a necklace of human teeth. A signed photograph of General de Gaulle confronts two religious paintings made with colored earth by the soldiers of the Conquistadores. A pair of Bolívar's pistols are displayed beside one of the earliest American sewing machines. There are also coins, Chinese fans, poisoned arrows and blowpipes, bits of clothing belonging to famous Colombians, autographed books, geological specimens, stamps. And there is an Indian mummy—the only one in existence with perfectly preserved male sexual organs. Its hands, according to custom, are raised to its mouth, so that it can eat.

In addition, Dr. Buenaventura has huge archives of state papers and other documents covering the whole period back to the Spanish Conquest. These include letters written by every one of the Colombian Presidents. He speaks with extraordinary knowledge of past generations, and even told Salazar of relationships in his own family which he didn't know about.

November 1.

Caskey spent the day before yesterday in bed, until suppertime, when he began to feel better. Salazar helpfully tried to arrange for us to fly to Popayán by a local air line. I was relieved when we were warned that this would be dangerous, because the winds were bad, and later told that it would be impossible, because the airfield at Popayán is flooded. The small air-lines have a very good safety-record in this country, and the pilots are said to show great skill in making forced landings; but just the same I'd rather be excused. . . .

Salazar also hired musicians, so that we could hear some native music. They were to come up to our room and play for us during the evening. This was certainly a charming gesture—though impractical; not unnaturally, the hotel manager objected. So Salazar sent the musicians off to serenade one of his girl friends.

Yesterday morning early, we left for Popayán on the *auto-ferro*. I felt terrible even before we started, and soon I was seized with the most violent stomach-cramps I have ever had in my life. Diarrhea and vomiting, often simultaneous, kept me in the toilet throughout most of the three-and-a-half-hour journey, with only occasional glimpses of the scenery, which was very beautiful.

One of our fellow-travelers was the girl who had just been elected Miss Cauca Department in a beauty contest. When we arrived at Popayán, there was a large crowd waiting to welcome her, including the Governor, troops, police and a band. The Governor has just returned from Cali, where he was staying at the Alférez Real. I'd met him there already, through Salazar. This was a real mercy, because, although somewhat harassed by his official duties, he found time to put us in charge of a police officer. Bent double with pain, like some hunchback of evil omen, I was hurried through the merrymakers and thrust into a cab, which got us into town well ahead of Miss Cauca's procession. The Governor had already reserved a room for us at the Hotel Lindbergh. I went straight to bed.

We had visitors, almost immediately. The first was Maestro Baldomero Sanín Cano, whom I should have mentioned earlier in this diary, because I first met him in Bogotá; he came to the *tertulia* at the British Institute and made me a speech of welcome. Sanín Cano is usually addressed as "Maestro" in deference to his position as the senior critic of Colombian letters. He is in his seventies but still immensely active and vigorous, though a little deaf. He reads all the latest writers, and his opinions about them are downright and unhesitating. He also continues to produce innumerable essays on all kinds of literary and historical subjects. His home is now here in Popayán. Need I add that he was born in Antioquia?

Next came Dr. Gregorio Hernández de Alba, head of the Ethnological Institute of the University of Popayán, and Dr. John Rowe, his colleague, from the Smithsonian Institution. As a matter of fact, I had a letter of introduction to Hernández from Lincoln Kirstein, but he didn't know this when he called; their visit was prompted by pure kindness, because they had heard that an American was lying sick in town. They sent me an English-speaking doctor named Guillermo Angulo, who cured me in a few hours with some stuff called, I think, *Enterovioformo*.

Kirstein described Hernández as "the man who invented ethnology in Colombia." He is in his thirties, slender and birdlike. He lived for some years in Paris, and acted as Colombian Consul there during the Nazi invasion and part of the occupation. Rowe is younger. He wears glasses, and looks like the nicer kind of American scoutmaster. Today, the two of them left for Silvia, a neighboring village, where they and some of their students are going to study an Indian All Souls Day festival. They have asked us to come out there on Monday and join them.

This morning, we walked in the town with Sanín Cano. He talked about the time he spent in England, before and during the 1914–18 War, when he taught Spanish literature at the University of Edinburgh and compiled an Anglo-Spanish pocket-dictionary. "Those were the happiest days of my life," he said. Actually, there is something rather British about his appearance; with his strong bulldog features and his walking-stick, he reminds me of a country squire. If there were a squire of Popayán, he would certainly be it; everyone here knows him and greets him deferentially as he passes.

This is a very attractive town—much the nicest place we have been in, so far. The streets are wide and clean, with comparatively little traffic. You hear the trotting of a pony as often as an automobile horn. There are a lot of university students strolling around, with books under their arms. The entrance to the University is right opposite our hotel, beside an old stone fountain and an eighteenth-century church. Nearly all the churches here are old, but many of them have been spoiled by tasteless modern additions and renovations; cheap statuary, commercial religious prints, imitation marble, imitation wood, cardboard cherubim and clouds. The intention is evidently devout; each new priest feels that he should contribute something extra. Actually, these buildings could only be beautified by drastic housecleaning.

Sanín Cano took us to see the home of his great friend, the poet Guillermo Valencia, who died in 1943. Valencia's work is dignified and melodious, somewhat in the manner of Robert Bridges. He wrote a famous ode to Popayán, and translated *The Ballad of Reading Gaol*. The patio of his house is entirely carpeted with growing violets. We walked through the lofty formal rooms, all opening into each other and furnished with stiff-backed Spanish chairs and family portraits. It is hard to imagine a man writing poetry there; perhaps the place has become dehumanized since his death. His study is a little more personal, however—despite the busts of Beethoven, Goethe and Wagner. There is a picture of D'Annunzio, Valencia's particular hero; and a nauseating lithograph of angels bearing away the souls of Christians martyred in the Roman arena, which at least proves that the Maestro wasn't ashamed to like what he liked. There is also an absurd but charming doll of the baby Christ, resting inside a split log lined with satin. This was presented by some local admirers. The shelves are full of French books. Sanín Cano says that Valencia was more influenced by French literature than by Spanish.

This afternoon, Caskey and I walked up the hill behind the town. To the north, east and south, the broken green plain is bounded by mountains. Somewhere hidden in the clouds is Puracé, a 16,000-foot volcano which smokes all the time, though it very rarely erupts. Last year, there were severe earthquake shocks here, but no loss of life. Seen from above, Popayán's blocks of houses fit together like a puzzle; long gray-tiled rectangles which convey the idea of ordered security, silence and sleep. This is a wonderfully peaceful landscape; like New England with exotic vegetable touches—the sharp-leaved fibrous agave, the feathery bamboo, the palm. And the altitude (between five and six thousand feet) is just right for the tropics; it produces perpetual mild summer weather.

This evening, Miss Cauca Department was crowned in one of the local movie-theaters. Most of the population turned out to watch the procession. There was much joking and good-humored jostling, but very little applause. People just stared. Perhaps the ceremony was too formal for the popular taste. It is a pity they didn't have a band. Miss Cauca walked between two officers with drawn swords, attended by six maids of honor with bouquets. A tall girl, pretty but not beautiful, smiling shyly and self-consciously. She wore a blue silk hood over her hair, which was a mistake, because you couldn't see her very well. Nearly all the guests were in evening clothes. After the coronation the Governor gave a party. We were invited, but didn't go. Our suits needed cleaning too badly.

November 4.

Yesterday we hired a car and drove up to Silvia to meet Hernández and Rowe. It is a summer resort, two or three thousand feet higher than Popayán, in an upland valley at the end of a narrow mountain road. The fiesta had started already by the time we arrived, but we found them without any trouble, for all the Indians were concentrated in and outside a big church on the square, and Rowe and Hernández were going around among them asking questions and taking notes.

"I'd like to burn this place to the ground," said Rowe bitterly, and he went on to explain that Silvia is a parasite community; it lives by overcharging the tourists and cheating the Indians. The Indians built the original town and were only turned out of it a little over a hundred years ago. The townspeople, who regard themselves as pure whites, look down on them, and would even like to break up their reservations, although they depend on the food the Indians produce.

These Indians are Guambia—formerly a very warlike race which violently resisted the Spaniards and was never entirely conquered. They live high in the mountains and work hard at farming. Rowe says they are still extremely independent; they like to be different from their neighbors. Ten years ago, the men started wearing kilts or skirts, largely because the authorities in Silvia had said they must come to town in pants. They always vote Liberal, because most other peasants vote Conservative.

The men have short glossy black hair, shocked up into an untidy tuft, and lively impudent black eyes. Some look strikingly Mongolian. Their mouths are a bit apelike. They smile readily and don't in the least mind if you examine their ornaments or their clothes.

Fashions in dress change frequently. At present, the men go hatless or wear town-made felts, but they make the hats for their women out of reeds. These are flat-crowned dish-shaped affairs, with a colored zig-zag pattern and tassels, held on by red strings at the back of the head. They must be very awkward to keep in place. They are always tilting crooked.

In exchange for the hats, the women make the men's black blanket-capes, or *ruanas*. They themselves wear cloaks of a deep bright blue with a cherry-red border, and wide black skirts. They have earrings and beads, as well as a whole bunch of silver crucifixes and ornaments hung around their necks under the cloak. These things are made in Silvia, where the Indians buy them for many times their value, along with household pots and pans.

There is a Franciscan convent school here, with a Swiss priest and nuns in charge of it. I talked to one of the nuns, who took a dim view of the Guambia. "They're pagans, really," she said. Technically speaking, this is no doubt true. They still make a cult of a legendary hero named Juan Tama, the Son of the Morning Star, who became chief of all the Indians and ended his term on earth by disappearing into a lake. Until recently, members of the Guambia community councils had to go in turn to the shores of this lake and spend one week there, to render an account to Juan Tama of their actions while in office. Also, they believe in witchcraft, evil spirits and the supernatural powers of certain animals and birds. A rooster crowing before daybreak is fatal to the hearer. The box turtle follows those who are about to die. If you strike a white dog, it will bite you later, in the after-life. When a rainbow appears, you must stay indoors and spit tobacco at it.

Most feared of all are the ghosts of the dead, and this gives the All Souls festival a special significance; it is a blend of Indian and Christian beliefs. The ceremony has nothing to do with individual grief. Rowe says that the Guambia mourn their family losses sincerely, without external show. But All Souls is a communal event, a social act of propitiation, and it is quite cheerful.

Each woman brings with her a little fiber bag containing bread, onions and potatoes. They arrange these on the floor of the church, and sit down around them in large circles, chatting and smiling, as though a meal were being prepared. On the piles of food they set lighted candles, one for each member of the family who has died within the past ten years. Meanwhile, the men crowd around the priest, waiting to pay for requiem masses and prayers. As each payment is made, the donor's name is called and a bell is rung.

Caskey was busy taking photographs, so I sat down on the floor among them and started writing in my notebook. Several people collected to watch, interested and quite friendly. Then the Swiss priest said some prayers. And the local Colombian priest preached a sermon—his second that morning. Rowe told me that the priest, in his first sermon, had informed the Guambia that they were better and more civilized than other Indians because they spoke Spanish. This was a stupid compliment, anyway, and it proved to be quite untrue. For the women had taken off their hats, and when the priest told them that this was unsuitable they obviously didn't understand him, and did nothing until their own mayor got up and translated. As soon as the Swiss priest began praying, off came their hats again. But, when the Colombian priest started his second sermon, every head was immediately covered.

The sermon was mostly a sales-talk about the forthcoming Church feasts—how nice they were and how much they would cost. There was also an attack on the Protestants, who were accused of not believing in the after-life and therefore not caring for the souls of their dead. Rowe said that this attack was really aimed at Mr. Smith, a Canadian Protestant missionary who has settled here and made some converts. As a matter of fact, attendance this year was smaller than usual; only about two hundred Indians came to the services. The Guambia blamed this on their poor potato-crop, saying that they couldn't afford the necessary offerings. It seems more likely that they are simply getting tired of Catholicism because it is so expensive. Perhaps they will turn to the Protestants, who are much cheaper. Perhaps they will go back for a time to their own cults, and later develop into orthodox Marxian atheists.

The onions and potatoes are being sold at the market today— the proceeds going to the Church. After the market, the Guambia take their bread back with them up to the reservation, where they hold a week's fiesta—their big holiday of the year. They drink fermented sugar-cane juice, chew coca, feast, dance, sing, and masquerade as various characters—including, I hope, the priest. Rowe says that their impersonations of white men are incredibly funny. But they will never impersonate any animal, lest they should be reborn as animals in the next world.

As we were coming out of the church, one of the Indians began to tease me, shouting, "Alemán! Nuremberg! Truman!" No doubt these were just words someone had read to him out of a newspaper; but, to my chronically guilty conscience, they sounded like an accusation. From the Indian point of view, no doubt, all whites are equally responsible for all the trouble in the world. However, everybody laughed pleasantly—so I laughed, too.

We ate lunch at an inn with Hernández, Rowe and some of their students. One of these was a Negro; another was a Guambia

Indian who is living in Popayán to help Rowe prepare a dictionary of their language. The Indian boy is a remarkable artist; he has made a lot of drawings to illustrate the meanings of words. The innkeeper made no objection to having the Negro eat with us, but the Indian had to eat in the kitchen. Later, we were joined by Mr. Smith, the Protestant missionary. He is a lively youngish man who wears a startling check suit and doesn't seem either worried or annoyed by the disapproval of the Catholics. After lunch, Hernández drove back with us to Popayán.

We had supper with Sanín Cano and Señorita Luz Valencia, one of the poet's daughters, at Bella Casa, a rambling old house just outside the town which used to be Valencia's country home. Luz Valencia is beautiful, and a charming person; we were both sorry that our Spanish and her English couldn't quite be stretched to make a conversation. However, Sanín Cano did enough talking for everybody. He is full of opinions and anecdotes. In Bogotá, he says, the milk was always sold diluted with water. One day, a pure-milk dairy was started but soon went bankrupt. It had been deliberately ruined by the directors of the water-works, who feared a serious drop in water-consumption. He also told us about a priest who collected Indian languages, and finally discovered a language which was spoken by only one man.

Today we visited the University and the High School. There are scarcely any real universities in Colombia; only professional schools, where they teach engineering, law, and sometimes medicine. Hernández wants to see the teaching of social ethnology extended to all parts of the country. Until this is done, he says, there will be no practical understanding of Colombia's acute racial problems, and hence no efficient social legislation. At present, he lacks field-workers; but soon he will have more of them and a much larger school, for the University is building new blocks in the suburbs. I think he is a wonderful man—one of those people, rare enough in any country, who are both able and disinterested enough to get the right things done in the right way, and thereby prove that greed and ignorance and stupidity aren't as hopelessly formidable as they sometimes seem.

The University has started several interesting museums—including one for ethnological studies, where we saw the small gold fish-hooks which are still used by some Indian tribes; and one for natural history, where I was surprised to learn that Colombia has its own rattlesnakes. At the High School we were introduced to the English Professor and had a long conversation with him, amidst a critical audience of his pupils. I felt terribly anxious for him, but I needn't have been. He didn't make a single mistake.

November 5.

Going into a bookstore this afternoon, I met Sanín Cano and Luz Valencia. She had been buying us some of her father's poems. Sanín Cano gave me his pocket-dictionary and a volume of his essays. The essays cover an astonishing amount of subjects: Alfred Polgar, Samuel Butler, Germán Arciniegas, Lord Northcliffe, Giosuè Carducci, Wilfrid Blunt, Georg Brandes, the Argentine Theater. As usual, I was humiliated—having nothing to give in return. Auden could have sat down and dashed them off a couple of sonnets.

We had coffee in the back of the shop, which is apparently one of Sanín Cano's favorite haunts. Presently we were joined by an American from Seattle, who is writing a thesis on "The Pure Indian in Colombian Literature." His findings: that nearly all of this literature treats the Indian as a picturesque curiosity, remote from Colombian life; that the best novel on the subject is *Andágueda*, by Jesús Botero Restrepo; that Zalamea's book is "dirtier than Zola."

Supper with John Rowe and his wife. They live in a suburban row of villas on the edge of town. Their cook has two children by a boy in the near-by drugstore. They aren't married, and he pays nothing toward their support, but she doesn't seem to mind.

Rowe gave us two monographs he has written—one on Inca Culture at the time of the Spanish Conquest, the other on the distribution of Indians and Indian languages in Peru. The great point he makes is that the Indians are still a nation—the Inca Nation. More of this later.

He also talked about the Motilones, the jungle Indians who live up near the Venezuelan frontier. They are hostile and very dangerous to all travelers. Recently, a missionary who was planning to go into the forest decided that he would have a better chance with the Motilones if he introduced himself in advance. So he had his photo taken, and hundreds of copies of it dropped all over the area by plane. The result of this experiment isn't yet known, as the missionary hasn't been heard of since.

After supper, we went with the Rowes to the Orféon Obrero, the local academy of music, where they were giving a program of folk-songs and dances. The performers were mostly working-class men and women who only have time to study in the evenings. They are certainly a credit to Maestro Pazos, their teacher. The singers usually began by humming the tune or vocalizing it without words. In one song, about the pan-pipes, they produced a weirdly beautiful effect by whistling. The orchestra was made up of drums, ocarinas and guitars.

There was one simple country dance which we all liked. It was performed by a single couple, a boy and a girl, and consisted chiefly of stamping, clapping and turns, shoulder to shoulder. Their bodies never touched, but the general effect was charmingly sexual and gay. The rest of the dancing was less interesting because less authentic. It represented the history and life of the forest Indians, in the form of a ballet. An Indian chief fires his last arrow at the Conquistadores, sinks down wounded and dies. A group of Indians drink a drug which produces visions, and go into a religious frenzy. This was noisy and energetic rather than impressive, and we weren't much surprised to learn that the chief dancer was famous for his impersonation of Carmen Miranda.

November 6.

Here we are in Pasto.

We left Popayán at five-thirty this morning, in a bus which was actually a truck full of wooden benches. The benches weren't fastened down—they didn't have to be; compact wedges of passengers held them firmly in place. We were more comfortable than the rest, however, because Rowe had somehow managed to reserve us the seats next to the driver.

The distance from Popayán to Pasto is 175 miles. This doesn't seem much to cover in a thirteen-hour ride—until you see the country. First there is the descent into the hot lowlands around El Bordo. Then the long grinding climb to La Unión, perched on its sheer-sided ridge. From there on in, the terrain resembles violently crumpled bedclothes. You enter tremendous valleys, and foresee twenty miles of your journey at a glance, for the road is scribbled wildly across them. The tilled fields on the opposite mountain-face look nearly vertical. The racing bus creaks and rolls like a boat amidst its clouds of dust. At the blind precipice-corners, with nothing but empty air ahead, I kept remembering the lines from *Casey Jones*:

> *He pulled up short two miles from the place,*
> *Number Four stared him right in the face,*
> *Turned to his fireboy, said "You'd better jump*
> *'cause there's two locomotives that's going to bump!"*

"Number Four" never actually did appear, though we had several breathtaking squeezes. Others, before us, had been less lucky. All along the way, you see crosses which mark the spot where someone went over the edge.

At length, long after dark, when your head swims and your back aches and you no longer care—you come over the top of a final pass, and there are the lights of Pasto in a shallow hollow below. Now we're resting after a good dinner at the Hotel Pacifico, a clean place, run by Germans. Tomorrow, we cross into Ecuador —that is, if the road isn't washed out. No one here seems to know definitely about this. They'll only go so far as to say it might be, considering the time of year.

November 8.

Yesterday morning, while we were walking in the town, we were accosted by a little man in a seedy black suit. "Psst!" he called after us, "Psst! Psst!" This Latin American noise never fails to irritate me, and anyhow we both took him for a guide or a pimp or a seller of something unwanted, so we shook our heads and ignored him. But now two other men appeared. They began chattering and plucking excitedly at our sleeves. I recognized the word "*Seguridad*," but it never occurred to me that these nagging pests could really be plain-clothes detectives. On the contrary, I feared that this was some kind of a trick which local crooks played on foreigners—perhaps a trumped-up accusation which would have to be settled with bribes. To avoid them, we went into a church where there were gaudy modern pictures representing the results of the Seven Deadly Sins.

When we came out again we were arrested, not forcibly but quite firmly, by a uniformed policeman with a bleak Indian face. He asked for our passports. We told him they were at the hotel. Then we must come to police headquarters. But couldn't we pick up our passports on the way? No. Why? Orders from his superiors.

Our journey so far has been so free of such incidents that I had almost forgotten to worry about them. When we registered in Bogotá we were told that the affair was settled, we needn't report our presence anywhere else in the country. In an hour and a half, we were due to leave on the mail-car for the frontier. I tried to prepare my mind for the worst; a big fine, probably. Or maybe even a week in jail, while they wrote Bogotá for instructions.

The people at headquarters were quite friendly, however. My desperation and my awful Spanish rather amused them. We were escorted back to the hotel, re-escorted to the police station. Our passports were passed from hand to hand, examined like priceless etchings, stamped and counter-stamped. Entries were made in ledgers. Names and numbers were copied with snail-like care. At the end of an hour we were free—and not one centavo to pay! Once again, I marveled at the zeal of officialdom, which will put itself and its victims to such pains for pure disinterested love of the regulations.

The mail-car arrived nearly two hours late, with one other passenger, a girl, who sat beside the driver. They started kissing and squeezing hands almost at once. We watched their love-making benevolently at first, happy to be on our way, in glorious weather, amidst magnificent scenery. But when, at Túquerres, the lovers retired into a hotel "to drink coffee" and didn't emerge for an hour, I began to get anxious. I asked what time the Ecuadorean frontier closed, explaining that we wanted to reach Tulcán that night. This, it seemed, was news to the driver. He had supposed we were only going as far as Ipiales, on the Colombian side. He agreed to hurry.

Nevertheless, it was close on five o'clock when we arrived in Ipiales, only to meet another obstacle; our baggage had to be passed through a customs office in the town before we could leave for the frontier. Meanwhile, our driver disappeared. We had barely half an hour to spare. We hired another car and made a dash for it.

Ecuador and Colombia are separated, at this point, by the Rio Carchi. The frontier post stands on a natural bridge, where the river gorge is pinched into a bottleneck. Behind it, Ecuador towers into the sky, a tumultuous and forbidding wilderness of mountains. Travelers have been using this road for hundreds of years.

We soon found that all our haste had been in vain. The real

customs and passport examination, we were told, took place in Tulcán and the offices wouldn't be open until tomorrow morning. Worse still, the only bus from Tulcán to the south left at 4 A.M., which would mean one day's delay under any circumstances. Worst of all, this was a Friday evening, and no bus ran on Sunday. No one knew of a private car which could be hired; and anyhow, it was agreed, this would be fabulously expensive. We seemed condemned to stay in Tulcán over the week end.

Last night, that looked like a horrible prospect. The town, which stands at over 9,000 feet, was dreary, dirty and icy cold. A few streets around its main square were dimly lighted, the rest were in total darkness. The only bright cheerful spot was a liquor store; but we didn't want to change our dollars at the local rates and hadn't enough Colombian pesos to spare for whisky.

We were put down at the Hotel Granada, a shabby wooden building with inside balconies around a central dining room. The bedrooms are like stables. Windowless, with great barn-doors closed by padlocks. The combined shower and toilet—the only one on the ground floor—is unfit for pigs. While we were eating a tepid greasy supper, in strolled the mail-car driver with his girl. On seeing us, he smiled without surprise but didn't offer a word of explanation or excuse. We neither washed nor shaved, brushed our teeth in bottled mineral water, and went sadly and shiveringly to bed at eight-thirty.

This morning, everything changed for the better. I discovered another bathroom upstairs which is fairly clean. The waiter smiled at us kindly; last night he scowled. A boy came to tell us that a private car is available, after all; it will take us to Otavalo for only seven dollars. The town still looks grim and dirty, but the big square is quite beautiful by daylight. The customs officials have made no difficulties, and we have just had our passports stamped by a courtly old gentleman with the beard of a great Victorian poet. We shall leave in an hour.

We are much impressed by the appearance of our fellow hotel guests. After a night in this sty, they emerged for breakfast looking clean, tidy and refreshed, in immaculate business suits. We have already heard it said that even the wealthiest Ecuadoreans take hotels like this one in their stride, and never dream of complaining. They have certainly mastered the art of travel. Much more so than the average Englishman or American, who will sleep anywhere if he has to, but always with a certain conscious pride in "roughing it."

November 9.

South of Tulcán, we bumped slowly over a high rainswept moorland—pale green, with scars of black earth where the road has been cut. It has an air of utter desolation, and is really the natural frontier between the two countries; a no man's land. Nobody lives there and nothing grows but a multitude of small cactus-like plants which stand limp-leaved in the blowing rain. "*Muy triste*," said the driver—and I think it is the saddest place I have ever been in. Caskey thought that Purgatory must be like this. You could imagine yourself helplessly rooted there, in forlorn unending awareness of the deeds which should never have been done and the words which should never have been spoken. . . . "But perhaps," I said, "at the end of every thousand years, one of those plants is pardoned and allowed to die."

Then we came down into a valley where the sun shone and the wet earth steamed in its warmth. It was pleasanter there, but I still felt depressed. This titanic landscape seems to have overpowered and degraded its inhabitants. Such places are only suitable for seers and giants; ordinary mankind is too small for them. The terrible cold mountains tower into the clouds while wretched villages huddle at their feet—miserable crowds of huts, with smoke-blackened interiors and crumbling adobe walls.

Some miles farther on, we entered a strange yellow region of gaunt eroded rocks. There were places where the road had been almost cut away from the hillside by sudden floods, or blocked by falls of earth. In Colombia, you often pass road-gangs at work, repairing the damage; here there was nobody. Yet this rough cart-track is the only link between Ecuador and the North, and a part of the grandly-named Pan-American Highway!

Down by the broad stony bed of the Rio Chota there is a village of grass huts inhabited almost entirely by Negroes. The huts are characteristically African, but the Negroes wear the dress of the mountain Indians and speak their language. Here, as at two other places along the route, a chain bars your way and you must stop to show your papers to a customs officer. Our driver, on these occasions, was very helpful and diplomatic. He didn't want our luggage or the car searched because he himself was smuggling some shirts, hidden under a blanket on the seat.

Not until you reach Ibarra does the countryside seem really populated. The town lies near a lake, amidst gardens and trees, with a great blue mountain beyond. The road between Ibarra and Otavalo is cobbled, and on either side of it there are adobe walls. Now we began to meet Indians returning from the Saturday morning market. The men wore long braided pigtails and red blankets and big hats. Some carried earthenware pots, nearly as big as themselves, on their backs. A few were incredibly drunk—drunker, said Caskey, than anyone else in the world. They wandered along with blissful visionary expressions on their faces, guided like cattle by their good-humored women. Many grimaced at us gaily and waved their hands.

The driver recommended a hotel called the Chalet Intiyan. This is an attractive little house, about ten miles beyond Otavalo, on the shore of a large lake. There is a German manager, so the food is good and the place is kept very clean, although the plumbing is temporarily out of order. When we arrived, our driver demanded an extra three dollars because, he said, he had only agreed to take us as far as Otavalo itself. We argued for a while and then gave in; the price was very moderate anyway, considering that we had come eighty miles over such a road and that the car wouldn't be able to return to Tulcán that night. As soon as the money was handed over, we were all good friends again and parted amiably.

Staying here are two Americans, a Major Hays and his wife. He is attached to the U.S. Air Mission in Quito. After supper last night, Major Hays produced a bottle of whisky, and the two of them told us about their life in Ecuador. Their attitude is more or less typically Army Abroad—it hasn't changed since the days when my father was stationed with a British regiment in Ireland, thirty-five years ago. They like the country—especially from the point of view of hunting and fishing—but are chronically homesick. They have a few Ecuadorean friends, but keep pretty much to their own circle of military expatriates, within which a semblance of American life is created with the help of bridge, baseball, tennis, U.S. magazines, imported bourbon whisky and cigarettes. The men have their job, which includes some dangerous mountain flying; Mrs. Hays described feelingly how she and other wives sometimes wait on the airfield, listening to their husbands' planes trying to find a way down through the overcast. The women have their unending struggle to "keep things nice," despite exasperating servants and dubious local food. Occasionally there are excitements—as when, during the recent revolution, two armies began to approach the city and looting was feared. And there is the constant threat of burglary. Robbers get into your house by poisoning your yard dog, but they are seldom armed. It is advisable to own a revolver and practice ostentatiously with it in the garden, so that all the neighbors may know you mean business. As for the police, they are more of a hazard than a protection. They are apt to ask you for your driving license and then confiscate it; you have to go down to the police station and pay a fine to get it back.

This lake—the Laguna de San Pablo—is calmly beautiful, amidst its mountains. The Indians used to regard it as sacred. There are a great many of them settled here; they even own small farms and are relatively prosperous. They bathe in the lake and paddle across it, kneeling on canoes made of bundles of reeds. This morning, there were crowds of white herons along the shore, and we could hear the Indian pipes playing all over the hillside. Major Hays and his wife went out in a boat and shot two birds which looked like duck but didn't have webbed feet. They left the birds on the steps in the garden for a few minutes, and they disappeared. The manager said that the Indians must have taken them. They steal everything they can lay hands on, useful or useless. And not merely from strangers. In each of their walled fields you see a straw hut on a platform, five or six feet high. This is a watchtower, in which the owner sleeps with his gun beside him while his crops are ripening.

From Otavalo you can reach Quito by rail-bus (similar to the autoferro) or by train. There is only one of each daily, and they both leave very early in the morning, although the trip is comparatively short. The rail-bus, which is the quicker, takes five hours. How are we to catch it? The manager has no car, and he says that if we order a taxi from Otavalo it probably won't arrive on time. Mr. Haskell, a Californian who lives next door, has another suggestion which we have accepted because it sounds romantic, though a bit complicated. His young brother-in-law will row us across the lake to a landing-stage at the far end. We shall be sure to find some Indians there, on their way to work, and they will help carry our bags to a village called Eugenio Espejo, where we can get the rail-bus. So we are to leave tomorrow, at 4 A.M.

November 10.

This morning, Mr. Haskell's plan seemed a good deal less romantic. It had rained hard earlier in the night and was still drizzling. The boat was a quarter full of water and had to be baled out; it leaked a little, anyway. And then there was all our baggage to get on board—the suitcases, my typewriter, the heavy overcoats which we hope will justify their existence when we get into the really high mountains—so far, we have only cursed them—and Caskey's camera-tripod, which he never uses and which is always tripping us up when we're in a hurry. So we started late.

A couple of dozen yards from the shore, in the starless darkness, all sense of perspective failed. The lake appeared to shrink to the size of a small pond and the mountains looked like mudbanks, ten or fifteen feet high. Only—the mudbanks didn't move. The boy rowed and rowed, as if in a vacuum. The rain fell. From time to time we scooped a few canfuls from under the seat. Nearly an hour must have passed.

Finally, as it began to grow light, the landscape imperceptibly adjusted itself and we drew in to the shore. An Indian was wading in the reeds, filling an immense jar with water. I, who was nearly twice his size, could scarcely have lifted it, but he signed to me to put a suitcase on the top. Another Indian appeared and was ready to help. He sat down like a camel in the mud while we loaded three bags onto his back; then he rose without so much as a grunt and the two of them started forward at a quick trot. We followed, carrying practically nothing but gasping for breath in the thin mountain air.

After we had walked about two and a half miles, I looked at my watch. It was 6.15 already. The rail-bus was scheduled to leave Otavalo at 6.10. I asked one of the Indians: "Eugenio Espejo—is it much further?" He grinned and pointed in the opposite direction. There had been some misunderstanding. They were taking us down into Otavalo.

We should miss the rail-bus, that was certain; and perhaps the train as well. However, there was nothing to do but hurry on. The path turned downhill and crossed the railroad track. We paused for consultation: would it perhaps be better to walk along the track itself? The Indians said No. We turned to follow the path. And at this very moment, like a miracle, the rail-bus appeared. We waved our arms frantically, hardly daring to hope that it would stop. It did stop. We scrambled thankfully on board.

That is the irony of travel. You spend your boyhood dreaming of a magic, impossibly distant day when you will cross the Equator, when your eyes will behold Quito. And then, in the slow prosaic process of life, that day undramatically dawns—and finds you sleepy, hungry and dull. The Equator is just another valley; you aren't sure which and you don't much care. Quito is just another railroad station, with fuss about baggage and taxis and tips. And the only comforting reality, amidst all this picturesque noisy strangeness, is to find a clean pension run by Czech refugees and sit down in a cozy Central European parlor to a lunch of well-cooked Wiener Schnitzel.

oil in the jungle

November 13.

THE PENSION ASTORIA, where we are staying, is out in the northern residential suburbs on a quiet back street called the Calle Texeira. It is a pleasant shabby villa, overgrown with vines, which stands in a garden of small pseudo-classical statues and flowering trees. It used to belong to one of the presidents of Ecuador.

Frau Schneider, the proprietress, is a large brisk vivacious lady from Prague. She has filled and furnished the house with an atmosphere of Jewish *gemuetlichkeit*. The rooms are crowded with knick-knacks, embossed ash trays, velvet cushions, carved wall brackets, family photographs. The cuisine is rich and abounding in delicious cakes.

In Prague, the Schneiders used to be comparatively wealthy. Now Herr Schneider works in a bank, for a very small salary. Frau Schneider says he worries a lot; she obviously doesn't. She is one of the few refugees I have ever met who seem entirely contented with their new home. "Every morning when I wake, I am so happy to be here. It is the climate—ah, wonderful! My husband says we have a whole new year every day: spring in the morning, summer at noon, autumn in the evening, and, at night, winter. . . . I give you plenty of blankets." The four young Ecuadorean maids who do the housework seem happy, too. They sing like birds as they sweep. Whenever one of them has waited on us, she darts out of the room, just in time to hide her laughter. We hear her giggling with her friends in a corner over the two foreign freaks, until Frau Schneider's good-humored scolding recalls them to duty. "Always I must be very strict," Frau Schneider tells us, smiling, "like a firm rider with his hands on the reins."

When Frau Schneider isn't controlling her staff, or cooking, she spends a great deal of time at the telephone. The Quito telephone service is about as reliable as roulette; it may take you three-quarters of an hour to get the right number. Also, you have to shout at the top of your voice. But Frau Schneider has so much vitality that she seems even to enjoy this, like a game.

The old central section of Quito is very much as I had imagined it: brown-tiled roofs, domes, church-towers, winding up-and-down streets filling a deep narrow ravine between the mountains. The best view is from the top of the Panecillo Hill with the snow peaks of the eastern range for a background—Cayambe, Antisana, Cotopaxi, all more than 18,000 feet high. This kind of beauty is so authentic, so immediately convincing, that you "recognize" it at once, like a famous masterpiece of which you have already seen countless reproductions, and murmur to yourself, "Ah, yes—of course . . . Quito . . ." just as you might murmur, "ah, yes—the Mona Lisa . . ."

The sidewalks are too narrow to hold the jostling crowd. People swarm across the streets, despite the ferocious tooting and the murderous speed of the traffic—modern cars cutting in recklessly on ancient overladen buses. (A chauffeur will sometimes cross himself before attempting this.) Everybody seems in a hurry, yet at the same time cheerful and relaxed. A pedestrian misses death by an inch and turns to grin at the driver.

Social contrasts are very distinct here. Even the poorest clerk (and all wages in Quito are pitifully low in relation to the rising cost of living) will somehow manage to afford the business suit, dress shirt and tie which are the marks of his caste. An obstinate barrier of pride separates him from the unashamed rags and patches, the dirty barefoot poverty of the manual worker. Wherever you go, you see the cargadores, the porters, bowed and straining under huge loads which are held against their shoulders by leather bands passed around their foreheads. Heads down, eyes lowered, they hurry forward with the dazed singlemindedness of beasts of burden. And then there are the pure Indians in their native costumes; the men with ponchos and pigtails, the women with wide petticoats and little hats, and their babies slung sideways behind them in bags. They come in from the country districts to sell their farm produce or the textiles and ornaments they make. They too are very poor, but not wretched. They laugh and chatter; a gay practical people living outside the boundaries of class pretension.

There are fifty-seven churches and monasteries in this city—

nearly all of them "worth a visit." So far, we have visited about six, and I doubt if we shall see many more. We are neither of us good tourists. We tire easily of so much splendor—of golden altars, carved choir stalls, intricately molded ceilings, murals painted on marble, crucifixes of silver and ivory, monstrances flashing with jewels.

In the chapel adjoining San Francisco there is a statue of St. Luke as the patron saint of painters, holding a brush, mahlstick and palette. In the monastic library of La Merced, I noticed a copy of *Mein Kampf*.

There are a great number of public statues, good, bad and incredible. The good ones are mostly modern portrait busts; I like particularly the head of Eugenio Espejo, the Ecuadorean patriot, which stands in front of the Espejo Hospital. The Bolívar monument is less successful. The Liberator, mounted on horseback, is surging onward and upward at the head of a group of followers and angels with enormous streamlined wings. The general effect is vaguely aeronautical, but, as Caskey says, they'll never get it off the ground. On the Plaza Independencia, there is a memorial to the heroes of the independence movement of 1809. At the foot of a tall column, the Spanish Lion is skulking away with an arrow in its back. Who fired the arrow? Apparently an enraged condor, the symbol of revolutionary Ecuador. Here, at least, the sculptor's intention is clear—whatever one may think of his zoology. But no one we have met can explain the significance of the girl called Insidia, in the Parque 24 de Mayo. Surrounded by an attentive circle of seals (one of which has been stolen) she is turning to confront a snake which had been about to bite her in the right buttock. In the same park, and even more enigmatic, are two stark naked heavyweight wrestlers, locked together and sprawling on top of an unfortunate dragon, which they seem in their excitement not to have noticed. To judge by the reptile's agonized expression, it is being squashed to death.

The worst of these efforts look like rejects from a late nineteenth-century Paris salon. French sculptors are, in fact, responsible for many of them. There is a well-known story about the time when the city of Guayaquil ordered from Paris a statue of some national hero and received instead a figure of Lord Byron, which happened to be in stock. It was erected just the same, with the hero's name inscribed on the pedestal.

The people we have met so far have been mostly Americans—

the U.S. Ambassador, Mr. Shaw and Mr. Herron of the Embassy staff, and Mr. Kessel Schwartz, the director of the American Cultural Institute. Schwartz, who is quite a young man, will be leaving his job here soon and going back to the States, because his wife's health can't stand the altitude. (Quito is about 500 feet higher than Bogotá.) Naturally, he is worried and depressed, so perhaps his attitude is unduly pessimistic, though it certainly makes a lot of sense. Schwartz feels that Washington doesn't appreciate the importance of cultural institutes at all, and thinks them a waste of time. His funds have been cut down so much that it is hard to operate. Ecuadoreans see this and say, "During the war, you needed us—you wanted our raw materials and you were scared of the Nazi influence down here—so nothing was too good for us. Now you don't need us, so you don't bother." Meanwhile, the Argentines, with the advantage of a common language and tradition, are making great progress. Recently, they sent Ecuador a portrait of Bolívar. It was brought on a training-ship full of handsome cadets who delighted all the girls of Quito and Guayaquil. And the country is flooded with Argentine publicity and propaganda.

A cultural institute is, of course, a propaganda center for the country it represents; but this is a kind of propaganda which Latin America can respect and appreciate. In the course of learning English, talking about England and the United States, listening to lectures and music, looking at pictures and maps and books, the Latin American comes nearer to the Anglo-Saxon than in any other way. Personal contacts through the medium of culture are always more valid than business contacts—no matter how much tact, skill and sympathy may be brought to the latter. Culture is enormously important to the Latin American. The least breath of it—the mere naming of the names of artists, authors or composers —excites his interest and arouses his enthusiasm. He is perfectly well aware that these things are a cloak for the angular realities of business and politics. Never mind; he likes cloaks, and is offended when you come to him in the nude. The head of every cultural institute is an ambassador of the most valuable kind—or could be, if his government would give him proper support.

If the United States isn't doing so well in this respect, there is no excuse; for plenty of money could be made available. Great Britain doesn't have the money, and must economize. So the British Cultural Institute in Quito will be closed at the beginning of next year. We have already made great friends with its director, Mr. Smith. He smokes a pipe, and is large, tweedy and very Scottish.

November 14.

Last night, Mr. Smith and his wife asked us to a party at their house where we met Mr. Mott, the manager of the Shell Oil Company of Ecuador. He has invited us to visit Shell-Mera, the company's oil-camp down in the Amazon jungle. We shall leave in two or three days.

This morning we spent with Smith and his secretary, Tony Mancheno. Tony is a charming and unusually intelligent boy, with a quiet thoughtful air and perfect manners. He is very sensitive where anything Ecuadorean is concerned, and I notice how he watches our reactions.

Today, we certainly had plenty to react to. First they took us to see the Manicomio, the old city madhouse. It is an enormous rambling building, which has been used for more than two hundred years as a combined poorhouse and lunatic asylum. In former times, the madmen were kept in underground dungeons. One of them is still charred and blackened by an abortive fire which an inmate started, sanely hoping to burn his prison down.

"Oh, how I wish he had succeeded!" exclaimed Dr. Cazares, smiling, as he showed us around. He and Dr. Jarrin, both young men, are running the Manicomio almost single-handed, with the aid of a few interns, male nurses and nuns. It is a truly heroic struggle. Cazares is in a state of half-humorous despair because of the lack of funds and the condition of the building. It is on the verge of falling into ruins, and has to be constantly patched and plastered. Once, he told us, he resigned from the job in desperation and went away, but his conscience called him back.

At present, the Manicomio has about four hundred patients. Jarrin and Cazares are getting quite good results with shock-treatment and analysis, but they have no proper facilities for occupational therapy—except for those who are well enough to do house-cleaning, or carpentry, or work in the garden. The old whitewashed patios have been brightened up with flower-beds, and a lot of the patients were sitting around them in the sunshine. Some of them sidled up to us as we passed through, and bowed with an exaggerated impudent politeness, slyly smiling, or plucked at Cazares' sleeve as they mumbled some incoherent request. Others crouched in corners, their faces obstinately muffled in blankets, sulky and depressive. A white-bearded man sat reading a newspaper, and from time to time uttered a yell, either of disgust or self-advertisement. And there was an Indian boy who laughed— not savagely, not frantically, but with a kind of idiotic cosmic mirth which included everybody; himself, ourselves, the asylum, Ecuador, the entire world. I couldn't help joining in.

Despite the smallness of the staff and the necessarily dirty habits of some of the patients, the whole place is kept wonderfully clean. All the floors were newly scrubbed and the bed-linen was fresh. Upstairs, walking along dark narrow passages, we peeped through spyholes in small strong doors and saw the violent cases— the terrible roarers and the formidably silent—lying with fists clenched and foreheads pressed against the wall. Each one of them is self-isolated, unimaginably alone.

In one of the large wards there was a Czech—a big haggard man with fair thin hair. For some obscure reason, he had attacked his brother-in-law, after seeing a vision of Christ in the clouds. He had just received insulin treatment, and lay exhausted. Cazares asked me to speak to him in German. He answered so weakly and faintly that I had to kneel beside the bed and bend down close to his pillow to hear him. I couldn't help wondering, as I did this, what would happen if he got a sudden spasm of energy and grabbed me by the throat. Our conversation was unsatisfactory. He complained of a pain in his heart. Cazares told me to assure him that this was nothing serious; his heart was quite sound. But the news didn't seem to cheer him. He began murmuring that he wanted to get out of this place and go back to Europe, but that he hadn't any money. Cazares said that he could leave as soon as he was well, and that his brother-in-law had already agreed to pay for the journey. But he didn't seem to grasp this, either. After a few minutes, we gave it up as a bad job.

From the Manicomio, we went on to the García Moreno Prison. It stands a little above the town, on the steep mountainside. Dr. Vizuete, the Governor, showed us around. He seemed to be a decent humane man, who hated his position. He told us that he had about 350 prisoners, the majority of them murderers. In

Ecuador, as in Colombia, there is no capital punishment. The maximum penalty for murder is sixteen years, with three off for good behavior. Perhaps this comparative leniency is due to a recognition of the nature of violence in a tropical country, where killing is very seldom premeditated. At any rate, it is a fact that most of Ecuador's murders are committed in the hot coastal region rather than in the high mountains. There are a few military prisoners in the García Moreno, and some women—nearly all infanticides—but we didn't see them.

A guard unlocked a gate, we passed through and were locked in. There seemed to be no guards and no regular supervision within the prison itself. The prisoners don't wear any kind of uniform. Most of them were out in the big courtyard, lounging, playing handball, or strumming guitars and singing. A few were in the workshops—quite voluntarily, we were told—making furniture or shoes. One of them spoke English, and soon a group gathered around us, asking questions: What did we think of Ecuador? What were we doing here? What was it like in the States? Their manner was casual and friendly. They didn't ask us for cigarettes before we offered them. They didn't pester us to buy the things they had made, although they had plenty for sale—shoe-brushes, mostly, and chess-sets. In fact, they were much better behaved than most of the people you might talk to on the streets outside.

Once a week, the prisoners can see their wives—not from across a table or through a wire screen in the presence of a guard, but in whatever privacy the building affords. Prostitutes are also allowed in, for the benefit of the bachelors.

In 1912, the great Liberal ex-President, Eloy Alfaro, was imprisoned in the García Moreno by his political enemies. His policy had been anti-clerical and often misunderstood by the simple devout masses; it was easy to incite them against him. Soldiers broke into his cell, shot him dead, and threw his body to the crowd. It was dragged through the streets, mutilated and burned in a public park.

It is a tragic irony that Alfaro was confined and murdered in a prison named for the man whose life-work he opposed and largely undid. President García Moreno, his predecessor, had given back to the Church most of the power it exercised during the Colonial Period, including press-censorship and control of education. He made profession of the Catholic faith a condition of Ecuadorean citizenship, and even passed a law consecrating Ecuador to the Sacred Heart of Jesus. During Alfaro's two terms of presidential office, all these measures were reversed. He proclaimed religious tolerance, permitted civil marriage, qualified women to hold public employment, and established a system of secular education. After a long struggle with the Vatican, he deprived the Church of its landholdings and expelled the religious orders from the country.

Leaving the Catholic problem aside, it must be admitted that both men did Ecuador much material good. Both of them built roads and harbors, improved public administration, helped commerce and agriculture. García Moreno planned the Guayaquil-Quito railway; Alfaro had it constructed. And both of them were murdered. García Moreno was assassinated at the beginning of his third term as president, in 1875. His murderer may perhaps have been inspired by the work of the famous Liberal writer, Juan Montalvo, one of García Moreno's most fearless enemies. At any rate, Montalvo thought so. On hearing of the President's death he exclaimed, with pardonable author's vanity: "It was my pen that killed him!"

Today, Alfaro's cell is a shrine, with a bust, memorial tablets, wreaths, and the national colors painted around the door. Many great men in all countries have been jailed at one time or another, but their monuments are put up elsewhere, in some dignified public place. Or else their prison has been turned into a museum, ennobled and denatured. Not so here. The cells along the gallery on either side of Alfaro's are still in use. His monument is for his fellow-prisoners, not the public—a daily reminder to them that one of Ecuador's heroes shared their life and condition.

Tony Mancheno was sincerely distressed by our visit. "We spend all our money on the Army," he said, "and we don't need one at all. Why doesn't the Government use it to improve places like this?" He was right, of course. A U.S. or British prison-inspector would condemn the García Moreno from the ground up. No doubt the food is poor, the accommodation inadequate and the sanitation primitive. No doubt the official approach to the problems of criminal psychology and social rehabilitation is hopelessly unscientific. And yet, strangely enough, I didn't feel nearly so ashamed and depressed as I usually do in such institutions. It sounds sentimental and reactionary to write this, but I keep remembering the look on those men's faces. Nobody had tried, even with the best intentions, to "understand" them. Nobody had studied them. Nobody had made them feel, however tactfully, that they were misfits or types or cases. Nobody had even told them that their crimes were the expression of certain social conditions, bad economic environment. No, I'm not sneering. I'm puzzled— just because I am firmly on the side of the psychologists and reformers. But the impression is too strong to be ignored. . . . Each of those prisoners had killed one or more human beings. Perhaps some were sorry; perhaps some weren't. But all of them looked like intact individuals, not criminals, not humiliated. You could picture them going back to their home towns and taking up life where they had left off, quite naturally, as a matter of course. . . . Certainly, the García Moreno is pretty bad. But I am afraid there are many cleaner, kinder, infinitely more terrible places in which people are forced to spend a quarter of their lives.

November 17.

Early this morning, we left for Shell-Mera Camp in a station wagon belonging to the Company. With us were Frank Bellew and Dr. Antonio Quevedo. Bellew is young, Scottish, married to an Ecuadorean. He is a Shell executive, making one of his regular tours of inspection. Quevedo, a guest like ourselves, is a prominent Quito lawyer. He has been Ecuadorean Minister to England, and a president of the League of Nations. He once refused a nomination for the presidency of the Republic, because he prefers to stay out of politics. He is in his middle forties, slight and wiry.

Unluckily, the weather wasn't very clear; Cotopaxi and most of the other peaks were hidden in the clouds. We headed south over the broken table-land, which somebody has compared to a horizontal ladder; the eastern and western cordilleras forming the sidepieces, and a succession of cross-ranges the rungs. At the top of one of these we passed a hut with a crucifix on it. For some superstitious reason, every peasant drops a stone inside it as he goes by. We also saw a bus called "Lenin." Most Ecuadorean buses have names—the fancier the better. Quevedo told us that, a few years ago, he had noticed several "Hitlers."

Bellew talked about the history and geography of the Shell-Mera project. It is situated in the Oriente, Ecuador's tiny share of the jungle wilderness which stretches across northern Brazil, all the way to the Atlantic Ocean. To the north, the Oriente is bounded by Colombia, to the east and south by Peru; but these are merely political frontiers. The only natural barrier, the double ridge of the Andes, lies along the west. Down its sides flow rivers which will sooner or later join the Amazon. Ecuador's cities and towns are all on the Andean table-land or down on the western coastal plain. The Oriente is still uninhabited, except by forest Indians and a few communities of villagers who live close to the mountains.

About ten years ago, the Shell Company got a concession from the Ecuadorean Government and sent their geologists down into the Oriente to make a survey. The report was favorable, but operations were delayed by the outbreak of war and they are only now beginning on a large scale. At present, two wells are being drilled, a third will be started next spring, and a fourth has already been temporarily abandoned. So far, not one drop of oil has been found at any of these places, but the experts are hopeful and they can produce cores of oil-soaked sand to support their opinion. There is certainly some oil in the jungle. But is there enough to make further investment worthwhile? If there is, Shell will have to lay a 300-mile pipeline, one of the highest in the world, over the Andes and down to the ocean in order to ship it out.

At midday, we reached Ambato, a pleasant town surrounded by flower gardens and orchards, and had lunch in a German restaurant where Shell's employees usually eat on their way to or from Shell-Mera. Here we picked up Notchey O'Keefe Starr, one of the oil drillers. Notchey's given name is North American Indian; everything else about him is Oklahoma-Irish. He is so perfectly "in character" for his profession that he could play himself in the movies—provided that his dialogue was strictly censored. His love-life and drinking exploits—or rather, the stories he tells about them—are the scandal and delight of the Shell Company. The stories began as soon as we were back in the car, and quickly reached such proportions that Bellew protested: "Oh, come off it, Notchey! You surely don't expect us to believe that?" "Listen," said Notchey, grinning, "if that's not true I'll kiss your ass in front of the post office, and I'll give you three weeks to collect the crowd."

On the outskirts of Ambato, Shell has a storage depot, and a radio station which keeps in constant touch with Shell-Mera, signaling the weather conditions at the top of the pass for the benefit of the Company's planes. After about twenty miles, the road begins to run downhill toward the gorge of the Rio Pastaza which forms the entrance to the Oriente. Just before you get to Baños, you cross a bridge over a narrow chasm cut by the river, hundreds of feet deep. Numerous travelers have fallen into this, and a few have been rescued, it is said, by the intervention of the local Virgin. Primitive murals in the church at Baños record these and other miracles—including the preservation of the town from fire during an eruption of Tungurahua, the near-by volcano. I particularly like the story of an old priest who fell asleep on his mule one night as he was riding to visit a farm on the other side of the chasm. The priest didn't know that the bridge had broken, but the farmer and his family did, and they were amazed to see him arrive safe and sound. In the morning, when they went down to look, they found that a slender tree-trunk had fallen across the mouth of the chasm. Over this, the divinely guided mule had crossed.

Baños looks rather like a town in the Alps, tucked away in a corner under wet green mountains. There are several curative springs of hot and cold water which have been used to fill swimming pools. You are shown a big tree beneath which Juan Montalvo (whose home was in Ambato) used to sit and dream up his pamphlets against García Moreno.

Below Baños, the gorge deepens between precipices covered with tropical forest which must be thousands of feet high. Even a magnificent 200-foot waterfall, exploding through a cleft in the lava bed, seems dwarfed by these huge dark jungle walls. There is one place called the Puente del Cielo where a mass of rock overhangs the road and water rains down on the roof of the car. Landslides are very frequent. Bellew showed us where a peasant's house and half of his upland pasture slid clear down to the river. He has obstinately built again, right on the brink of the disaster. Men from Shell-Mera are constantly at work on this road. It has to be dug out or remade somewhere nearly every week.

Then there are side ravines through which other rivers pour down to join the Pastaza—the Rio Negro, the Rio Blanco and the Rio Verde, which actually is a light brilliant green. One of these was the scene of the only fatal air-accident a Shell pilot has had, so far. A Grumman amphibian took off from Shell-Mera with an extra heavy load because, at the last moment, some men were put on board who had fallen sick and had to be rushed to a hospital in Quito. When the Grumman entered the Pastaza gorge, a thick fog closed in. The pilot must have missed his way, for he turned up a side ravine. Weeks later, after the wreckage and the bodies had been found, another Grumman, with exactly the same load, was sent out in clear weather to determine the cause of the crash. They flew into the ravine and began to climb, but at 12,000 feet the aircraft would go no higher and they had to turn back. This was the point at which the other Grumman must have hit the precipice wall in the fog. And, to add to the tragedy, they were only fifty feet from the top!

Shell-Mera Camp lies on the bank of the Pastaza, at the opening of the plain. This is high ground still—more than 3,000 feet above sea-level; the days are only pleasantly warm and the nights are cool. We arrived shortly before sunset. The Camp is a big, well-lighted, solidly built town of huts, workshops and hangars, with a military atmosphere of order and tidiness. Our room in the bunkhouse is cleaner and more comfortable than most hotels. Only a few years ago, the site was swampy virgin jungle.

We had supper in the noisy mess-hall, amidst a crowd of engineers, drillers, company officials, pilots, radio-men and geologists —British mostly, but with a sprinkling of Ecuadoreans, Americans and Dutch. Afterwards, we went around to visit Mr. Humphries, the general field-superintendent and boss of the camp. He is a genial man with a pipe and a close-cropped mustache; the sort who can say "No" with a pleasant smile. Humphries and his immediate subordinates live on a street of villas which has the snugness of a tropical suburbia, complete with wives, children, gardens and dogs. There are people who will grow up remembering this place as their childhood home.

Bellew asked us to sign our names in the visitors' book. Notchey Starr has written:

> Here's to the boys with oily clothes
> That all the girls knows.

We can hear him in the next room, right now, shouting and wrestling violently with a small muscular English pilot who is very drunk.

November 18.

Breakfast, and preparations for flying. The morning aspect of the camp resembles a large-scale military operation; everybody has his job and is busy—hurrying from hut to hut with papers, bending over maps, hammering in the shops or tuning up the aircraft engines. Bellew, Quevedo, Caskey and I stood around on the airstrip, waiting to start. It is hardly a mile long, with the mountains at one end and the jungle at the other. It was a beautiful morning, with a light breeze blowing.

The Company has eight planes here: two Dakota transports, two Bristols, two Grumman amphibians, and two old tri-motor Fords which are only used for emergencies. The Grummans fly to Tiputini, keeping along the Napo River, on which you can put down almost anywhere, if necessary. Tiputini is 206 miles east of Shell-Mera, the farthest of the four field-camps, and the one where drilling is to be started next Spring. Taisha and Ayuy, the two we were going to visit today, lie more to the southeast, comparatively close together, seventy and fifty-three miles from Shell-Mera, respectively.

The chief problem in flying down here is the weather, which is very treacherous, constantly changing. Somewhere over the area, it is nearly always raining. Great storms build up with extraordinary rapidity. Within half an hour, fog can shut down and close an airfield altogether. So Shell-Mera has to keep in continuous radio-communication with its field-camps and all its planes. The planes fly back and forth between the camps, all day long; there is no other means of transportation or supply.

Our Dakota was called the Star of Sangay. Its pilot, Mr. Atkinson, is a big man with a black pirate's beard, which he grew after sandfly bites had festered and prevented him from shaving. Notchey joined us just as we were about to leave, suitcase in hand; Taisha is where he works. I was glad of his wisecracks and his big-brotherly presence, for I was feeling a bit nervous. The revolver hanging from Mr. Atkinson's belt ("Just in case of any difficulty"), the paper to be signed, renouncing all claims on the Company for damages ("One of these silly formalities"), the bare well-worn interior of the aircraft, piled high with crates of canned food, spare parts and flour sacks; all these combined to create an atmosphere of emergency and adventure. Bellew and Notchey realized this, no doubt—although, to them, the trip must have seemed about as thrilling as a city bus-ride—for they did their tactful best to reassure us. Up to the present, there has never been a fatal accident on these routes; only a few minor mishaps before the airstrips had been properly leveled and drained. Suppose the weather turned nasty? We carried enough gasoline to fly to Ambato or even Quito. Suppose an engine failed? Our Dakota could get home easily on one. Suppose, just for the sake of argument, that both engines . . . ? Well—successful crash-landings *have* sometimes been made under similar conditions. There were iron rations and a shotgun on board. And, anyway, that was one chance in a million.

As the plane roars into the air, and the river and the toy huts of Shell-Mera tilt away beneath its turning wing, you get your first extensive view of the Oriente. The foreground is broken country—ridges so steep that the trails must skirt them, hollows fleeced with mist—and all crowded and richly carpeted by the tall slim-stemmed jungle vegetation, without the smallest patch of bare earth anywhere in sight. Beyond, the ocean of forest is spread smoothly to the horizon, a green unbroken ring. And beyond the horizon—three thousand miles of trees. . . . The sun was shining, with big bright clouds in the sky. But away in the distance, over what looked like a tiny area, a veil of rain was falling.

About halfway to Taisha, Notchey pointed out to us a little airstrip belonging to the mission-station. A few months ago, two of the missionaries made a forced landing among the tree-tops; their plane was so small and light that they weren't seriously injured. One missionary twisted his knee. The other, who was unhurt, went off to look for help. He reached Shell-Mera eight days later. He went straight to the doctor's office.

"Is the Doctor in?" he asked the nurse who opened the door.

"No. I'm afraid he isn't."

"Oh. I see. Thank you . . ."

The nurse looked him over more closely and became aware of his torn clothes and bleeding limbs. "I say," she gasped, "have you been in the *jungle?*"

"Yes," answered the missionary mildly, "I have."

He was put to bed and a search party was organized. On the eleventh day, the other missionary was found, alive. This story is told at Shell-Mera with sardonic professional amusement at the carelessness of amateurs. "They trusted in the Lord, so they didn't bother to clean their spark-plugs."

Within three-quarters of an hour, we were circling over Taisha. From the air, the field looks like a neat rectangular piece cut out of a very thick rug. The camp is named for a local Jibaro Indian chief. Taisha himself was one of the first people we met after landing. He was a little smiling man, in a striped athletic shirt and cotton pants, with long hair reaching to his shoulders. Jibaro families live in one big hut divided into sections. A chief's importance is measured by the number of his wives.

The Jibaros are one of those tribes of head-hunters about whom so much has been written by sensational journalists. And it is quite true that they still cut off and shrink their enemies' heads, by a special process, to the size of a small apple. You can see and buy these heads in Quito—though many of them are fakes, and some, it is said, are prepared by medical students from cadavers in the dissecting room. Strangely enough, they are not in the least repulsive. The hair on them stands up soft and furry, like a cat's, and the eyelashes, which have remained their normal length, look more beautiful than Garbo's. Their facial expression shows no pain or contortion. The eyelids are closed.

The forest Indians hunt their game with long blowpipes and small featherless wooden arrows which look like skewers. The arrows are dipped in Curare, a vegetable poison which paralyzes the game as soon as it is hit. The Indians are said to believe that the secret of Curare was given them by a god, who stipulated that it must never be used against human beings, on pain of a terrible curse. If true, this is extremely suggestive. It means that some great leader among them conceived an idea similar to that of atomic control.

The Jibaros, like the Yumbos on the Napo River, are quite friendly to the white man. Taisha has always co-operated with the Shell Company and some of his relatives actually helped to build the airstrip. Only the Aucas, who keep themselves hidden in the jungle, remain relentlessly hostile to all strangers and kill them at sight. Their hatred probably dates from the period of the rubber raids when prospectors murdered and tortured hundreds of forest Indians. If you are traveling in Auca territory, you may find a row of their spears driven into the earth across the trail. This is a warning. You had better heed it and turn back.

A young Ecuadorean petroleum engineer drove us out in a jeep to the oil well. It is six or seven miles from Taisha field, at a place called Cangaime. We had hard work staying in our seats, for the jeep went very fast and the road was like a river-bed full 'of mud and broken rocks. It has been literally smashed through the jungle by bulldozers; the trees on either side of it are twisted and piled upon each other as if a tornado had passed that way. In contrast to the freshness of Shell-Mera, the atmosphere is like a steam-bath. The humidity is around ninety, and the soil and the foliage are dripping wet. Sandflies and mosquitoes started biting us at once. Our necks and wrists were soon spotted with large itching lumps, which have already begun to fester.

The tall derrick stands in a hollow, amidst its drilling and pumping machinery. Here, the noise is terrific. Somewhat dazed by the din, I tried to listen to Notchey's shouted explanations. They were about to put another joint or section onto the drill stem, the revolving steel arm which does the drilling. At present, the drill stem has penetrated to a depth of about 700 feet, which is a mere beginning; wells are often drilled to eight or ten thousand feet before they strike oil or are abandoned. Meanwhile a boy with a hosepipe was manufacturing mud from the red earth of the hillside. This mud runs down a trough into the well-hole, where it acts as a lubricant, and is continuously pumped out again to be examined for traces of oil.

As we walked back to the huts where the engineers and drillers live, Notchey told us that they very seldom see any wild animals here; they have all been frightened away. The huts are built of palm-wood, and are as comfortable as they could possibly be under the circumstances. We had lunch with two Dutch drillers and the young engineer, whom Notchey calls "Ecuador." Notchey teased the Dutchmen. There was a lot of that good-humored bitchery which you usually find among experts. He also accused Ecuador of suffering from sex-frustration. Everyone agreed, however, that it is better not to have women in the camp. After six months, said Notchey, you didn't need them any more, and your intellect improved. Then you were "as happy as a pig in the sunshine."

I was glad to see them so cheerful. Personally, I should hate to stay in Cangaime for a single week. There is something oppressive and sinister about the place, even by daylight. All around the clearing, the dark living tangle of the forest stands up like a prison wall, an obscure vegetable consciousness, unfriendly to man and his works. Left to itself for a few months, it would begin to throttle

the road, to close in upon the huts, to coil up the derrick, to creep
among the engines. In five years, Cangaime would have vanished,
as a ship is swallowed by the sea. . . . What strength you would
need to live in a place like this! And how much I admire Notchey,
with his tall stories and dirty jokes. He is one of those people who
make life more bearable for all their companions.

When we returned to Taisha there was a group of Jibaro Indians standing on the airstrip. Some of them had war-paint on
their faces. One, who looked very young and innocent, carried a
rifle. He spoke Spanish in a soft modest voice, keeping his eyes
averted from our faces. He had been in Quito and Guayaquil, he
told us, but preferred to live in the jungle; his home was near
Ayuy. Just now he was returning there, after an act of vengeance.
Members of a hostile tribe had murdered his father, so he had
killed three of them. No—he hadn't taken their heads. Where had
this happened? Bellew asked. The boy made a slight vague gesture
toward the trees: "Eight days from here."

Nevertheless, he was afraid that his enemies might have followed him. It would be dangerous to continue the journey on foot.
Might he fly to Ayuy? Bellew said that he could, but not in our
plane because it was full already. It was the Star of Altar this time,
and its pilot was the boy who created the disturbance with Notchey
last night. He wore a sweater and khaki shorts, and smoked a
cigar with an air of extreme boredom.

The flight from Taisha to Ayuy only lasts ten minutes. There
were several Indians in the plane with us, and none of them
seemed in the least nervous; already they take flying as a matter
of course. The Macuma well, near Ayuy, is the one which has been
temporarily abandoned, and the camp itself, run by a skeleton
crew, looks untidy and shabby. We didn't stay there long.

As soon as we got back to Shell-Mera, Mr. Humphries drove
us in his car to Puyo, where the road ends and the jungle begins.
Like the neighboring village of Mera, it has grown enormously
since the Company's arrival and is rapidly turning into a tourist
resort. A new school has been started, and the Shell employees are
organizing a Red Cross drive to build a hospital. There is a restaurant run by German refugees which is said to bake the best choco-
late cake in Ecuador.

On the way home, both Altar and Sangay became visible. Altar
is a huge broken crater, deep in snow. Before its top blew off, only

a few hundred years ago, it may have been the highest mountain in the world; it is now around 19,000 feet. Sangay is still active, and expected to become more so in the near future. At night, you can sometimes see the glowing lava spilling over its lip; by day, there are puffs of black smoke. We didn't get to see the lava, because Sangay clouded over soon after dark.

This evening, Humphries showed us his colored movie-films. He has some very exciting shots of the run down the river to Tiputini, taken from the plane as it skims low over the water with the jungle-banks racing past. At Tiputini, the Napo is so broad that you can put down right across it. The Grumman is tied up to a big landing-raft called a balsa. The other day, an Indian woman was sitting on the balsa washing her clothes when a water-boa put up its head, grabbed her baby from beside her, and carried it off. The boa-constrictors live in the trees until they reach their full size, then they take to the river. Humphries says that you sometimes meet them swimming, when you are in a canoe. You can hear them coming from a long way off, for they make a tremendous splashing with their tails.

The men who built the airstrips had to trek out to their proposed sites on foot. Until the strip had been cleared, all supplies had to be dropped by plane. Humphries has a film which shows pigs and sheep sailing down through the air, their orange parachutes open above them, against a dark blue sky. The animals seem to have taken these jumps very calmly. Within a few moments of alighting, the sheep had already started to graze. Incidentally, the parachute landing-ground at Taisha is already overgrown with vegetation, after a few months of disuse, to a height of five or six feet.

November 19.

This morning the weather showed what it could do. A solid bank of cloud swept in from the jungle, shutting down the field and grounding all planes. And it rained in torrents. Bellew showed us around the Camp; the sawing-mill, the bakery, the pumping-station by the river, the electric plant, the workers' bunkhouses, the control tower, the boxing rings and the handball courts. On the airstrip, the mechanics were running the engines of the aircraft; this has to be done every day, if they aren't being flown, or they would rust in the humid atmosphere.

There are night schools for illiterate workers and a day school for the employees' children. The day school is taught by an English girl named Brenda Nicholls who, during the war, used to be an expert on codes. She is an intelligent happy-go-lucky person who likes wandering around the world and trying her hand at various unusual jobs. She says she is writing a novel about Shell-Mera. I hope she will finish it. This place, with its blend of the suburban and the exotic, of domesticity and danger, would make an absolutely ideal setting.

A sign on a notice-board in one of the offices: "Sawn-off types please use stool."

After lunch, the weather cleared and we flew to Arajuno. This is the oldest-established and nearest of the field-camps, thirty-one miles away. By air, you get there in twenty minutes. On foot, the journey would take you four hard days; the jungle is so thick that you can't use a mule. Dr. Quevedo was a bit nervous because our load included several large drums of gasoline. I sat down with my back against one of them and resolved firmly not to think about it.

Arajuno is a much more attractive place than Taisha or Ayuy because it is not entirely enclosed by trees. From one side of the camp you get a wide view over the Arajuno River. Many of the field-workers live on the other bank of the river and have to cross it by canoe. When the water is high, they occasionally get drowned. Some relatives are at present suing the Company for damages.

The Auca Indians are another hazard. Several men were working at the end of the airfield when a flight of spears came out of the forest. A Negro boy was hit. He cut the spear in half with his machete, so as to be able to run away, but two more spears followed and killed him. They never saw the Aucas at all. It is no use chasing them, for they can run incredibly fast through the jungle. On another occasion, the Aucas raided a store near the camp, killed two men, stripped off their pants and waved them at a passing plane. If the Shell pilots fly low over an Auca encampment, the Aucas will all throw spears up toward them. Fifteen men have been killed by the Indians, at one time or another, since the Company came to the Oriente.

After we had looked around the camp and driven out to see the oil well, we sat on the cliffs above the river, waiting for the plane to take us back. Dr. Quevedo talked about Ecuador. Geography has divided the country psychologically; the people of the coast have become quite different from the people of the mountains. If there is a presidential election, each section will have its own candidate. (Next year, for example, the Coast will back Trujillo and the Mountains Galo Plaza.) There is an economic, rather than a color problem—for blood-mixture extends right up into the ruling class. It is the caste-system which still prevails, the bad legacy of the Colonial days. Contempt for the Indian, where it exists, is really nothing but fear of a great under-privileged majority. Ecuador is still suffering from the effects of being exploited as a colony by Spain. She was only allowed to produce what Spain needed, and the national economy remains unbalanced in consequence. As for the so-called revolutions, they have usually been attempts by some small clique to grab political power. In order to win popular support, they had to be camouflaged by slogans. But people are getting increasingly suspicious of the slogans, so there is a hope that such coups may become impossible. The last one flopped, and its leader went into exile in Argentina.

Quevedo is, of course, very pro-Shell. He thinks it will be a national disaster if the Company doesn't find oil here. If the project succeeds, the settlement of the Oriente can only be a matter of time. Towns will grow around the wells, roads will connect them, great areas of the jungle will be cleared for agriculture, the forest Indians will be absorbed into the population, and Ecuador will gain hundreds of square miles of economically valuable territory.

I asked Bellew about labor relations. He is strongly in favor of unionization, but thinks that the unions are badly run; they don't relate their demands in different branches of industry. Their newspaper *Subsuelo* is circulated and read in Shell-Mera; it criticizes the Company freely and often nastily. But there has been no real clash, as yet. The union leaders are apt to get very excited about small details, and sometimes they make themselves ridiculous. For example, at one of the field-camps, the union leader complained to the company representative that they didn't get enough soup. So they went into the kitchen to investigate. There seemed to be plenty of soup for everybody. The union leader at once changed his ground: "The plates are too small." "Then why," said the company representative, "don't you ask for a second helping?" "I'm a mechanic," said the union leader, "and I come from work with dirty hands. Because the plates are so small, my thumb gets in the soup." "Well," said the company representative, "why not wash your hands?" This left the union leader without an answer. The workers who were listening to the argument all laughed, and the matter was dropped.

This evening, we had a drink at the club which is owned and operated by the Shell-Mera pilots—most of whom were in the Royal Air Force during the war. It is called Ye Finger Welle Inn, and is built out of the fuselage of a dismantled Budd plane, with a bar, a piano, seats from old aircraft and curtains of parachute material. Torn neckties—relics of the favorite R.A.F. tug-of-war game —hang from the ceiling. The place was rather quiet; tomorrow will be a big night, in celebration of Philip's marriage to Princess Elizabeth. But the pilot in shorts was complaining loudly that Shell's air-transport wasn't being sufficiently publicized. "We carry fifty per cent more than B.O.A.C. Then why the hell don't we shout about it?"

November 20.
Today, we drove back to Quito in the station-wagon. The first piece of news we learned on arrival was that there has been a fight in the García Moreno. One of the prisoners—nicknamed El Chino because of his Mongolian features—was stabbed to death by another. Maybe we actually saw and spoke to both of them.

into peru

November 26.

THIS IS A CHARMING CITY. I wouldn't mind spending six months here, or even a year. Not that I should ever care to live permanently in the high mountains. But here the Andean sadness is no more than a faint shadow in the mind. And on clear days, when part of the great dazzling avenue of snow-peaks is visible, your heart really rejoices. Strangely enough, we neither of us suffer from the altitude as much as we did in Bogotá. Perhaps we are getting acclimatized. Or perhaps its effects are offset by our more cheerful mood.

I wrote earlier in this diary that Frau Schneider belonged to the rare type of contented refugee. But this type seems to be common in Quito. The Schneiders tell us that there are now 436 Czechs in the city. When the war ended and travel became easier, only fifty left for the United States—despite their reputation here as the modern Eldorado—and only ten chose to return to Czechoslovakia—although the Czech Government will pay the fare of any of its nationals who want to be repatriated.

And then there is the case of Hippi Seckel, an old friend of mine from pre-Hitler Berlin days. Hippi likes to travel, and could easily settle in the States if she wished, but she says that she would rather make her home in Quito than anywhere else in the world. Before the war, she lived on the island of Minorca until Franco, under pressure from the Nazis, ordered all refugees to leave. They were told to embark in a certain ship, without knowing its destination. When they were already at sea, they discovered that the ship was bound for Italy, where they were to be handed over to the Gestapo and taken back to the German concentration-camps. The ship docked at Genoa and the other refugees were arrested, but Hippi and her brother climbed into a locked toilet

102

and hid there until they sailed again. Some of the crew were friendly, and they were allowed to go on to Marseilles where they disembarked and later began their journey to Ecuador.

Hippi now runs a small shop in Quito where she sells leather goods. Like many refugees who come to Latin America, she has had to find herself a new profession. Two of her friends, one an artist, the other formerly a night-club entertainer, have established a successful business as couturiers—the first of its kind in the city. Wealthy ladies who used to buy their clothes while on holiday abroad are now their clients and obey their decrees about the latest fashions. And this reminds me of another German refugee in Colombia whom I forgot to mention. A photographer by trade, he found that he couldn't make a living with his camera in Bogotá, so he went around the larger stores offering his services as a window dresser. The storekeepers had never even heard of such a creature. "Why should we bother about our windows?" they asked. "If people want to buy something, they come inside." The refugee pointed out that many potential shoppers are undecided, and have to be lured to the counter. The storekeepers were dubious, but they agreed to give him a trial. That was ten years ago. There are now a dozen window dressers in Bogotá—and, incidentally, the refugee has gone back to his photography.

We have heard it said that the European refugees are unpopular in Ecuador. This is very natural. Change is always unpopular, and the refugees represent change. They are a disturbing element. In the course of their own struggles to start a new life, they set up new and stricter standards of business enterprise and efficiency which challenge the old easy local ways. And if this is true of the refugees, who are poor and few, it is obviously much truer of the North Americans, who are rich and many. You find the same situation, the same psychological conflict here as in Colombia. The foreigners bring money and technical skills, and very few of them could honestly be called exploiters. Their operations are a force toward better labor conditions and higher wages generally. Nevertheless, they are foreign, they are different; and their mere presence is somehow a reproach to the native patriot. Why, he feels, can't Ecuador be doing all these things for herself?

The worst of it is, the foreigner just cannot help being bossy, or at best benevolently schoolmasterish. He has his own ideas of efficiency, his own methods of doing things; it is hard for him to accept another tempo, another approach. Deep down in his heart, he is apt to have a slight sense of grievance. He has come to this country—it isn't home, and he is sometimes lonely and uncomfortable—and he feels, in his wistful, less reasonable moments, that he has made a sacrifice. He would like just a little gratitude. Now and then, he gets it. More often, his thanks are only of the polite official sort. He is chilled and discouraged. The Ecuadorean, needless to say, cannot share his point of view. "These people," he thinks, "are here because they want something. I admit that they are helping my country, but they are helping themselves first. If they don't like the customs and conditions here, well—there is an excellent plane service to Miami, every day. . . ."

I don't see how this conflict can be resolved, with all the goodwill in the world, except by time and the gradual process of economic change. By degrees, the people of the country will take over the projects which the foreigner started. When that process is completed successfully, it will be time to talk of friendship, and even, perhaps, of gratitude.

Meanwhile, many beginnings have been made. During the past years, the Ecuadorean Government, with the help of an architect and money from the Institute of Inter-American Affairs, has been building a fine mental hospital. Very soon, the more hopeful cases can be moved out there, and the Manicomio will have a lot more room to spare. A maternity hospital, also, is nearly finished. And there are other public works in hand—all part of a great master-plan for Quito, which will extend and redistribute government offices, clinics, school zones, residential and industrial sections into the wider areas of table-land north and south of the overcrowded ravine in which most of the present city lies, leaving the old town as an intact historical monument in the center. But this is a project which it may take fifty years to realize.

The workmen are busy on the new Casa de la Cultura, and some of its rooms are already in use. This is going to be one of the biggest institutions of its kind in Latin America. It will have a theater, lecture and concert halls, accommodation for visitors, an art gallery and an international library. Oswaldo Guayasamín and Diógenes Paredes, two of Ecuador's most distinguished modern artists, are doing murals for the entrance.

Quito has always been a city of painters. During the seventeenth and eighteenth centuries its art-work became an industry and its pictures and statues were shipped up and down the western coast, to Santiago, Lima and Bogotá. Great native artists emerged —Miguel de Santiago, Nicolás Javier de Gorivar, and the sculptor Caspicara. But Spain and Italy imposed themselves absolutely, in form, conception and subject matter, and perhaps the only trace of a native Indian influence is to be found in a certain pagan splendor of drapery and ornament. Nowadays, the tendency is reversed. The subject matter of modern Quiteño painting is predominantly Indian, its forms are often based on motifs from the Inca and pre-Inca cultures, and its only occasional debt to Spain is a debt to Picasso—if you can call Picasso Spanish.

This is true even of a foreign-born artist like Jan Schreuder, whom we have met several times already. Schreuder is a Dutchman who has settled in Ecuador, not merely in a physical sense but emotionally and aesthetically. His style owes something to Rouault, but it is hard to imagine him painting anywhere but here. This country is his whole subject matter; the magnificent gloomy weight of its landscape, the darkness and mystery and intensity of its living faces. He is good because he doesn't forget that he is a stranger, a European. He doesn't pretend to see things with an Indian consciousness. He isn't a fake. His portraits have the excitement of a genuine human encounter; the blue eyes of the artist looking deeply and inquiringly into the black eyes of his model.

We have also visited Guayasamín. He is in his late twenties, and of an untidy trustful childlike appearance; the sort of person you make friends with immediately, with or without the aid of the Spanish language. His large expressive face and eyes are at once cheerful and tragic. In the evenings, we are told, he likes to play Indian folk-songs on the guitar and weep.

I think Guayasamín's best work, so far, is in his portraits and smaller watercolors and drawings. His murals are too conscious of their social significance and much too close to Orozco. Orozco and Rivera are, anyway, the "natural" foreign influences on any South American painter who concerns himself with social problems and native Indian themes. Their political philosophy provides an aesthetic idiom for those who can no longer find inspiration in the idiom of Roman Christianity. The agony of the masses is substituted for the agony of Christ. The peasant mother takes the place of the Virgin and Child. God the Father—in one of

Rivera's own murals—has given up his central station to the figure of Karl Marx.

Guayasamín is also a sculptor of great talent. In the tiny courtyard behind his studio, surrounded by the neighbors' laundry hung out to dry, stands his huge gaunt plaster statue of Hermano Miguel —the priest who founded many of Quito's first schools. This is later to be cast in bronze and set up in a new public park. But how, we both wonder, will they ever get it out into the street?

Through Guayasamín, we have met Humberto Navarro, the poet and journalist, Jaime Valencia, the painter and architect, Luis Moscoso, the painter, and Leopoldo Moreno, another architect, who is one of the leading spirits in the execution of the Quito master-plan. These men and a few others—all in their early thirties or younger—have founded a group which they call Los Contemporáneos, The Contemporaries. They meet every Saturday in Guayasamín's studio, and they have just started to publish a magazine.

The Contemporaries insist that they aren't just another artistic clique. They don't want to found a mutual admiration society or waste their time attacking other groups or individuals. Their aim is to create and promote a genuinely indigenous modern Ecuadorean art. But first the ground must be cleared. They are greatly dissatisfied with the present state of Ecuador's painting, sculpture and literature. In general, they say, it suffers from three faults: a cult of the past, a blind imitation of contemporary foreign models, and a lack of technique. "We stand looking backward like statues of salt. We know more about Homer and Vergil than about Valéry and Claudel—more of Sophocles than of Sartre." They want to achieve, as they put it, "a modern classicism, a classicism of the twentieth century . . . a national art without provincialism or folklore." In other words, the group hopes to develop a kind of sensibility corresponding to the peculiar blend of races, traditions and social forces which makes the life of Ecuador what it is today. Certainly they are proud of their Spanish ancestry and the legacy of Colonial Quiteño art, but they do not wish to fossilize into ancestor-worshippers and antiquarians. Certainly they are proud, also, of their Indian blood, but they do not yearn for the days of the Inca culture; they have no desire to lose themselves in a cult of native folk-tales, charming superstitions, picturesque costumes and quaint dances. Certainly they recognize the influence of the

great Europeans, but they will not allow Quito to become a mere
annex of Paris. Their problem is, of course, the problem of all
artists everywhere—to learn the lessons of the past and apply them
creatively to the circumstances of the present. Only, in Ecuador,
the problem is especially difficult because past and present are
both so complex. By the same token, Los Contemporáneos, if
they succeed, may produce work which is more subtle, original
and powerful than that of their less handicapped neighbors. Well
—good luck to them, anyway.

November 28.

Yesterday morning, we revisited the Manicomio to watch
Cazares and Jarrin administering shock-treatment. They wanted
Caskey to take some photographs. As for Mr. Smith, he is a
frustrated doctor, like myself; neither of us would ever miss a
chance to see anything medical.

Jarrin and Cazares use an Offner machine, an apparatus not
much larger than a typewriter. The electrodes connected to it are
placed on either side of the temples, and the patient has to be
gagged. Today the patients were all women. They stood in line,
waiting their turn, chattering and laughing. Not one of them
showed the slightest anxiety. After the treatment is over, you
don't remember it. The actual shock only lasts a fraction of a
second—otherwise it would be fatal—and then the convulsions
begin. The arms stiffen and shoot out, the body writhes, the
pointing fingers move slowly through an arc, the eyes bulge and
stare. Finally, all the limbs relax, and the patient lies quiet and
unconscious. I noticed how, in several cases, the palms of the
hands came together and were folded on the breast in an attitude
of prayer.

Sometimes, they use Metrazol injections instead of the shock.
Metrazol induces fear, and, unlike the shock, it is remembered.
Cazares says that this is psychologically valuable in certain cases.
In non-medical language, you might say that there are some kinds
of mental illness which represent the ultimate degree of sulking.
And sulking can sometimes be cured by a hard kick in the pants.

Later, we saw the Czech patient. He has practically recovered
and is quite logical. He will leave the Manicomio in a few days,
and soon start his journey back to Europe.

That evening, there was a Thanksgiving party at the U.S. Embassy. Mr. Simmons, the Ambassador, and his wife are both very charming and intelligent people who completely give the lie to everything I wrote earlier about American officials. They remained in an outer room all evening, welcoming or saying good-bye to their guests, and this was truly tactful; it left the rest of us free to indulge in an uninhibited national festival which would have fascinated the Guambia Indians. I only wish Hernández had been there to take notes. All I can report of my own and everybody else's confusion is the following dialogue between Caskey and a fellow-citizen, whose name I never knew.

He: "Hello, there."
C: "Hi."
He: "Will you drink with me?"
C: "Sure."
He: "Let's drink to the U.S.A."
C: "That depends what you mean by the U.S.A."
He: "Oh . . . Well, then—let's drink to the Union of Soviet Socialist Republics."
C: "That depends what you mean by the Union of Soviet Socialist Republics."
He: "Never mind what I mean . . . Will you drink to Ecuador?"
C: "That depends what you mean by Ecuador."
He: "Do you know what you mean by Ecuador?"
C: "I know what *I* mean by Ecuador. But I don't think you know what you mean by Ecuador."
He: "Oh—you don't think I know what *I* mean by Ecuador? You don't think so, eh?"
C: "No. I don't."

At this point, trouble might have started, if the other party hadn't been firmly removed by his wife.

November 30.
I have just finished this translation of a poem by Humberto Navarro—"Ballad of Absence."

> *High wall of distance between us two*
> *Nights without end and without beginning*
> *The ocean widening day by day.*

Colonial doorway, Cartagena

David Arango loading firewood on the Magdalena River

Paco Lara entering the bullring, Bogotá

A boy of the savannah, Colombia

Guambia Indians

On the Square
Silvia

The plaza from the tower of San Francisco, Quito

The cloisters from the tower of San Francisco, Quito

Prisoners making shoes at the García Moreno, Quito

Jibaro Indians at an airfield in the jungle, Ecuador

The painter and sculptor Oswaldo Guayasamín, with his children and his statue of Hermano Miguel

Bamboo tenements, Guayaquil

On the plateau: the railroad to Cuzco

Pottery sellers,
Pucará

Street photographer outside cathedral, Cuzco

The gorge, Machu Picchu

The sundial, Machu Picchu

Outside the church, Pisac

A village
mayor, Pisac

Country girl,
Pisac

The ceremony
of the staffs,
Pisac

Dancing women, Copacabana

Indians at prayer before the crucifix on the hilltop, Copacabana

An angel conquering a deadly sin, La Diablada, Oruro

Entry of the Devils,
La Diablada,
Oruro

Carnival masks, Oruro

Carnal womanhood, an angel, and friends, Oruro

Dancers at the prefect's reception, Oruro

Unmasked devil, Oruro

Pepinos, Oruro

The Sangay volcano, Ecuador

Reed boats, Lake Titicaca

South American vista

Christ with thorns

Faces on a pyramid

Birds at the market

Gaucho, Argentina

Elbows propped on the gunwale of my loneliness,
Here I watch, like an old mariner
Disenchanted, the boat grow distant
Once again, through the dewdrop of a tear.

How it rises—the salt line of the water—
To the last horizon of my tenderness!
How I long to send my message to you
Sheltered in a seagull's wing!

Being a writer in Quito is economically very difficult. The best most of them can hope for is to get their work printed in the newspapers or literary magazines—an excellent one is put out by the Casa de la Cultura. There are no publishers except the Government offices. If you want to bring out a book, you must buy your own paper. Nearly all the money it earns will go into production costs.

December 1.

Today I talked at the British Cultural Institute, about Hollywood and the film industry. The rooms are already being dismantled. The library is to be sold to Shell and taken down to Shell-Mera Camp. Poor Tony Mancheno is very sad, particularly because Smith will soon be leaving for a job in Argentina. Guayasamín came to my lecture and sat right through it. Knowing that he wasn't understanding a word, I found this gesture of solidarity very touching.

December 3.

More about Ecuador, from various informants: mostly American.

The country's real problem is shortage of labor. Ecuador's economy will remain basically agricultural, even if Shell finds oil in the Oriente. Its coastal region is one of the most fertile in Latin America. But its inhabitants lack energy, owing to the climate, and the weakening effect of various diseases. Infant mortality is very high throughout the country, and syphilis is widespread. The pre-natal clinic in Quito found, during the first half of this year,

that over 17% of its patients were positively syphilitic, not including doubtful cases; comparable figures for U.S. and British
clinics run between 2 and 7 per cent.

Twenty years ago, Ecuador practically had a world monopoly
of the cacao crop, until it began to be attacked by a parasite called
the witchbroom. This produced a major economic crisis. Absentee
landlords came hurrying home from Paris, and many were ruined.
Experts have now evolved a cacao plant which is not subject to
the witchbroom disease, but now West Africa also grows a lot of
cacao, and rice has become the principal crop. Banana plantations
are also a possibility, but no foreign firm cares to invest too much
money in them as long as the political situation is still so uncertain.

Political feeling is predominantly anti-clerical and Socialist;
the Conservatives have no real chance. The Church is a powerful minority, but is kept in check by legislation which has followed
the lines laid down by Eloy Alfaro. The Army is anti-clerical and
independent; it does pretty much what it likes. Great potential
revolutionary forces exist, in the mountain Indians and the working-class populations of Quito and Guayaquil, but these, so far,
have never been co-ordinated and organized. If sections of them
do revolt from time to time, they are apt to follow leaders who
don't really represent their interests.

At least half a dozen Quiteños have said to me: "I hope you're
not going to write about us the way Ludwig Bemelmans did?" To
which my answer was: "I won't, and I don't want to—but I wish
I could." Bemelmans is an author whose work I sincerely envy.
He is far too mature and humane to sneer at anybody, and I think
that The Donkey Inside was his way of saying how much he loved
Ecuador. Only—Ecuadoreans don't think so. For them, Bemelmans has become the symbol of the foreigner who comes to Ecuador and sees it as a beautiful riotous joke, a quaint endearing land
of irresponsible revolutions, eccentric characters and picturesque
screwball customs. Every country can be viewed from this angle,
of course—the United States not least. The point is that the
United States, in its power and its glory, needs to be laughed
at; Ecuador, in its poverty and weakness, doesn't. It isn't that
Ecuadoreans can't take a joke; they have plenty of humor. But
a joke isn't what they want just now. They want intelligent understanding. They want to be taken seriously. Indeed, it would be far

more friendly to criticize them—even brutally—than to treat
them as lovable, ineffectual and absurd.

Ecuadorean pride is certainly oversensitive, and naturally so.
Every thoughtful man and woman in the country is aware of its
shortcomings; they analyze them much more thoroughly than
any outsider can. They aren't ashamed and they have no reason
to be, because they are working toward what is better. During the
past years they have accomplished a lot, but the job ahead of them
is enormous. So they have to believe in the future, and their pride
is a part of their belief.

The moral is: if you are a Bemelmans, pick on someone your
own size—say, Russia.

Tomorrow we leave for Guayaquil, by train. I am very sorry
to be going. It is sad to have to say good-bye again to Hippi, after
such a short reunion. And we have both become fond of Frau
Schneider, Mr. Smith and Tony Mancheno. Today, we went down
to the British Institute for a last visit. Jorge Carrera Andrade was
there to meet us, which was not only an unexpected honor but a
real pleasure; he is as sympathetic as his poetry. In a few weeks he
will be leaving for London, to become the Ecuadorean Ambassador; this is a particularly admirable example of Latin cultural
diplomacy. Why can't the British ask T. S. Eliot to go to Quito?

December 6.

We left Quito the day before yesterday, just as dawn was
breaking. This meant getting up at 4 A.M., because Frau Schneider
had warned us that we shouldn't otherwise find seats in the observation car, on account of the crowds traveling down to
Guayaquil for the Inter-American football games. This proved
to be a false alarm; the car was half-empty.

The weather was only fair. But as we were leaving Riobamba
the clouds thinned away, and there was Chimborazo in all its
splendor, with the sunlight on the snow. There is nothing to say
about it. There it stands; the formidable old masterpiece. I
thought of W. J. Turner's poem:

> *The houses, people, traffic seemed*
> *Thin fading dreams by day,*
> *Chimborazo, Cotopaxi*
> *They had stolen my soul away!*

He wouldn't have been disappointed. I wished he could have been with us.

Despite what the guidebooks tell you, there was no roast guinea-pig for sale at any of the stations where we stopped. I read J. B. Trend's *Bolívar and the Independence of Spanish America*. What a depressing story! Bolívar said, as he lay disgusted and dying: "The three greatest *idiots* in history have been Jesus Christ, Don Quixote and—myself!"

We had been looking forward to seeing the Nariz del Diablo, where the train descends the sheer face of a precipice by means of a series of switchbacks. But it wasn't much of a thrill, after all. The engine-driver was unexpectedly cautious. And the gorge is so brown and barren as to be almost ugly. We reached Durán, the terminal, long after dark and were ferried across the river to Guayaquil.

Guayaquil is so different from Quito that it's hard to remember they both belong to the same country. The city is spread along the western shore of the estuary, fringing it with parks, tumbledown shipping offices, piers and small colored craft which lie stranded on the mudbanks when the tide is out. It seems very flat and low, right down on the water-level, half awash in the lazy heat. The houses are large and mostly wooden, with louvre-shutters on the windows, hinged at the top and opening outward. They are built out over the sidewalks on pillars faced with corrugated iron, to form arcades. Here, at noon, you see men sleeping, and cacao beans laid on the ground to dry. The whole place is unusually clean and there are few bad smells. Once a notorious pest-hole, full of malaria, yellow fever and bubonic plague, it was finally disinfected during the early years of this century. The cure appears to have left it somewhat exhausted.

Only at night, as in Cartagena, does the city become really lively. Hundreds of Costeños crowd the streets and fill the cafés. They are noticeably better-looking and more attractive than the people of Quito, perhaps because they have a larger admixture of Negro blood. At night, too, the slums look beautiful, for their houses are made of split bamboo and lights shining out through the cracks give them the appearance of lanterns. The inner structure of these dwellings is very odd and complicated; there are all kinds of platforms at different levels, connected by stairways and ladders.

We are staying at a Polish pension called the At Home, which is quite adequate in every way. The only disadvantage is a rooster—not the property of the management—which lives at the bottom of the air shaft between this building and the next. It must be very dark down there, for the rooster has no fixed hours and crows whenever it feels inclined, at any time of the day or night.

Any traveler visiting this town should certainly inspect the cemetery, which stands at the foot of a small hill, amidst gardens and superb palms. It is dazzling white—whiter than Heaven itself could ever be—and filled with an assortment of angels, columns, wreaths, busts, mausoleums and crypts such as you could hardly find equaled anywhere outside the Père Lachaise in Paris. And then there is the monument on the waterfront commemorating Bolívar's meeting here with San Martín, in 1822. As large as history, but somewhat weak at the knees, the figures of the Liberator and the Protector are exchanging a languid handshake. "My dear," Bolívar seems to be saying, "you must be *dead*. . . . Aren't those Peruvians *awful?*"

As we were sitting outside a café, yesterday evening, I was jerked forward by what I thought was a violent kick in the seat of my chair. I turned, but there was nobody behind me. Then I became aware that the shop signs and hanging street-lamps were swinging to and fro, and that a number of people had run out of the houses onto the sidewalk. It was a mild earthquake. They are frequent all along this coast. One in Lima the other day did a good deal of damage, and there were a lot of casualties.

The U.S. Consulate here keeps a file of letters from travelers who have made unusual or complicated journeys in this part of the country—giving prices, times, mileages, and useful hints on police and customs regulations. According to one of them, we should proceed to Tumbes (the most northern town on the coast of Peru) in the following manner: Take a boat across the Gulf of Guayaquil to Puerto Bolívar. Then take a launch called the *Faraón* (which is captained by an old man with cataract in one eye) to a village called Hualaca (?). Then hire a burro for the baggage and walk two or three miles until you reach the Peruvian frontier. From there you can get a ride in a truck to Tumbes. . . . We have written all this down carefully. But, somehow, it sounds like one of those wonderful cooking recipes which never *quite* work out.

December 9.

Well, we got the boat to Puerto Bolívar all right. It sails at ten o'clock in the evening, and you spend about eight hours on the water. The boat was very crowded, so we stayed on deck, in the bows, dozing uneasily. Toward dawn it grew bitterly cold and we were glad of our heavy overcoats. It seemed strange to be needing them here, at sea-level, only two or three degrees south of the Equator.

Puerto Bolívar is a large dirty village in a clearing of the jungle, which grows thickly along this shore of the gulf. Its cane houses are built on platforms above the swampy ground. Dozens of pigs root in the mud and wallow in the stagnant pools. We looked around in vain for the *Faraón* and its old captain. Nobody seemed to know of either. However, there were several trucks waiting to take passengers to Machala, a small town about five miles inland. We decided in favor of the trucks.

But first we had to get permission to leave Ecuador. This permission must be obtained twice if you are traveling south; once in Guayaquil, once in Puerto Bolívar. So I went and sat in the customs office for an hour, waiting until the two officials had explored every avenue of local gossip and were bored enough to take an interest in our passports. Meanwhile, all the trucks had left except one, which we caught just as it was driving off.

Another long wait in Machala, where it grew steadily hotter and hotter. We sat on the steps of a store, not daring to walk around lest we should miss some chance of transportation. Nobody paid much attention to us. Nobody could tell us anything definite about buses or trucks. But I pinned my faith on a large fat man who had firmly announced that he must get to Tumbes that night. He looked purposeful.

Around mid-day, a truck arrived and off we went. The border country is uninteresting; bald, barely arable patches of cultivated land, amidst sandy wastes. Here, the rich jungle lowlands of Ecuador begin to give way to the coastal desert which stretches, almost unbroken, down through Peru to the north of Chile. We forded a river at full speed in order to rush up the opposite bank, which was steep and muddy, and later crossed an open railroad bridge, balancing delicately on two narrow planks laid alongside the track. Near the frontier, there is a big army camp, with a very

striking monument in the middle of its parade ground; a giant
hand holding a torch.

The frontier itself runs through an arid wilderness. It is
marked, at this point, by a cluster of huts, a bridge over a small
stream trickling along a concrete channel, two national flags, two
kinds of soldiers, and many neutral goats. This is like a frontier in
a children's book. The abstract idea of a frontier, reduced to its
simple wretched absurdity and thereby exposing all other frontiers for what they really are—a public nuisance. Angry and sweating, we dragged our baggage from examiner to examiner and were
finally permitted to stagger with it across the bridge to meet more
examiners on the other side. After much argument between the
fat man and the soldiers, our truck was allowed to follow us,
empty. It was now, apparently, decontaminated of dangerous
Ecuadorean radiations, and could take us on to Tumbes. Actually,
as we discovered later, yesterday's formalities were less strictly
observed than usual, because of the fiesta which is going on in
Tumbes. Ordinarily, Ecuadorean travelers are somewhat unwel-
come. There is still much bad feeling between the two countries.
Now and then, the frontier is closed altogether for several days at
a time.

There is usually another customs examination halfway between the frontier and Tumbes, but this was somehow sidetracked
for all of us by the fat man, who evidently had influence. Instead, we stopped at a hut and drank Chicha, a variety of corn
liquor, with the customs officials, ceremoniously passing a gourd
bowl of it from hand to hand. I didn't like the taste, and only
sipped. Later, I wished that I had taken enough to get properly relaxed, for our driver, urged on by a party of soldiers who had
joined us, decided to finish the trip at a speed befitting the occasion. I sat down on the floor of the truck, preferring to foresee
nothing of the immediate future, and tried, quite unsuccessfully,
to fix my mind on what is eternal. Several times, I thought we
must surely be airborne. The soldiers treated the ride as a serious
sporting event. As each new hazard approached—a twist in the
road, a flooded hollow, or a car coming in the opposite direction—
they talked together with anxious excitement, weighing our
chances. At a particularly alarming bump, one of them was thrown
headlong into my lap. Caskey crouched beside me scowling

crossly, as he always does on the rare occasions when he is scared. When Tumbes finally came into view, the soldiers greeted it with shouts of "La Meta! La Meta!"—the goal!

When we arrived, it was late in the afternoon, and the fiesta was at its height. The central square was lined with market-stalls and crowded with people. Two bands were playing, one at either end. We didn't stay to see the sights, however, but set off at once in search of rooms, having been warned already that the town was overflowing with visitors.

Although Tumbes is a remote little place, it has a beautiful and quite inexpensive hotel—one of the several which the Government has recently opened in different parts of the country. (Peru is much more tourist-conscious than Ecuador. The Peruvian Consul in Quito even gave us travel folders when we went to him to get our visas.) We tried this government hotel first, and were told there wasn't a free bed in the building. So I left Caskey with our baggage in a café on the square and started out again, with the fat man and two more of our fellow-passengers, to continue the hunt. One of these was a local boy who had a grandfather in town, a very polite old gentleman who appeared to be living in a sort of tent which was also a henhouse, behind a store. The grandfather had a long conversation with the fat man, of which I caught only the frequently repeated words "muy suave," very smooth. In my ignorance, I supposed this to refer to the kind of beds we wanted, and thought he was being unnecessarily particular. Only later did it dawn on me that the fat man was asking where he could buy horses—"suave" also means gentle, quiet—and that he wasn't interested in beds at all. As for the grandfather, he didn't know of any, and assured us that every inn in town was full.

Meanwhile, the fourth member of our party had stopped to chat with two girls who were leaning over the balcony of what was probably a brothel. Soon he went inside, and the boy and I were left alone. Our next attempt was at a cockpit—cockfighting is very popular here—where the manager was extremely kind. All he could offer us, however, was the floor of his living room. By this time, I was tired enough to accept anything gratefully; and yet the image of the government hotel kept appearing before me, like a vision of paradise in the midst of all this squalor. I asked the boy to go back there with us and talk to the proprietress. This he did, and his speech to her was worthy of an infinitely more heroic situation—one phrase I remember was: "The human body will stand just so much and no more." It moved the proprietress deeply. She agreed to let us sleep on couches in the ballroom. There were several of these, and Caskey and I tried for a long time to persuade the boy to join us, as our guest. But he wouldn't. I suppose he felt shy in such grand surroundings. He wrote down his name on a piece of paper—which I have already lost—and disappeared out of our lives. I wish there was some way to thank him. He was marvelously patient and goodnatured—and he even understood my Spanish.

Our couches had one drawback. An engagement party was being held in the ballroom that evening, so we couldn't occupy them until it was over. We went back to the café on the square. (In view of what I have written elsewhere about Latin American morals, I must record the fact that we had left our bags there in a corner, unguarded, for quite a long time while we were washing at the hotel. None of the bags lock—and nothing is missing.) A dance band was playing what it called "*el Buggi Buggi.*" One of its members came over to say that they were about to "dedicate" a tune to us and hoped that we should "return this courtesy"— which meant that we had to buy them all drinks. Then we wandered around the market, which was a little disappointing. We had hoped for some beautiful Indian pottery, silverwork and woven materials. But most of the goods for sale were cheap ugly city stuff. Later on, there was a fine display of fireworks. After this, we returned to the hotel and stared reproachfully in through the ballroom windows at the engagement party, which was very formal and well-dressed. My social conscience becomes very sensitive whenever I find myself on the wrong side of the tracks, and I moralized severely on the selfish ostentation of the Peruvian upper class. How dare they sit there drinking champagne in the midst of all this poverty and filth and disease? How dare they advertise their private happiness in the face of so much misery? How dare they, in other words, keep us out of our beds? Well—they did dare. The party continued until two o'clock this morning, when the management ended it by turning out the lights. By that time, we had already been dozing for several hours in armchairs in the lounge.

Today we have been given a room, in which we have already caught up on most of our lost sleep. Tomorrow morning, at 8 A.M., we leave for the south on a bus.

December 11.

Here we are in Trujillo, about half of the distance down the coast between Tumbes and Lima. We arrived here this morning, at dawn. There is very little to be said about the trip; even its discomforts and annoyances were no more and no less than we had expected. Our passports were examined six times at various police stations en route, but quite quickly and without undue fussing. The scenery is mostly uninteresting desert. The road might be worse; a good deal of it is even surfaced. During the night, however, we struck some patches of really cruel bumps. I kept dozing off and waking to find my head hammering against the side of the bus, like a woodpecker.

This is a beautiful quiet spacious city. It was founded by Pizarro, and has many old churches and mansions with pictures painted on the walls of their courtyards. It lies about two miles inland, in an oasis, with sandy desert all around and stark naked stone mountains which rise straight up out of the plain. We are staying at another of the government hotels. It is larger and even more comfortable than the one at Tumbes. The hotel stands on a big square which has a ridiculous fountain (School of Rodin) in the middle of it. The central figure is posed in such an extraordinary position that his arm, holding a torch, looks like an extra leg doing a high back-kick. All around are groups of muscle-men in a state of agonized disintegration.

December 13.

Yesterday morning, we hired a car and drove out to see the ruins of Chan-Chan, which are three miles from Trujillo. Chan-Chan was the capital of a pre-Inca kingdom which once extended over three-quarters of the coastal area of Peru. It is now a vast desolate maze of courtyards, mounds, narrow lanes and massive earthen walls which are gradually losing their outlines and melting back into the landscape. Here and there, you find some small remnants of sculpture; patterns of men and weird evil-looking birds. Everything else has been taken away by the conquering Spaniards and the modern archaeologists. Even the graveyard has been dug up and picked over; the earth is littered with bones, skulls still tufted with hair, rags of burial garments. And, as if this ancient necropolis were not sinister enough already, Chan-Chan was recently used as an execution-ground. During the early nineteen thirties, the Apra Party in Trujillo unsuccessfully attempted an armed rising. Its ringleaders were captured, taken out here and shot against the earthworks. Many of them are now scrawled with Aprista emblems and slogans—for the Party has become powerful and can openly honor its martyrs. One inscription reads: "Let our dead teach us how to be free."

In the afternoon, we went to Chiclín, where there is a sugar plantation and a famous private museum belonging to the Larco Herrera family. Actually, the museum is more public than private. They have guides to show you around, and there is no trace here of the surrealistic disorder of Dr. Buenaventura's collection at Cali. Nevertheless, the pottery section is fascinating. Here you see hundreds of Inca and Chimu *huacos*, those sculptured drinking-vessels which look like remote ancestors of the Toby Jug. More than any other artifacts, the *huacos* seem to give you an insight into the psychology of these early cultures. There is something nightmarish about them. Every kind of individual and occupation is represented: rulers and servants, cripples, prisoners of war, animals and demons, peasants tilling the soil, soldiers fighting, lovers copulating, women in childbirth. The portraits are startlingly expressive, verging on caricature; they remind you somewhat of Rowlandson. Such a lively, energetic ugliness. No sweetness or gentleness in any of these faces. No ideal of male or female beauty. The leaders are stern and grimly dignified; their subjects are humble and humorous and sly. You can picture them grinning with furtive satisfaction when a neighbor stepped out of line and got punished.

While we were in Tumbes, we made friends with a very attractive and good-natured girl named Sarita Cisneros. She was there because her job is to inspect the government hotels; and now she has arrived here. Sarita has introduced us to the Pisco Sour, an alarmingly potent drink which is made by mixing Pisco, the local brandy, with lime-juice, beaten egg-white, sugar and Angostura bitters. Caskey, in his cups, is apt to get argumentative.

Last night in the dining room, when the Piscos had done their work, he leaned over and smacked my face—neither of us can now remember why. Luckily, I didn't smack him back, so the incident passed off without creating a public disturbance.

December 14.

At six o'clock this morning, we left by bus for Lima, a journey of about 350 miles. I hate to keep on complaining about South American drivers, but this ride was really something to remember. What is very curious is the complete fatalism of the passengers. Many of them are obviously nervous, but they accept homicidal speeding as a necessary condition of travel; they would never dream of insisting that the car should slow down. I have a theory that bullfighting has something to do with it. Just as the *torero* is expected to work as close to the bull as possible, so the chauffeur feels in honor bound to graze the side of every passing vehicle. When two cars are approaching each other from opposite directions, they will both hold the middle of the road until collision seems inevitable, and then swerve sharply apart. This swerve corresponds to the pass made by the bullfighter's cape over the horns of the charging animal. And, like the pass, it isn't always successful.

The road is paved all the way; it would be pleasant to drive along, at a reasonable speed. But the sand which borders it becomes a danger when you are going too fast; if your wheels touched it even for a moment, the car would overturn. This is probably why there are accident-crosses in several places where the highway is straight and level. There are a few green valleys along the route, but most of the landscape is a moonlike desert, with vast sweeps of sand, sometimes broken into wind-waves, extending right down from the jagged mountains to where the dim rollers burst sparkling out of the ocean fog and foam over the empty shore.

I noticed an Army officer reading what I at first thought was a battered U.S. comic book. Then I saw that it was Dante's *Inferno*—very suitable literature for such surroundings. At one spot in the midst of the wilderness, with no living creature or habitation in sight, a passenger asked to be put down. He got out of the bus, stretched himself, and looked around with an air of unmistakable satisfaction, as if to say: "Home at last!"

A few miles north of Lima, the road winds around a succession of enormous sand cliffs, falling sheer to the sea. It has to be swept clear of sand many times a day. It is far too narrow on the curves, and almost entirely unfenced along the precipice side. This is the worst hazard of the whole trip, but it is also the last. Once you are safely past it, you are almost certain to reach Lima alive.

We did so, at five-thirty this afternoon. Now we are in the Hotel Maury, a stuffy old place, shabbily grand in the style of the eighteen sixties, and famous for its sea-food. We have the highest bedroom I have ever seen anywhere in the world.

lima and arequipa

December 18.

THE DAY after our arrival here, we moved from the Hotel Maury to a pension in the seaside suburb of Miraflores. It is run by Señora Lily Cisneros, a cousin of our friend, Sarita. She is a big elegant lady, shrewd and talkative, who is related to several of the leading Lima families. On our first evening, Señora Cisneros took us to a party at the house of a wealthy collector named Osma—a fantastically splendid and, to my mind, absolutely uninhabitable establishment furnished throughout with priceless treasures of Spanish Colonial art: paintings, altar-pieces, jeweled crucifixes, etc. The atmosphere of cocktails and streamlined would-be-Parisian society women made it impossible to examine anything seriously. We exchanged silly jokes about the guests in a corner and were tempted to smash or steal something, just to break the spell of such magnificence. Nevertheless, I could see that Osma was no mere dilettante. He really knows about his collection and loves it for its own sake, not for the impression it creates.

Miraflores is, for the most part, a rich residential section, with boulevards of big villas standing in tropical gardens. There are flowers everywhere; Lima is famous for them. Geraniums are even used as danger signs, stuck in poles to warn drivers that men are at work on the roads. A great many British and North American families live here; the ice-cream parlors are full of their children. Upper-class teen-age Peruvian boys in this neighborhood dress like U.S. high-school students, but are too tidy to be quite authentic. There are also a lot of Chinese—as there are in all the towns we passed through on our way down the coast. They usually own restaurants or small provision-stores. They are said to be well-liked because they often marry Peruvian girls. The Japanese aren't because they don't; they are much more clannish.

Miraflores is frequently compared to Beverly Hills, California. There is some superficial resemblance, certainly, but the climate and mood of the two places are quite different. Beverly Hills is bright and cheerful and unsubtle, boldly illuminated by the healthy sunshine. The town is like an advertisement for itself; none of its charms are left to the visitor's imagination. Nearly all its houses, even the grandest, are built to be looked at from the street; for a movie star's home is also the property of his fans and democracy implies the right of every citizen to stand and stare. In Miraflores, luxury retires behind walls and guards itself with ferocious dogs. And the climate is melancholy and languid. A ceiling of cloud hangs over Lima throughout the year, seldom breaking for more than a day or two at a time. In winter, from June to November, the humidity rises so high that the air almost drips, though actual rain is very rare. Fog from the cold Humboldt Current keeps stealing in over the gray water and piling up against the bare brown cliffs. Standing there and looking out to sea, you feel the gentle overpowering sadness of the Pacific—that same sadness which invests Hong Kong, San Francisco and the islands of Japan.

From Miraflores you drive four miles into the center of town along the Avenida Arequipa. The Arequipa is a more or less officially recognized race track. No speed limit is enforced, and it is better not to trust too much to the stop-lights if you are crossing it on foot. Pizarro's original city, laid out in rectangular pattern around the Plaza de Armas, remains very much as it was in Colonial days. The streets are noisy and narrow, and every block has an individual name in addition to the name of the street itself —the Egg, the Seven Sins, the Seven Syringes, and the Devil's Pocket are the examples quoted by our guide-book. The rest of central Lima resembles the duller parts of nineteenth-century Paris; there are spacious avenues and handsome parks, but the oddness and charm of Quito are lacking. However, this is beyond comparison the most imposing city we have seen in South America so far.

Yesterday we went to call on the U.S. Ambassador, Mr. Prentice Cooper. He told that he had recently succeeded in settling the repayment of a sixteen-year-old loan made by American investors to the Peruvian Government. Others before him had tried to do this, but they had always failed because they carried on the negotiations in Washington, not in Lima—which offended the leaders of the Peruvian Congress and made them refuse to ratify the agreement. Mr. Cooper went direct to the Congress and got it through. But now the bondholders in the United States are complaining that the new rate of interest is too low, although they haven't been receiving a cent in all these years. Mr. Cooper feels injured by such ingratitude. When we sympathized with him, he invited us to lunch. I'm glad he did so; otherwise I might have been stupid enough to dismiss him as a fairly ordinary type of Southern politician (he used to be Governor of Tennessee); the kind who believes that you can solve any international problem by straightforward small-town business methods.

At lunch, another and much more fascinating side of Mr. Cooper's character was revealed; he is a passionate naturalist. In his garden, he has a jaguar, an ocelot, a vicuña, a deer and a heron. The heron lives on the patio, where there is a pool, and the deer and the vicuña are kept inside a fenced paddock; otherwise the jaguar would kill them. It is a beautiful creature of lithe furtive movements and lightning turns, half-timid, half-dangerous. It will attack three or four large dogs without hesitation and chase them off the grounds; the ocelot it bullies but tolerates. The Ambassador plays with it fearlessly. They stalk each other among the bushes, the slinking cat and the small gray-haired man. The jaguar crouches, snarls, pretends to spring, then suddenly rolls over and lets itself be petted. We didn't join in this game, but I cautiously patted the vicuña; if you annoy them they will kick, bite and spit. It seemed to like my jacket, which is almost the same color as its own coat but of much inferior quality.

Mr. Cooper used also to keep a boa-constrictor and two condors. But the boa had to be gotten rid of; it was always trying to get at the other animals, or escaping and terrifying the neighbors. The condors flew away, which is a great pity; perched on the roof, they must have given the house the air of a Charles Addams drawing in the New Yorker.

One of Mr. Cooper's best qualities as an Ambassador is that he is genuinely interested in Peru. He has made several trips into out-of-the-way parts of the country, including the site of a spectacular earthquake, where the landscape has been ripped wide open for miles. He described how a party of his friends were riding along a narrow trail in the high mountains when they saw three condors and fired at them. The condors disappeared—to get help, apparently—for they returned a few minutes later with twenty-five others, and all of them swooped down upon the pack-train. In the confusion, two horses fell over the precipice; their riders jumped clear just in time. Condors will peck the eyes out of cows and then drive them with their wings off the edge of a cliff; the cows get killed and the condors eat them.

December 19.

This morning, I went to see Mr. John Harriman, the head of the British Cultural Institute; they have a beautiful old house here and quite a good library. Harriman knows Latin America well; he lived many years in Colombia. He is enthusiastic about Latin Americans in general; he finds them so open, spontaneous and affectionate. He has no use for the kind of Anglo-Saxon who doesn't get along with them; the fault, he thinks, is entirely the Anglo-Saxon's—he is cold and domineering, and has the wrong approach. It's nice to hear someone say this. It merits a big entry on the credit side of the South American ledger, because Harriman is obviously an experienced and intelligent person.

He told me a charming story to show just how spontaneous Colombians can get. At a village near Medellin, during a fiesta, he saw a procession come out of the church carrying a figure of Christ. The figure was wearing a Boy Scout hat. Meanwhile, the band played: "I Can't Give You Anything But Love, Baby." The band didn't know any sacred music, and the hat was probably the best they could find. So, after all, why not?

Later, we talked to an American pilot—a friend of Mr. and Mrs. Knox, our fellow pension-guests—about commercial aviation in the Andes. The planes he usually flies are designed to have a maximum cruising altitude of 16,000 feet. Above this, they are no longer so reliable, but they often have to climb to 22,000. The radio doesn't work well over the mountains, and the maps can't be trusted; the height and position of a peak may be wrongly given. So all flying must be contact—you don't go where you can't see. In consequence there are many delays and unscheduled changes of route which make the passengers, who have no idea of these difficulties, complain indignantly. They would do better to remember that the air-line has had no fatal accident since 1940.

As for the pilot himself, he seemed to be taking his job very calmly. "If I'm flying from Peru to Brazil or from Kansas City to Los Angeles, that's all the same to me. I'd rather land up in Los Angeles, though. It's what happens after you get there that matters."

Nowadays, you can take comparatively cheap South American round-trips by plane; down the eastern coast to Argentina, over the Andes into Chile, then back up north to the States. Of course you are quite free to stop over anywhere along the route if you have the time, but many people haven't. They try to cram the whole continent into an annual vacation which would be barely long enough for a visit to a single city. This kind of total travel is likely to become more and more popular, until we have a generation which has seen all the world's principal airports—and nothing else. At the Hotel Maury I met a dazed American lady who was suffering so severely from travel-indigestion that she seemed uncertain where she was, where she'd been, or which way around she was going.

December 28.

A lapse in my diary-keeping. Christmas is partly to blame, with its hangovers. Also the climate; Lima makes you feel lazy and weak. They say you should take extra vitamins. There aren't enough in the vegetables because the weather is so cloudy.

We ate an authentic U.S. Christmas dinner, thanks to the kindness of Mr. and Mrs. Tauch. (He works in the Civil Aeronautics Administration, and is the brother of one of Caskey's friends in New York.) The Tauchs invited their gardener to bring his children in to see the Christmas tree. The gardener refused because, he said, it would only make them sad that they hadn't one of their own. So Mrs. Tauch fixed up a miniature tree and sent it over to them, with presents. Like all decent foreigners here, the Tauchs feel guilty and helpless in the presence of the miserable poverty which is right outside their gates. Just now, Lima has a serious food shortage. You see breadlines standing in front of many of the poorer shops.

The Tauchs also asked us to a pre-Christmas party at which we met many other members of the U.S. colony here. Chief topics of conversation: the possibility of war with Russia, the fall of the dollar, Peruvian dishonesty. People in South America are apt to be very pessimistic about the European situation, and no wonder; their knowledge of it comes largely from the most alarming kind of U.S. journalism. The fall of the dollar happened quite recently, just before our arrival. It used to be worth 16 to 18 Peruvian soles, now it has dropped to 9.80 because the Peruvian Government is trying to economize on its imports. Mr. Knox doesn't think this devaluation will last very long, but at the moment there is a big scare. U.S. residents here have become accustomed to having a lot of spending money. Married couples have wonderful collections of solid silverware. Silver is cheap in Lima, anyway, and as most of them are connected with the Diplomatic Service or the Army they will be able to bring it back into the States duty-free when their jobs are finished.

Peruvian dishonesty is a subject which comes up again and again. Even those foreign residents who love Lima most will tell you how hub-caps and windscreen wipers were stolen from their cars, how post-office employees will tear the stamps off unregistered mail and then destroy the letters, how their subordinates lie and cheat and are generally unreliable. What shocks me is the indulgently patronizing tone in which these anecdotes are usually told: it's tiresome, of course, but all rather charming and amusing and quaint—a Latin American custom—nothing to be done about it. I feel much more respect for the attitude of Mrs. Knox, who says hotly: "What can you expect—as long as everybody is underpaid?" But that isn't the whole answer. It isn't only the starving who steal or the underpriviliged who are dishonest. A better economic set-up would improve things, no doubt. But how are you to get one as long as nobody can be trusted to cooperate? The whole basis of social organization is rotting away. Bolívar exclaimed in his despair: "Here, in this country, no one can live. Too many crooks." And he certainly wasn't referring to Colombia only. I suppose one must ultimately blame the Conquistadores; their original crime haunts this unfortunate land like a curse. Oppression degraded the oppressed, as it always does, and their cynical self-contempt was bequeathed, as it always must be, to the heirs of the oppressors. The Spaniards brought Christianity, which might have been a great cohesive force—but the Catholic Church was hopelessly compromised by the policy of imperial Spain. South America nationalism necessarily implied anti-clericalism, and so, in due course, the baby was thrown out with the bathwater, leaving an empty and dirty tub. Who is going to get into it? But that brings me to politics. I don't want to write about them yet, until I have talked to some more people.

Among the Americans we have met I must also mention Mr. Parsons, a geologist. He has written a very interesting if rather improbable novel about an imaginary colony of white settlers in a remote Andean valley, deliberately hiding from the rest of the world. Parsons has an excellent opening, describing a plane crash in the high mountains and a subsequent journey on foot by its two survivors, down through the gorges. Reading his manuscript I realize how very useful a practical knowledge of geology can be to a novelist; it makes his descriptions of landscape exact and scientific. He isn't reduced to those wearisome adjectives of magnitude— big, great, vast, huge, tremendous, enormous, gigantic—which are nothing but emotive noises inviting the reader to do all the work. They are the plague of most travel books, including this diary.

We have also been seeing a good deal of Cyril Donnelly, who is First Secretary of the British Embassy here and acting as Chargé d'Affaires while the Ambassador is away. Donnelly has a whole group of literary and artistic Peruvian friends: the poet Emilio Adolfo Westphalen and his wife, the painter Fernando de Szyszlo, the dramatist Sebastian Salazar Bondy and the painter Alicia Bustamante who presides over a *peña* or club at which we have met a number of others. Westphalen's poetry is surrealist, and quite beyond the grasp of my Spanish. He is the editor of *Las Moradas*, the best literary magazine in Peru. Both he and his wife, who is a painter, are remarkable for their physical beauty. At moments, his face looks so intelligent that it seems almost transparent—a thin golden mask covering a melancholy and subtle lucidity. His manners are gentle and diffident and extremely polite. He is always punctual in keeping his appointments with us —a virtue most unusual among Limeños, as we are already beginning to discover.

Fernando de Szyzslo, like Salazar Bondy, is a young man— tall and dark, with an air of romantic fanaticism. His style and subject matter are still obviously influenced by Picasso, but he has an original and exciting sense of color. Donnelly thinks him the most promising of the younger painters.

Señorita Bustamante's *peña* forgathers in what looks like a dark uncomfortable little shop, full of modern Peruvian peasant art and ceramics. We only wish her collection were really for sale. It has been brought together from all over the country; and, since each town specializes in certain objects, you would have to travel for months to duplicate even a part of it. Best of all, we like the *retablos*, which are made by a craftsman in Ayacucho. Small shallow boxes with doors, they look like household shrines but aren't necessarily religious; some of them contain village scenes, groups of peasants and animals, crudely carved and brilliantly colored. They would fascinate any child.

The atmosphere in the *peña* is lively. Comparing it with a similar gathering in London or New York, you notice that women are treated more definitely as members of the opposite sex; the traditions of Latin gallantry are upheld, even among bohemians. We drink pisco and eat little meat pies. A novelist sings folksongs. Everybody is anxious to talk to us, but language difficulties make the conversation somewhat disjointed—a series of direct statements without connection or elaboration: "Peru is a very sad country." "The best American poet is English and the best English poet is American." "I once made love in the Vatican Library."

January 1, 1948.

Yesterday, Westphalen took us to visit Dr. Basadre, the head of the National Library. This is a magnificent place, not yet quite finished; it has been under construction since the fire which destroyed the older building, six years ago. At that time, the Library owned about a hundred thousand books. They had never been catalogued, and a group of young students were just starting work on this project when the disaster happened. It is suspected, but has never been proved, that the fire wasn't an accident, since the catalogue would probably have revealed that many rare volumes and manuscripts had been stolen and sold to collectors abroad. Dr. Basadre is now appealing to libraries and universities all over the world to help him get another collection together.

We went on to see Dr. Porros, who works at the Ministry of Foreign Affairs. A very amusing man. In his office, there is a map of Peru which seems to confirm all the Ecuadorean accusations of land-grabbing; the Peruvian frontier has moved northward and westward right up to the Andes, like a rising tide. When I remarked on this to Dr. Porros, he laughed and said: "Ah—you musn't take that too seriously. What else can you expect, in the Ministry of Foreign Affairs? We love the Ecuadoreans, so we want to come closer to them. We believe in *rapprochement.*"

At lunch, we talked about Pizarro, whom Porros greatly admires. He thinks that *The Conquest of Peru* is unfair to Pizarro, and has the startling theory that Prescott was prejudiced against the Spanish invasion because he regarded it as an infringement of the Monroe Doctrine!

Last night, we went to several parties, ending up at the home of some people we didn't know at all. I asked a man to show me the Southern Cross, which we have never seen. He took me out onto the balcony and solemnly pointed to a cross of electric lights, on the roof of a neighboring church. The whole evening was like that; silly but not gay. Much talk, as usual, about Russia and war.

A charming domestic custom practised by an American couple here: before drinking their first Martini they kiss each other, as a pledge against quarreling later. This technique seems to work. Whenever we have seen them at a party they have always been on the most affectionate terms.

Dr. Porros talked a good deal about politics, yesterday, and this reminds me that I had better try to summarize what we have heard from various informants. Short of open civil war, the situation in Peru at this moment could hardly be worse. It is a complete deadlock, and one doesn't see how it can possibly be ended except by violence.

The present trouble started a year ago, when Dr. Francisco Graña, the owner of a Conservative newspaper called the *Prensa*, was shot dead as he was leaving his office. The Right Wing immediately blamed Apra, the People's Party, for the murder, and several Apristas were arrested. Apra is very strong in the Congress but it doesn't have the necessary two-thirds majority to form a quorum. The Rightist representatives have boycotted Congress; so Congress can't meet.

If Apra really had anything to do with the Graña murder, this was a terrible piece of folly. The scandal has lost them a lot of votes and popular support. Also, their members have been forced to withdraw from the cabinet, in order to leave President Bustamante free to conduct the investigation. Bustamante has filled up the cabinet posts with Army men, who used to be ministers under General Benavides, the last dictator. The general impression seems to be that Bustamante is an honest man trying hard to do his job in accordance with the constitution. But since he can only act by grace of the Army, which is by nature extraconstitutional, his position is hopelessly compromised. It is even possible that the Army itself is split. No one knows to what extent Apra has infiltrated the rank and file. This will only appear if it comes to actual fighting.

The Communists, a comparatively small party in Peru, hate Apra so much that they have allied themselves with the Right, which optimistically imagines that it will first liquidate Apra and then dispose of them later. The Right and the Communists together have managed to block a deal which would have opened up the Sechura, the northern desert, to Anglo-American oil interests. The Communists are, of course, anti-U.S. Apra, which is pro-U.S. and anti-U.S.S.R., supports the Sechura deal.

We have heard many opinions of Victor Raúl Haya de la Torre, the Apra leader. On the whole, they aren't favorable. He is accused of being a snob, a phony, a ham. It is said that he gets an erotic pleasure out of public speaking. Once, before addressing a mass meeting on the Plaza San Martín, he looked up at the moon and two tears rolled down his cheeks. These tears—"the tears of Haya"—were much written up in the Aprista press, and described as "two diamonds." In his youth, he was a gossip columnist. He has evolved an Aprista philosophy which he calls Historic Space-Time. One lady described "his primitive sharp way of listening, with his full profile turned toward you, like an Indian who listens to the noises over his crops and thinks, 'This must be the east wind,' or to the cry of a sheep lost far away on the plateau." However, all our informants agree that he has great personal charm.

These accusations aren't of much significance from the political point of view. What is more serious is the suggestion that Haya is quite ruthless and habitually works through violence. It is said that he has his own bodyguard and storm-troopers, that his enemies are threatened over the telephone and if necessary removed. His party is tightly organized—far better than any other in Peru—and nothing is done except by his personal order. This means that if Graña was really murdered by Apristas, Haya must have been directly responsible.

January 4.

Today, we drove up into the mountains with Cyril Donnelly. The Andes rise so steeply from the narrow coastal plain that you can reach an altitude of over 15,000 feet at a railroad station less than 100 miles inland. The building of this railroad during the eighteen-seventies, under the direction of the American adventurer, Henry Meiggs, involved the most complicated engineering problems (61 bridges, 66 tunnels and 21 switchbacks) and a huge expense of manpower and money. Seven thousand workmen died of a mysterious fever accompanied by warts, which was traced to the bite of a sandfly called the Verruga. A young doctor, Daniel Carrión, injected himself with the poison in order to study its symptoms, died, and became a national hero. It was finally discovered that the Verruga is localized in a relatively small area, between three and eight thousand feet, and that it only bites at night; so the problem was solved as far as the railroad workers were concerned—they merely had to be moved out of the danger-zone before sundown. But the Verruga pest hasn't yet been exterminated—although a government medical commission is working against it—and the flies have lately been reported in other parts of the country. There is a theory that their poison may come from some plant on which they habitually settle.

We picnicked in a green sub-tropical valley, right in the midst of the Verruga belt, and then drove on, climbing the steepening curves of the road to a little town. In the cliff above it, is wedged an enormous threatening fragment of rock; if this is ever dislodged by an earthquake it will almost certainly destroy the railway station. On the rock, Apra has painted its name in bold red letters. The Party, ably assisted by the Communists, has done its best to disfigure Peru in this manner—though its efforts seem puny when compared with those of the big advertising firms in the States.

Climbing higher, you enter the black wet cloudy gorge of the Rio Rimac. It is as narrow as Wall Street, and the bare windowless precipices are more horribly claustrophobic than downtown New York. The river rumbles and roars over the rocks, like traffic. And from somewhere high overhead, amidst the fog, you hear the desperate little whistle of a train, puffing along a ledge, emerging from a tunnel, or crossing the abyss over bridges which look as thin as matchsticks. The most gruesome part of this natural slum is appropriately called El Infiernillo, the Small Hell.

Meanwhile Donnelly talked, most interestingly, about Churchill and Roosevelt and Bevin and his own work at Whitehall during the war. This is what I remember most clearly about our excursion. Tourists carry their own conversation along with them, like their sandwiches, and can only spare a few moments for the scenery between mouthfuls.

January 5.

Today, we bought our airplane tickets to Arequipa. You can fly there in about three hours. The alternative—a sixty-hour bus-ride along the coast—is too unpleasant to be considered.

Another meeting with Westphalen. He introduced us to the painter, Ricardo Grau. Grau is an ardent Aprista, and he promises to arrange for us to meet Haya de la Torre. He and Westphalen seem to be good friends, although Westphalen doesn't share his views and is a Liberal—a tragic and honorable position in this land of violence. I asked him about police spies and informers. He said that there were none now, but that they flourished under the regime of Benavides. Westphalen himself was arrested at that time and imprisoned, but he wasn't beaten up. When he talks of these things, he seems very gentle and weary. He is the kind of man who will accept torture and death if his conscience shows him no other way out, but unwillingly, with a sort of apologetic embarrassment.

January 6.

All along the shore south of Lima there are wonderful beaches; they are known by the number of the nearest kilometer-stone on the coastal highway. This afternoon, we drove out to Beach Fifty-five with Donnelly, a Belgian painter named Maes, and Greta de Verneuil, a Swiss lady whom we met at the

Bustamante *peña*. Beach Fifty-five is protected from the Pacific rollers by a natural breakwater of big rocks. On the reef between two of these, a rich Lima family is building a villa—a squat ugly place with a lighthouse tower. The sea foams dramatically around it through a gap, bursting against the rock opposite and cannoning back under a narrow footbridge. There are a lot of seabirds, and the roof will soon be rich in guano deposits. (Which reminds me that, on our first day here, we saw a newspaper headline: "Guano Alone Can Save Peru"—a pronouncement almost as grim, in its own way, as Churchill's blood, toil, sweat and tears.) Donnelly, who is a strict aesthete of the old school, was much shocked by the villa. Bad taste, he said, was worse than immorality.

Presently the sun set, striking across the barren shore and the little mud-cube houses, which look like the very earliest dwellings of settlers on some hitherto uninhabited planet. The pale mouse-colored desert behind them darkened into splendid folds of crimson. And then came the afterglow, with clouds flashing like splinters of crystal, against glimpses of sky which were a very old bright innocent blue, such as you see in the paintings of the primitive Italian masters. The whole performance struck us speechless, until Donnelly objected that it was really going too far and getting a bit vulgar.

January 7.

While we were sitting in the bar of the Bolívar Hotel this afternoon, some boys on the street below were distributing leaflets. They had a banner showing a frog with a Stars and Stripes stomach which was swollen with dollars, inscribed "The Greatest Congressman." A man who was passing looked up at the window, recognized me for a gringo, and said malevolently: "Now the dollar is worth ten soles. One day the sol will be worth ten dollars."

Today is the anniversary of Graña's murder. There are a number of memorial demonstrations being held, including one at his grave in the cemetery. Feeling is said to be running high against the Apra Party, and violence is expected. Meanwhile, the Apristas have conveniently found something else to hold a meeting about: the centenary of the birth of Manuel González Prada—a free-thinker and temperamental anarchist, of whom Haya de la Torre, in his youth, was a disciple. González Prada would certainly never have approved of Apra, but the Party now claims him as its great forerunner.

We decided to go to this meeting, which was being held in the Casa del Pueblo, the Apra headquarters. It is a large cheerful building, decorated with posters and graphic charts illustrating social problems. There is a cost-price workers' restaurant and an open-air auditorium. We were received with the greatest friendliness—perhaps owing to a misunderstanding, which I didn't correct, that we were representing *Time Magazine*. We even got seats on the platform. I hope this won't compromise Henry Luce.

Unfortunately, Haya himself wasn't present. The guest of honor was González Prada's widow, described by an acquaintance as "a bitter old Voltairean who hates everything." Actually, she seemed dignified and rather touching. She has written a life of her husband which you see in all the bookstores. It is called *My Manuel*, and has a nauseating jacket design: the tiny figure of a woman with her arms raised adoringly toward the gigantic granite face of the great man. His eyes are closed like the Buddha's, and over his head the star of Peru burns.

The meeting passed without interruption. If any hecklers tried to attend it, they must have been stopped at the doors. The audience was highly disciplined, applauding every Party slogan with organized rhythmic clapping—one-two-three, one-two-three. The speakers on such occasions are not expected to say anything startling or novel; their function is somewhat like that of orchestra conductors, and their success or failure depends upon their ability to create dramatic pauses, exciting crescendos and brilliant climaxes of applause. Also, the element of physical contact is very important. There was one muscular young man who began by stripping off his coat and rolling up his shirtsleeves. By the time he was through, we were all stimulated and pleasantly exhausted, as though we had taken part in a friendly mass-wrestling match.

January 8.

This afternoon, Grau took us to see Haya. He is very different from what we had been led to expect—not nearly such a conscious charmer. (Unless, indeed, this very absence of charm was a refinement of technique—since, as we have so often been told, he prides himself on being all things to all men.) He is in his fifties, powerful, short, fattish, with thin hair and a great eagle nose. His features are somewhat Indian. He looks tired and battered by Life. His eyes are old and shrewd. He speaks excellent English.

We talked first about his time in England, to which he fled after the unsuccessful rising at Trujillo, when many Apristas were shot and the Party went underground. He became great friends with old George Lansbury (this is certainly a strong point in his favor) and Lansbury actually intervened on his behalf when he later returned to Peru and was imprisoned.

I asked about Gaitán. Haya replied cautiously that Gaitán was his good friend, but had no real program. "We have always had a clear program," he added, "right from the earliest days. You know, we began as an educational movement. We built ourselves up by opening night schools for the workers. Apra is a great proletarian college, and I am its dean."

He is in favor of letting U.S. enterprises into the country. "The American oil people up at Talara have done everything for their workers that Apra could wish. Of course there are also foreign firms where the working conditions are bad, but even these have a negative value; they compel Labor to organize and become more conscious of its rights. . . . The agricultural conditions in this country are our real problem. The Conquistadores deliberately ruined the irrigation-system which the Incas had built up. Now the governing classes own all the land on the higher mountain slopes and they keep the water for themselves. Apra has prepared an irrigation scheme for the whole coastal region, but they'll never consent to it unless they have to; if more land were opened to cultivation, the peasants would have the opportunity of working elsewhere and so be able to demand higher wages."

(Haya didn't go into any further details about this irrigation scheme. Maybe it is workable. But a British expert told us that it is very difficult to see how the Peruvian desert could be cultivated. Rain-making by plane, as it is practised in the States, doesn't work well here because the temperature is too high. And dams are liable to get cracked by the frequent earthquakes. An earthquake followed by a landslide recently polluted Lima's water supply by dumping arsenic into the river.)

I alluded, rather hesitantly, to the Graña murder. Haya seemed perfectly willing to discuss it. He made the obvious defense that Apra had had most to lose by the crime. In his opinion, it was committed by private persons for non-political reasons, probably under great provocation. According to Haya, the chief witness for the prosecution is a boy who has been examined while under the influence of the "truth-drug," and his testimony has varied on different occasions. "No doubt you have seen your American film 'Boomerang'? Well—this film has just been banned in Peru. We believe the reason is because it shows how an innocent man can be convicted on purely circumstantial evidence, if the authorities are interested in finding him guilty."

I asked his opinion of President Bustamante. "Bustamante," said Haya," has been a disappointment to us. Apra supported him, and our votes were responsible for his election. We thought he was a strong man—but he is only a legalist, a jurist. You have heard of this Senators' strike—how the Right is boycotting Congress in order to tie our hands? The President should insist that these Senators must either return to Congress or lose their salaries. But he won't do this, because he says that there is nothing specifically written in our Constitution about Senators' strikes. What does that matter? Our Constitution says that Senators are expected to do their jobs conscientiously. Isn't that enough?"

Again rather hesitantly, I questioned him about the Party's record of violence. Haya became quite passionate: "What about our opponents' record? Who do you think started this violence? Can I tell these boys, these young courageous men, that they must not fight back, that they must allow themselves to be beaten and imprisoned and murdered?" Calming down, he became vaguer, less direct: "Naturally there have been some incidents . . . things we regret. Every political party has its hot-heads. Now and then, they get out of hand. . . ."

We parted cordially. As he drove us home, Ricardo Grau praised Haya with great emotion and obvious sincerity. He was such a wonderful man, and so misunderstood. "You must tell the truth about him," Grau said. I promised that I would try to be fair. And I have tried. The trouble is that I still don't quite know what to think of Haya. I suppose I'd flattered myself that a personal contact with him would reveal everything, and it hasn't. Caskey feels the same way as I do. Probably it is only the absolutely honest and the utterly corrupt who can be so easily recognized. If Haya isn't as great as his own social program, he certainly isn't as small as his enemies' opinion of him. Did he really order Graña's murder? I very much doubt it. Would he be quite incapable of giving such an order? I doubt that, too.

January 9.

This morning, at 7 A.M. we set off for Arequipa. It is desert nearly all the way, with a few straggling green threads of valleys following the courses of rivers. From above, the landscape looks like crusty yellow bread, with round loaf-shaped hills dimpled as if by the print of a cook's thumb. At one point, you see marks on the sand, forming huge triangles, like roads leading nowhere. Nobody knows who made them or what they mean. They are hundreds of years old, probably. It never rains here, so nothing washes out.

On your left, the broken rampart of the Andes towers up, with its hard gleaming snow peaks; on your right is the soft gray emptiness of the Pacific, the silent water-hemisphere, beyond the limits of the human world. Poised between these three sterile immensities—mountain, desert and ocean—the droning plane seems to shrink and become tiny as an insect. Now and then it swivels and bumps insecurely on the hot uprush of air from a deep gully. Even on a fine bright morning, like today, nature feels hostile here. I never quite relaxed until the first good earthy bounce of the landing gear on Arequipa's stony airfield.

"Of course," our friends in Lima told us, "you'll stop at the Quinta Bates. You can't come to Peru and not meet Tia. She's the most famous woman in South America. If she likes you, she'll do anything for you. If she doesn't—well, she'll have you out of the place in twenty-four hours." And they went on to describe how Tia, then a young girl from upstate New York, had married an Englishman and followed him out to a mining-camp in the High Andes, where he died; how she had settled in Arequipa and has spent the rest of her life there, becoming, in course of time, not only a great-grandmother but also an "honorary aunt" (hence her nickname) to hundreds of guests who still send her letters from the corners of the earth; how she has entertained the Duke of Windsor, Henry Wallace, General Pershing, Noel Coward; how she is the real boss of Arequipa, no matter who is in office; how she charges hugely or nothing at all, according to her opinion of you; how she detests tangerines and scorns corsets. All this filled me with misgivings, for I dread "characters," and I had more or less decided to stay at the government hotel and avoid her, despite Caskey's protests. But when we arrived at the airport and had to scramble for a taxi, and the driver said "Quinta Bates" without a question mark, I thought only of getting a quick wash and breakfast, and gave in.

Now, I'm very glad I did. Tia is much more impressive and less tiresome than her legend. A handsome majestic old lady in her advanced eighties, she greeted us with the informal graciousness of acknowledged royalty: "Where are you from, son? All right—make yourselves at home. Ask the boys for anything you want." Her house is like her personality—old-fashioned, rambling and full of souvenirs. Vines grow all over it, and there is a garden on the roof where you can sit and look downhill over the roofs of the city or uphill toward the mountains. The food is delicious; especially the ice-cream, which is almost the best I have ever tasted anywhere. The beds have silk quilts on them, and the bedrooms are supplied with fleecy pre-war towels, pens, ink, writing-paper and novels by Edith Wharton. The plumbing is hardly of the latest pattern—but everything is kept so clean and hot water is so quickly produced by the many efficient houseboys that you feel that this lack of modernity gives an added sense of safety and snugness. It is like staying with your grandmother—no, I should say your great-grandmother, or perhaps, to be on the safe side, your great-great-grandmother—for one of Tia's grand-daughters, who is here with her, already has children of marriageable age.

According to our guide-book, there is a legend that Arequipa got its name in the earliest Incaic times, when runners who were bringing fish in relays from the sea to the Inca's palace in Cuzco asked if they might not stop here to get their breath. "Are quepay," they were told—which means, in the Quechua language, "yes, rest." I hope this is true, because "yes, rest," perfectly conveys my feeling about the place. There is something delightful in the atmosphere, something soft and lucid, soothing yet stimulating, which immediately invites you to remain, settle down and work. I hadn't been here ten minutes before I began getting ideas for my next novel, which I have scarcely even thought about in weeks. They say that Noel Coward wrote a whole play while he was staying in this house. No wonder.

Although Arequipa is 7,500 feet above sea level it doesn't seem high, because it lies right under the inner Andean rampart. The upper end of its steep valley is closed by three huge mountains, Chachani, Misti and Pichu-Pichu. Misti is an extinct volcano. The smooth soaring lines of its cone carry your eyes up it in an instant and make it look deceptively accessible; you imagine that you could easily reach the top in two or three hours. The sun shines here most days. The gardens of the city are always full of flowers. The old Colonial churches and mansions look as if they were built of sugar-candy; actually, it is pink and white volcanic rock. Outside one of the churches is a large crucifix of a kind I have never seen before. Instead of the body of the dead Christ, the cross is hung with emblems of the Passion—the robe, the winding-sheet, the spear, the skull of Golgotha, the thirty pieces of silver, the cock that crowed to admonish Peter, and the head with its crown of thorns.

January 12.

Tonight we are leaving for Cuzco, after a peaceful all-too-short visit which we have spent mostly reading and lying in the sun on the roof. Does Tia approve of us? More or less—to judge by our very moderate bill. When Caskey asked her to let him take her photograph, she changed into her best dress and put on plenty of lipstick, which was certainly charming of her. On the other hand, since we have been here, she has only once asked us to sit at her table in the dining room. Tia's real favors seem to be reserved for young U.S. Army men and air-line pilots. One of the latter is staying here now. He describes the hazards of landing at some of the smaller airports in Southern Peru. There is one place which it is wise to prepare for by putting rocks in your tail. Otherwise you may not be able to stop in time, and risk running off the end of the strip, which is far too short, smack into the foot of a mountain.

The morning after our arrival here, we saw Tia in action. A man, comparatively well-dressed and rather drunk, stumbled into the sitting room, fell on his knees before her and poured forth a mixture of English and Spanish: "Mother! Mummy! Madrecita! Three days I eat nothing! *Tres dias!* Mother! Give me bread!" He clutched at her skirts. Obviously, he was rather enjoying his own performance.

"Get up," Tia told him, neither impressed nor alarmed— people wander in and out of the house all day long, and she must be quite accustomed to strange visitors—"Don't lose your dignity like that, son, for heaven's sake!" Then, fishing in her purse for money, "Here—take it. It's the widow's mite. Now be off with you!"

Many of Tia's benefactions seem to have been achieved by bullying important persons into giving her protégés jobs. Speaking of the local dignitaries of Arequipa, she told us: "They're all afraid of me. That's because I've got 'em bluffed. *I'm* afraid of *them!*"

on the plateau

January 13.

We left Arequipa by train at 10 p.m. yesterday evening. This line—the Southern Railway—runs up from Mollendo on the coast to Puno on Lake Titicaca, with a branch northward to Cuzco. It is the longest and, I believe, the oldest in the country. Our sleeping-car was as old-fashioned, clean and comfortable as Tia's house, and if we didn't sleep very well in it that was only because of the suddenly increased altitude. Crucero Alto, the highest point along the route, is nearly level with the top of the Matterhorn.

When day broke, we were already over the pass and down on the *puna*, the 12,000-foot-high plateau which includes Lake Titicaca and extends far into Bolivia. It is flat open country, covered with rough bright green grass and dotted with small ponds and marshes. As long as the sun is shining, it has a spacious spring-like air. When the clouds gather, it seems unspeakably mournful. Bitter gusts sweep across it from the snowfields of the great mountains. From this elevation they look like mere hills, rising beyond the rim of the plain. This landscape is very much as I imagine Tibet.

Around breakfast-time, we arrived at Juliaca, where you change trains for Cuzco. It is an almost purely Indian town of low brown earthen buildings. In the raw brightness of early morning, it looks very humble, dirty and desolate. Outside the station, women were selling blankets, scarves, sweaters and pointed woollen caps with ear-flaps. We bought two of the sweaters. They are decorated with rows of llamas and peasant girls in wide skirts, gaily colored, like paper cut-outs on a nursery wall.

Up here, you become overwhelmingly aware of the presence of the Indians. Cuzco was the capital of the Inca empire, and the *puna*, despite conquest and expropriation, is still their native land.

142

You see them, singly or in groups, all over the plain. Some of them are working on patches of arable field, others watch their herds of cows, sheep, llamas and vicuñas. In the extraordinary clarity of the atmosphere, every living figure seems significant and dramatic; the skirts of the Indian women, brilliant pink, deep orange or red, are visible as sharp spots of color even in the farthest distance. These people, like the Chinese peasants, have an uncanny air of belonging to their landscape—of being, in the profoundest sense, its inhabitants. It would hardly surprise you to see them emerging from or disappearing into the bowels of the earth.

A village called Pucará is famous for its pottery. Little clay bulls—fantastically garlanded, with their tails curling over their backs—cost about a dollar and could be resold in New York for twenty-five. And there are a variety of other animals, pitchers, pots and dishes set out along the whole length of the station platform. Not all the wares are of equal merit; you have to choose carefully and very quickly, for the train only stops seven minutes. Caskey and I scrambled back on board as it re-started, clutching an armful of bulls, a horse with a small snakelike head and another very beautiful yellow one, which looks oddly Chinese. We only hope we can get them back home unbroken.

Then the train climbs slowly, past a huge glacier, to the watershed at La Raya. Two streams part here—one to join the Amazon, the other to fall into the Pacific, via Lake Titicaca. It is unpleasantly high—over 14,000 feet—and even while sitting still in the coach we got headaches and felt slightly sick. As the descent begins, the stream thickens to a mountain river, red mud-water mingling with its slatey blue. The valleys become green and fertile. They have been cultivated for hundreds of years, and you can still see the Incaic fields, terraced and sided with masonry, which climb the mountain slopes like wide stairs. Boys came capering up to the train, waving their arms and shouting; they wore black woollen masks with long sinister hanging noses and eyeholes outlined in scarlet thread. At one of the stations, we watched a tall thin Indian youth creep up and stealthily pin a tuft of vicuña wool to the seat of his friend's pants; this he did with the utmost gravity and care. Farther down the platform, a tipsy little woman and a group of men were drinking pisco; she held the bottle to each man's lips in turn, as though she were feeding babies. These faces were straight off the huacos we saw in the museum at Chiclín; the same long high-bridged noses and half-open juglike lips. Near by, a tethered group of llamas disregarded the noisy scene. They are the most disdainful of creatures, stepping delicately and capriciously, arching their aristocratic necks. Caskey, with his camera, went rather too near one of them—it had strands of colored wool in its ear, which marked it as the leader of a pack-train. It gave him a cold rude stare, drew back its upper lip, and spat.

Throughout the journey, we noticed several sorts of Indian headgear. Around Juliaca, the women wear a white top hat with a pink or gold band; further on, you see a kind of garden hat with side-flaps; beyond this, a flat hat with circular patterns on the crown. The men usually wear battered felts, with woollen caps under them for warmth.

An Indian boy got onto the train and offered to sell us a little marble bull. Two of our fellow-passengers, American Protestant missionaries, told us that this was one of the household gods which the Indians still surreptitiously worship, despite their professed Christianity. You very rarely have the chance to see them.

We arrived at Cuzco shortly after six, this evening, and are staying at the government Tourist Hotel, which is large and clean and quite comfortable, except for a shortage of hot water. We have already complained to Sarita Cisneros about this. To our great joy, her tour of inspection has brought her here. Her liveliness somewhat counteracts the dismalness of the weather, which is wet and very cold.

In the lounge, there are some beautiful and absurd Colonial religious paintings. My favorite represents an angel, a fairylike little girl with a sword and golden butterfly skirts, who has her foot coquettishly planted on a sprawling demon. The demon, who is old enough to be her father, is obviously loving it. He is leering and caressing her foot with the enthusiasm of a boot-fetishist.

There is a pet deer which wanders freely about the rooms and passages, no doubt giving the staff a lot of extra work cleaning up its droppings. Sarita warns us that it will eat any manuscripts, photographs or letters which it finds lying around. It also cleans out the ash trays, and many of the guests feed it cigarettes. If it gets frightened, it kicks viciously and skids all over the polished floor.

Cuzco is right on the trans-Andean tourist trail. This hotel is full of tourists. The majority are North American—middle-aged women schoolteachers, mostly. Grimly devout, complaining but undaunted, they make their way over the mountains from Lima to Buenos Aires—gasping in the high altitudes, vomiting and terrified in planes, rattled like dice in buses, dragged out of bed before dawn to race along precipice roads, poisoned with strange foods, tricked by shopkeepers, appalled by toilets.

Machu Picchu on its precipice, about seventy miles north of Cuzco, is one of the principal stations of this great *via dolorosa*. Several excursions there are organized every week during the season. Soon after our arrival, today's returning pilgrims began to limp into the lounge and boast of their hardships to scare us newcomers. "*Well*—! I wouldn't do that again for ten thousand dollars!" "I couldn't stop the brute, but the guide just laughed and told me to hang on tight." "Muriel's mule was the meanest of the lot. It ate grass, *right on the edge*, and wouldn't budge." "When mine started to *skid*, I just shut my eyes. I thought, oh, boy, this is the *end!*"

January 15.

There is no sense in my trying to describe Cuzco; I should only be quoting from the guide-book. In fact, after two days' sightseeing, I am so bewildered by impressions that I scarcely know what we have actually seen and what we have read. What remains with you is the sense of a great outrage, magnificent but unforgivable. The Spaniards tore down the Inca temples and grafted splendid churches and mansions onto their foundations. This is one of the most beautiful monuments to bigotry and sheer stupid brutality in the whole world.

Present-day Cuzco is almost unchanged since early Colonial days, and probably a lot dirtier. The narrow cobbled lanes stink like sewers, the courtyards are littered with garbage, and the houses are mostly quite unfit for human habitation. You are warned against typhus-lice in the market. The Indians are pockmarked, filthy, wretchedly poor. The women look prematurely old. They squat on the damp ground, arranging and rearranging their wares. Nearly everybody has something to sell, even if it is only two or three onions or a handful of beans.

This raises a question: what on earth is to be done with a living historical monument? Evacuate it, and it hardens at once into a fossil. Modernize its interiors and its plumbing and it will turn, more slowly but just as surely, into a self-conscious death-mask. And yet the alternative is unthinkable—to condemn thousands of people to a life of squalor and disease for the pleasure of the archaeologists and romantically-minded tourists.

Today, we went up the hill above the town to see the ruins of Sacsahuamán, the Inca fortress. Its walls are built of huge ashlars cut with almost incredible precision and fitted together without mortar. The biggest blocks weigh twenty tons. How were they moved from the quarry? Probably with little bronze crowbars; the Incas had no wheels. Why were they brought here? Perhaps to satisfy some deep psychological need for weight and mass; perhaps, also, to make extra work for the compulsory labor service to which every taxpayer was subject. The emperor Huayna Capac is said to have had a hill moved from one location to another because he couldn't think of anything else for his men to do. If you weren't dragging rocks around, you were probably serving in the Army, working in the mines, tilling the fields, waiting on the nobles, or running with fish or messages along the roads. Relays of Inca runners could travel from Lima to Cuzco in three days. During the Spanish Colonial period in the seventeenth century, the mail was carried on horseback and took twelve.

Any failure in these duties was apt to lead to atrocious punishments—having a large stone dropped on your back, being hanged by your feet, brained with a club or thrown over a precipice. The nobles were somewhat better off; their minor backslidings were merely punished by public rebuke and loss of office. Nobles, however, are more liable to commit high treason; and the penalty for that was imprisonment in a dungeon full of wild beasts and poisonous snakes. Nor should the favorite wives and servants of the Emperor be unduly envied. When he died, they were expected to volunteer to accompany him. They were made drunk during a public dance and strangled.

If you didn't have the luck to be born an emperor, you were probably safest and most comfortable as a priest. Divination, it is true, is a risky business, but if the omens prove to have been misleading you can always blame somebody else for an unconfessed sin. A little knowledge of astronomy enables you to perform the annual miracle of "fastening the sun" at the solstice and bringing it gradually back to cause a new spring and summer. The many religious ceremonies must have provided the Inca priests with all kinds of perquisites, the leavings of sacrifices. And then there were the temple women, specially chosen for their beauty.

Most of the above information comes from John Rowe's book, which I have been re-reading. Rowe, obviously, has a considerable affection for the Incas, as well as a great respect. The respect is easy to share. They were certainly an impressive people. But they fill me, personally, with a kind of horror. I find them, as we used to say during the Evelyn Waugh Period, madly ungay.

The best thing you can say about the Inca culture is that it offered absolute security to all its members—in exchange, of course, for absolute obedience. It was a culture of mass, of authority, of order. A culture based upon natural law; materialistic, reasonable, and, within its graded social limits, strictly just. A mountain culture, solid, magnificent and somber. Much ritual, little spirituality. Much gold, little elegance. Much feasting, little fun.

The relation of conquered to conqueror is always interesting. Did the Incas "deserve" the invasion of the Conquistadores? Hardly. Only fiends could merit such a punishment. All the same, one can't think of them simply as a harmless peaceful nation overrun and butchered by bloodthirsty adventurers. The Incas were imperialists, too. At the height of their power, they had subdued all the other tribes of Peru, and conquered the Bolivian highlands, most of Ecuador, northwestern Argentina and northern Chile. Their leaders seem to have had no motives for making war except ambition; land wasn't needed, and many of the conquered tribes were so poor that they were at first an actual economic liability. Compared with the Spaniards, the Incas were merciful, but, like the Spaniards, they imposed their own religion and their own language. They also moved populations around from one part of the empire to another, in order to guard against national uprisings.

Incidentally, Rowe points out how amazingly lucky Pizarro was to arrive exactly when he did. If he had come only one year later, he would have found the civil war over, Atahuallpa securely in power, and all the armies of the Incas united against him.

Today the Indians, neither rulers now nor servants, form a large undigested mass in the stomach of the body politic. Are they sullenly resigned, obstinately rebellious, or merely indifferent— still suffering from cultural shock? Would they like to be educated? Would they prefer to co-operate in the national life? Or are they simply waiting, quietly and without impatience, for the white men to go away? At present, there is no official education given, and no official business transacted, in the Quechua language. This means that if you don't speak Spanish (and 35% of the population doesn't!) you are automatically debarred from the schools and law-courts, not to mention the holding of any kind of government job. The fact that the Incas had no written language makes this boycott doubly effective. Quechua can now be written down, but the Indians themselves will have to be taught to read it. As long as the present situation exists, Peru can only be described as a Spanish colony. And Bolivia, from all accounts, is even worse.

We talked about all this with a bookseller here who is a Communist. But our conversation didn't shed much light on the problem, despite Sarita's skill as an interpreter. The bookseller's mind seemed to be chiefly occupied by his hatred of Apra. He accused them of empty promises; while they were in power, he said, they had done nothing. And anyhow, he added, they were fascists. I asked him about his own Party's programme. He replied: "We believe in deeds, not words." Pressed to be a little more specific, he said that the Communists would break up the big estates and give the land to the Indians. I agreed that every progressive party would naturally want to do this; it is no more than elementary justice. But how was the Communist Party going to deal with the racial question? What about Spanish versus Quechua? What was to be the relation between education and the Church? Perhaps I fired these questions off too quickly, for the bookseller only answered the last of them. "Our Party," he said, "has no interest whatsoever in the religious problem." This remark struck me as being either so incredibly stupid or so brazenly hypocritical that I lost all desire to continue the discussion.

January 16.

Today we visited Machu Picchu.

A rail-bus takes you nearly all the way there—switchbacking over the hills north of Cuzco, crossing the farmlands of the Anta Valley, descending into the roaring jungle gorge of the Urubamba. After chilly Cuzco, the atmosphere here seems tropical and oppressive. The gorge is so deep that you can see very little of it from the bus; to explore it properly you would have to use a plane.

We drove by car from the little terminal station to the bridge which crosses the rapids. From here, right under the Machu Picchu cliffs, you can scarcely see anything of the ruins above. Mules were waiting to take us up the winding trail to the summit. "Yours is the best," our guide told me, "but you've got to watch him." I grinned weakly, remembering the alarming tales we had heard at the Tourist Hotel. We set off in single file—quite a large party. There was Sarita, laughing and joking as usual; Caskey, sitting slumped on his mule with the relaxed boredom of an old cowhand; Al Johnson, a young American who is gathering material for a Ph.D. thesis on some Latin cultural subject; Señor Penard, an Argentine gentleman traveling with his sister and another lady, meticulously dressed and extremely polite; and another Argentine, stout and jolly, who sang.

Although the trail is very steep and parts of the slope are nearly vertical, the ascent is not at all unpleasant. The many bushes and shrubs which cover the cliffs give you a comforting, if false, sense of security. You feel that you could easily grab something if you were to roll over the edge. But what a breathtaking place! You seem to be climbing into a larger world, a landscape built by titans in a fit of sheer megalomania. From the narrow saddleback on which the ruined city stands, the precipices plunge headlong into the raging brown river, fifteen hundred feet below. Looking up makes you even giddier than looking down, for all around the valley are black snow-streaked mountains looming over you through the driving clouds, and right ahead, at the end of the ridge, towers an appalling berg of rock, like the fragment of a fallen moon. This is called Huayna Picchu. The Incas, who must have been able to climb like flies, built a watchtower on top of it, to guard the approach to the citadel.

Nobody knows for certain how old this city is. It may have been inhabited by the earliest Incas before Cuzco became their capital. It was certainly used as an Alpine Redoubt by the last emperors, after the Spaniards had overrun their country. It had a very holy temple. There, when all else was lost, the surviving Chosen Women of the Sun were probably hidden. If so, the Spaniards never found them. One by one, the priestesses aged and died. Centuries passed. The city was forgotten. And then, in 1911, the American archaeologist, Hiram Bingham, following a devious trail of local rumors, made his way up to the ridge and saw enough to excite his curiosity. Next year, he returned with a party of assistants. Cutting through undergrowth swarming with deadly snakes, and thick jungle vines, they gradually uncovered the great amphitheater of terraces, the palace, the temples, the storehouses and the sacred sundial. And Machu Picchu was added to the known wonders of the world.

Our guide had been out drinking the night before and had a severe hangover. He was very cross when I insisted on an English version of his lecture, since our group was predominantly Spanish-speaking. It was pretty vague anyhow, a confused rendition of Bingham's conjectures and theories. I didn't really care. This site is too stupendous for any architecture. Even the Parthenon would seem unimpressive here. The Incas' masonry is a miracle of technical skill, but I can't help thinking that their buildings must have resembled municipal washrooms or public tombs. I liked best one curiously-shaped little altar in a cave. It looks like the step on which you put your foot to have your shoe shined.

Caskey, meanwhile, had gone scrambling up the mountainside to take pictures. I talked to Al Johnson about the Latin American character. He had been a flying instructor during the war to a group of South American pilots. They were quite a handful, he said. Two of them quarreled about something, and one challenged the other to an air duel with machine guns. This was discovered and prevented at the last moment. Johnson found the Brazilians and Argentines the most efficient, the Argentines the most difficult and aggressive, the Peruvians the craziest and the Ecuadoreans the nicest.

During lunch at the small government guest-house, it rained heavily. Sarita, who had planned to spend the night there, decided that she had inspected it sufficiently and would return with us to Cuzco. We drank an infusion of coca and later chewed some of the leaves, without getting the slightest kick. I believe the Indians mix it with another plant to bring out the effect of the cocaine. They all chew here, as they do in Colombia and Ecuador. Meanwhile, the manager of the hotel sang folk-songs to us with the maximum of expression, in a grand operatic style.

Then we started downhill. This was a lot less agreeable, especially as the rain had made the trail dangerously slippery. There was one particularly nasty place where you had to slide down a steeply inclined surface of bare wet rock, and then pull up sharp to make a hairpin turn. I soon discovered what the guide had meant about my mule. It must have been the one that Muriel rode. At each twist in the path it paused, chose a bush which was barely within reach, and craned its neck down over the abyss to eat it. There I sat, looking into emptiness; a precipice gains greatly in drama when you see it over a mule's lowered head. This I didn't so much mind. But the stout Argentine, who was riding behind me, had a sadistic sense of humor; with a great shout of "Vamos!" which echoed around the gorge, he would give my mule a well-aimed kick, making it plunge, scramble for a foothold and go slithering down the track. I could have killed him gladly, but I had to laugh, lest I should lose face with the Penards, who were in front of me, riding elegantly, like English gentlefolk. It was nice to reach the bottom.

These mountains are full of legends. Here is one of them: An Indian lost a cow belonging to his master. He searched for days, in vain. At last he came to a wood in a high upland valley. As he was about to enter it, a strange man appeared and told him: "You cannot pass. It is forbidden." "Have you seen our cow?" the Indian asked. "Yes," said the stranger, "we have seen your cow. You will not find it. But take this to your master instead, and he will forgive you." And the stranger gave the Indian a little cow made of pure gold. Later, the Indian returned with his master and the other servants to the place but the wood had disappeared.

I suppose this story reflects an Indian belief that somewhere, somehow, the Incaic civilization survives, waiting to manifest its power when the time is ready.

January 17.

Every morning, we are wakened by a burst of explosions. Boys are letting off rockets and firecrackers in different parts of the town. I remember how they used to do this when I was living on Tenerife. It may be a kind of Latin psychological safety-valve. Perhaps if real trouble were brewing, if a civil war were about to break out, there would be mornings of ominous silence.

We went shopping with Sarita Cisneros. She wants to buy one of the Spanish Colonial paintings which are still to be found in private houses here. As we were crossing the square in front of the Cathedral, we were accosted by a polite, charming boy who looked like a college student. He told us that he knew of a family who had pictures for sale and offered to take us to their home. We agreed. When we arrived, the lady of the house astonished us by flying into a violent rage. "Get out of here," she told the boy. "How dare you show me your face—after what happened last time? We don't want any more trouble. Get out!" There was much arguing back and forth, after which the lady calmed down and Sarita explained the situation to Caskey and myself. It seems that the Government has passed a law forbidding foreigners to buy and remove antiques from the country or even from Cuzco itself. (This doesn't, of course, apply to Sarita as a Peruvian citizen.) This law is certainly quite reasonable, but the local police have turned it into a racket. They employ *agents provocateurs*— this boy is one of them—who waylay foreign tourists, urge them to buy something and promise to arrange a secret sale. In due course, the tourists are denounced to the authorities and heavily fined. The boy didn't seem at all ashamed of himself. Proudly, he showed us his official permit to ply this dirty trade. I'm only sorry I can't remember his name and write it down here, as a warning to the unwise.

January 18.

Today we made the Sunday morning excursion to Pisac; Sunday is market-day there, and a whole fleet of cars is mobilized to take the tourists over. The drive is less than twenty miles but unpleasantly memorable; for the road, as it descends into the Pisac valley, narrows to a winding ledge along the mountainside, only just broad enough for a car and broken in several places by small landslides.

The market is too tourist-conscious to be really attractive, but it isn't much more expensive than Cuzco, and you can buy very handsome peasant jackets there and several sorts of hats. There were a lot of cheerful little boys playing around the square. When they find themselves near a tourist, they screw their features into agonized grimaces and start to beg for money with a penetrating professional whine.

The church is half in ruins, with a big hole in the roof at the west end; an inconvenience to worshippers on wet days but a boon to photographers on sunny ones. You can take pictures of the service and the congregation by natural light. The Indians enter the church in an orderly procession and kneel on the earth floor. When the Host is elevated, they blow conch-shell horns. The priest preaches in Quechua. When Mass is over, he interviews the mayors of the neighboring villages, arranging what offerings he shall receive from each: a lamb, or a pair of chickens, or a basket of eggs.

Every mayor carries a ceremonial staff of office, decorated with silver bands. The priest blesses these staffs. Then one of the mayors takes them all in the crook of his arm, kneels down and says a prayer, while the others stand round. Each mayor comes forward in turn, walks a circle around the staff-holder and approaches to receive his staff. Both men kiss it before it is taken away. This must be one of the many pieces of Incaic ritual which have been adopted into the practice of Indian Christianity.

I disliked the drive home even more than the drive to Pisac, especially as we were now keeping to the outer edge of the road. As the Penards weren't in the car with us and there was no need to act brave in front of Sarita, I frankly shut my eyes and asked Caskey to tell me when it was all over.

One of the Protestant missionaries we met on the train came to see us later in the day and stayed to supper. A decent man in his own way; hardworking, honest and charitable—except where the Catholics are concerned. He started off by telling us a story about a ranch in Bolivia, near a town where he himself had worked for many years. An Indian on this ranch found a small image of a Christian saint in his field. He took it to the local priest who said that this was a miracle and that the Indian should build a shrine on the spot, at his own expense. So the Indian went to the ranch-owner to ask for an advance on his wages. The owner asked to see the image. It was stamped "made in Germany." The priest had buried it there himself. He was forced to leave the district in disgrace.

This story is true, no doubt, but the missionary went on to generalize from it. According to him, nearly all Catholic priests in South America are greedy, lazy and corrupt. Most of them are the fathers of children, and they squeeze exorbitant offerings from their congregations in order to support their mistresses. They also make use of the confessional to put erotic ideas into the heads of the young. His venom knew no bounds. Exactly the same thing, he said, was true in the United States. Caskey, who was educated at a Catholic school, got very angry and told him he was a liar. The missionary climbed down at once, and admitted that he had merely read this in a book. But he added that the Catholic Church always became corrupt in countries where it had gained the upper hand.

Whenever I think about this subject, I am reduced to furious, impotent despair. Even if you discount fifty percent of all criticism, it can't be denied that the Church in South America is a disgrace to Catholicism, and that the conditions in some parishes are bad enough to satisfy the producer of a Russian anti-religious movie. But I loathe the prudery of the average Protestant, who judges nothing but external behavior, refusing to see that the Catholics, even at their worst, have much to teach him about the value of sacraments and the psychology of prayer. And how dare a comfortably married minister sneer at the backslidings of would-be celibates? He simply doesn't have their temptations. As for the militant atheists of the Left Wing, their smug stupidity appalls me. It is all very well to brand certain cults and legends as superstitious, and to attack the political crimes of the historic sects, but have they never stopped to ask themselves what religion itself is for? How in the world do they imagine they can make their free democratic community function when they have removed the whole spiritual basis of consent? Don't they know anything about human nature? Do they really think that justice and public ethics can operate in a vacuum? No—they are too busy getting on with their revolution. They take it for granted, with an optimism which is mystical in the worst sense of the word, that the fundamental problem will somehow solve itself.

There are now between three and four million Protestants in South America, and the movement is growing. According to our missionary, this growth isn't the result of direct anti-Catholic propaganda. When a Protestant minister comes to a district, he simply announces meetings and then goes ahead with his work. He leaves his congregation to get around gradually to the idea that there are differences between the Catholics and himself. Our missionary thought that Protestant competition was actually having a stimulating effect on the Catholics, forcing them to set their own house in order. He said that a group of Maryknoll Fathers had been sent down from the United States to put some energy into the local priests.

The Protestant missionary emphasis is, of course, on works rather than on faith. They build hospitals and schools. They get the Indians to clean up their huts and make windows in the walls. (There is no word in the Quechua language for "clean.") They insist that their parishioners must stop drinking alcohol and chewing coca. As soon as possible, they leave the preaching to native assistants, who, naturally, can make a far greater impression on their fellow Indians.

All this is admirable, but I can't help feeling—this is mere unsupported intuition—that Protestantism isn't really suited to the Indian temperament. I believe that the Indians are very devotional; their psychology demands sacraments, shrines and images. The Protestants accuse the Catholics of withholding the word of God, because they edit and interpret the Bible. But the Protestants themselves fall into the opposite error of saying that every line of the Bible is equally inspired and literally true, which must be very confusing for new converts. And as for interpretation, there is no more dogmatic interpreter than your Protestant fundamentalist. His teaching bristles with adroitly twisted quotations. Also, I believe that Protestant ethical standards are far too rigid when they are applied to a primitive people. When so many actions and habits are labeled as sins, how can you expect an Indian to distinguish between what is really wrong and what is merely socially inexpedient or injurious to his health? Where is the difference between telling a lie and smoking a cigarette? The Catholics are much more sensible about this. Which reminds me that Rowe notes a very interesting fact in his book; that intoxication was a ritual act among the Incas—they only got drunk during religious ceremonies, on prescribed occasions. The early Spanish missionaries, therefore, attacked drinking as a pagan cult, not as a vice. Rowe adds that ritual intoxication is still practised among the highland Indians. I wonder if the Protestants are aware of this? I doubt if it would seem at all significant to our missionary. A sin is a sin.

January 20.

We left Cuzco yesterday morning, at 7:30. The train only goes once a week, so it is always crowded. If you don't get a place in the buffet car you are out of luck, because meals are only served there. Also, its big padded leather seats—like armchairs in a shabby old London club smoking-room—are much more comfortable than the ordinary first-class hard benches. The hotel guests were all advised to send bellhops down early to the station with their bags. The little boys brought the bags down all right and put them in the baggage-racks, but they were quite unable to hold seats against the ruthless mob of the tourists. Caskey and I got places only because we came down on the first bus. Opposite us in the train, an American lady was screaming with rage because she had found some strange baggage over the seat which she had seized. "Get it out of here!" she yelled at the intimidated bellhop, who obeyed her reluctantly. "Leave everything to me," she told her friends, "I'll fix it. How dare they put things up there!" One of the friends, who seemed to have slightly more civilized instincts, was somewhat conscience-stricken when she found that the baggage belonged to Al Johnson; he had been very polite and attentive to them while they were in Cuzco. Johnson, with his usual good-nature, went off uncomplainingly to sit in the first class. When the time came for lunch, the Penards courteously gave up their places to some of the excluded travelers. A French party did likewise. The American ladies didn't budge.

Halfway up the gradient to La Raya, the train's wheels started to skid, the locomotive began to snort desperately, and I thought we should never get over the hump. We did, however, after a couple of false starts, and came rattling down the other slope so fast that we caught up with our schedule and arrived in Juliaca dead on time. There had been a big storm, and the ground was covered with hailstones. We reached Puno just as the sun was setting. The lake and the shore were flooded with an unearthly golden light which melted rapidly into darkness. It was like coming a moment too late for a vision.

The steamers which cross Lake Titicaca from Puno to Guaqui in Bolivia are surprisingly large—especially when you consider that they had to be brought up the Andes in sections and reassembled here. The pieces of the oldest one (which is still operating) came on mule-back, the others by train. All the boats were built in Britain; and they look, and smell, very like the steamers which cross the English Channel. This trip is a good deal longer, however. The run from Puno to Guaqui is nearly a hundred miles, and takes the whole night.

Caskey and I got a clean freshly-painted cabin and had an excellent dinner on board. The tourists were all very cheerful; perhaps the altitude had gone to our heads, a little. One of them told us, by way of light table conversation, that the Indians were apt to have sexual intercourse with their llamas and that many of the llamas had syphilis. In consequence, he said, there used to be a law forbidding a man to herd llamas without his wife. Everybody, including the ladies, found this very amusing.

The crossing was absolutely calm. Soon after dawn, I went up on deck. We were still a good distance from the land. The snow-mountains were pink where they faced the sunrise, the great lake was icy black, the pure thin air was bitingly cold. When you breathe it in deeply, it seems to possess you to the very tips of your toes and fingers. You feel transformed, triumphant, almost demonic; an inhuman creature riding high above the world of cities and men. It wouldn't be difficult to go mad in this country. It is the perfect setting for delusions of grandeur.

We docked at Guaqui soon after breakfast. The customs officials were inclined to be tiresome about Caskey's camera and my typewriter; they gave us a lot of instructions about the permits we should have to obtain in La Paz. We scarcely listened to them, for a porter was throwing the bag with the Pucará ceramics around in the most carefree manner, and our hearts were in our mouths. As soon as we got on board the train we unpacked it; nothing was broken.

Beyond Titicaca, the red earth of the plateau looks sodden and heavy; it is watered by many swampy streams. The Indian huts are roofed with a shaggy smoke-blackened straw thatch. On the gable, there is often an ornate tin cross which has to be blessed by a priest (for a fee, of course) every year or two, or it will lose its efficacy. You pass the ruins of Tiahuanaco—a monolithic gateway and some broken terraces and roofless walls; all that is left of the capital of an early empire about which almost nothing is definitely known. A highly dubious claim has been made that this was the cradle of mankind in the Western Hemisphere. Archaeologists love to poke around it, and many of its stones have been carried off and deposited in foreign museums.

Sixty miles from the lake the plain suddenly ends. You look over its edge into a deep horse-shoe valley and there is La Paz, fourteen hundred feet below. The view makes you gasp, for it is backed by the enormous snow-peak of Illimani, which fills the sky to the south. Illimani is rather higher than Mount Pelion would be if it were piled not on Ossa but upon Mont Blanc.

We got to La Paz at one o'clock this afternoon. I am writing this in our bedroom at the Hotel Italia.

titicaca and la paz

On the whole, the Italia is greatly to be recommended. It is cheap—far cheaper than the big pretentious dreary Sucre Palace, which gets most of the tourist trade. Its rooms are clean. The food is quite good. The service, however, is a bit erratic, not because the staff is lazy but because nobody has any fixed duties. If you ring a bell there is either no reaction at all, or else five people come running to answer it. The two Italian owners and the Viennese manager are desperately eager to please; they keep colliding with each other as they rush back and forth between the kitchen, the bar and the dining room, stirring pots, making out bills, pouring drinks and carrying plates, in a state of permanent crisis. The plumbing is sanitary but strange. When you want to take a shower you must call the boy who has the key to the switchbox of the electric water-heater. This looks like a very early radio set; it has two bulbs on it which glow ominously. The shower is turned on, the boy throws the switch and the water begins to heat and spread out over the bathroom floor in a large puddle. You have to finish washing before it becomes scalding and/or causes a serious flood.

Another good feature of the Italia is its view. The hotel stands high, and our bedroom window overlooks two-thirds of La Paz. It is a smallish city, with five or six semi-skyscrapers, one beautiful church, San Francisco, and one handsome boulevard, the Avenida 16 de Julio—usually called the Prado. There is very little Colonial architecture. Most of the buildings are modern and have corrugated iron roofs. There is a standing government order that these must be kept painted; they are not. Many of the side streets are so steep that you can scarcely hold your footing on the worn pavement. The Paceños have learned to slither down it in long strides, like skaters. What with the altitude, the gradients, the scarcity of

159

elevators and the shortage of taxis, you spend most of the day painfully out of breath, and envy the Indians, whose enormous lungs enable them to trot uphill without the least sign of strain.

The nights, so far, have been wet and deathly cold. Clouds drift up the valley and fill the streets until the city looks as though it were on fire. Actually, fire is a very minor hazard here; at 12,000 feet there isn't enough oxygen to feed a big blaze. La Paz is the only capital city in the Western world which has no official fire department.

Social distinctions follow the contours of the landscape, but in reverse order. At the top of the town, on the steepest part of the slope, is the suburb of Villa Victoria—terrace upon terrace of crude adobe houses, inhabited almost entirely by pure Indians. The *cholos*, or half-breeds, tend to live lower down, according to their economic status. Descending further, you come to the business section, the government offices, the restaurants and the university. And below these, the wealthy residential district begins, with its villas and walled gardens, extending down to Obrajes in the bed of the valley. This last is very disappointing, if you are looking for elegance. Some immense fortunes have been made in Bolivia; and, even today, with greatly increased taxation, there must be many rich men. Leaving aside all ethical considerations, all criticism of means, one must at least demand this of great wealth: that it shall create a style, a sophisticated luxury, a larger way of living—even if only for the few. Granted that the Indians have been robbed and exploited, granted that graft has been taken and government funds stolen—where are the fruits and flowers of crime? In Paris, perhaps, or Buenos Aires or New York. Certainly not here. La Paz has no palaces, no Versailles or San Simeon. It hasn't even a casino or a decent night club.

We spent most of the day before yesterday getting our papers in order and paying calls. The Viennese manager took us and Al Johnson, who is also staying at the Italia, down to police headquarters for our residential permits. On the way there, we passed through the Plaza Murillo, where the Cathedral, the Government Palace and the Capitol stand. The façade of the Government Palace is still pitted with bullet-holes made during the 1946 revolution. Rather furtively, the manager pointed out to us the particular lamp-post from which President Villaroel's body was hanged. More about this later.

The immigration office had an atmosphere of slightly plaintive leisure. We felt like tiresome, tactless intruders. The official who dealt with our passports uttered a profound sigh as he reached wearily for his rubber stamp. Over his desk was a notice: "Don't shake hands—it wastes time." We were watched incuriously by a group of Army officers in highly polished boots. You see uniforms wherever you go, in La Paz. The privates wear sandals, and look slovenly and ragged. The officers are dapper and dashing, like musical-comedy heroes.

Getting the permits didn't take long, but it seemed that registering our typewriter and camera would be a much more serious business. The official advised us to consult a lawyer. Our manager knew of one, and took us around to see him, in a dingy little office which looked like an abortionist's. There was much talk of fees. Caskey, suddenly indignant, decided that we were being exploited and should ask for advice at the U.S. Consulate. I wasn't very optimistic about this; consuls are busy people, not apt to sympathize with your minor worries. But this one, Mr. Morton Pommerans, proved to be a brilliant exception. On hearing our story he picked up his hat, took us down to his car, drove us to the Customs House, and settled everything in fifteen minutes. There was nothing to pay. I was so overwhelmed that I could hardly thank him. Unfortunately, this ornament to his profession is leaving for the States in three weeks, to go into private business.

Next, we called at the British Legation and introduced ourselves to Harold Osborne, the commercial first secretary, a friend of Cyril Donnelly's. Osborne is a musician, a collector of musical instruments and an enthusiastic photographer. He used to teach the philosophy of value at Cambridge and has written several books. Then we went up to the American Cultural Institute, which has the two top floors of an office building, with a superb view of Mount Illimani, and met its director, Frederick Drew, and his wife. Drew is new to this kind of work; he used to be in the insurance business. He is young, good-looking and energetic; very eager to make the place a success. Finally, we called on Kenneth Wasson, who knows Lincoln Kirstein, looks like a less formidable version of General Marshall, and makes documentary movies. All these people seemed genuinely glad to see us, and we began to feel that our stay in La Paz was going to be very pleasant.

The Wassons invited us to dinner that same evening. Mrs.

Wasson, who is French, has a fine collection of Indian silver and ceramics, including some exquisitely made silver fish with jointed tails which are designed to be worn as brooches. At my request, Wasson told us a lot about the 1946 revolution. I'll fill out his account with some information we have since obtained from other sources.

The trouble really began in 1943, when Colonel Gualberto Villaroel overthrew the regime of President Peñaranda and established a military dictatorship. This was a normal South American coup d'état, quick and bloodless. For some time, Villaroel's government wasn't recognized by the U.S. Then it declared its support of the allied war effort and Washington accepted it. Gradually, it became more and more repressive. Villaroel wasn't a bad man, but he tolerated a sadistic Chief of Police—a sensitive, cultured person, "whom you'd expect," as Wasson put it, "to go home every night and listen to Mozart." Perhaps this is what he actually did; but he spent the day supervising executions, tortures and illegal arrests. A favorite trick was to make prisoners swallow lubricating oil. Paceños, who are none too squeamish, began to get disgusted; they were particularly shocked by the murder of a popular old senator named Luís Calvo, who was beaten and thrown over a precipice.

As so often in South America, it was the university students who led the final revolt. They raided police headquarters and seized arms. After several days of sporadic street-fighting, the Army began to join them; soldiers wore their caps backwards as a sign that they had changed sides. The rebels brought some of their dead and laid them on the sidewalk outside the U.S. and British legations, shouting, "What are you going to do about it?"

By this time, most of the other members of Villaroel's cabinet had taken refuge in various foreign embassies. (Owing to the uncertainties of political life in the Latin Hemisphere, all South American ambassadors recognize the mutual right of sanctuary.) Villaroel's private plane was waiting for him, up at the airport on the plateau, but optimism or obstinacy kept him in Le Paz, at the Government Palace. He was alone there with a single aide-de-camp on Sunday July 21, when a great crowd gathered outside, on the Plaza Murillo. All kinds of people took part in the demonstration —soldiers, students, clerks, workers, Indian women in shawls, upper-class ladies in fur coats. The Palace doors were forced open by a light tank, and the crowd rushed in. The President and his aide were shot, mutilated, thrown from the balcony, dragged to the lamp-posts, hanged. You can still buy sets of photographs which illustrate the whole scene, including horrible close-ups of the corpses.

The Archbishop behaved badly. He was probably the only neutral person with enough influence to have stopped the bloodshed. But he was scared—so scared that he wouldn't even allow Villaroel's body to be put in the crypt of the Cathedral. Finally, the foreign diplomatic corps had it buried.

Meanwhile, the cabinet members remained marooned in the embassies. Parties of students used to picket these buildings; and one minister was even bold enough to stick out his tongue at them and shout insults from an upper window. Later, when feeling had calmed down a little, the ministers were smuggled out of La Paz and taken abroad, where they are still in exile.

But the Chief of Police had been caught. For some weeks he stayed safe in prison. Then the crowd broke in, seized him, and carried him right across town to the fatal Plaza, where he was told to make a speech in defense of his life. This he did—after first asking for a bottle of Coca-Cola, which was given him—but the speech failed to convince. So he, too, was hanged.

After the death of Villaroel, the homes of his friends and associates were looted—sometimes for the mere sake of smashing, sometimes very systematically; there was one man, for example, who carefully unscrewed and collected doors. When order was restored, and the new government called upon the population to give up the stolen arms and ammunition, there was hardly any response. To this day, La Paz must have many a private arsenal. Here is a true story: A gentleman, who had openly sympathized with Villaroel's regime, thought it prudent, when the revolution broke out, to leave the capital for several weeks. When he returned, he was horrified to find that his study was in ruins, with the furniture shot to pieces and bullet-holes all over the ceiling. Undoubtedly, he thought, the revolutionaries must be out for his blood. This was a warning to him to stay away. He had better take the next plane into Peru. . . . And then the man-servant, seeing his master's distress, apologetically confessed. There was no cause for alarm. It was just an accident. A piece of thoughtlessness. He had gone out and left his small children alone in the house. They had found his tommy-gun—and it was loaded. "And so you see, Señor . . . Well—you know what children are. . . ."

In the course of this journey, quite a number of different people have told us how difficult and tiresome it is to get a visa for Argentina. According to them, you had to show all kinds of certificates, pay for a special medical examination, and then wait several weeks. One informant added that the Argentine Consulate in La Paz was particularly unpleasant and obstructive, because of anti-American sentiment.

Well, yesterday morning, in the shower-room, I got talking to a little bald bright-eyed smiling man who introduced himself as Dr. Mosquiera, an urologist who had been working in New York and was on his way back to his native Buenos Aires. He had been very well treated in the States, he said, and wanted in future to do everything possible to help North Americans. That afternoon, by the purest chance, we met him again at the Argentine Consulate. He greeted me like an old friend, introduced us to the Vice-Consul, and apparently so much impressed him with our importance that we are to have our visas at once, without any formalities. This certainly seems to be our lucky town.

This morning, Al Johnson left for Chile. He had a piece of luck, too. A precious notebook, containing a lot of data he had collected, disappeared two days ago. Naturally, he was very unhappy about it. We said good-bye to him and went to the U.S. Consulate to ask for our mail. A clerk, who recognized us as Johnson's friends, produced the notebook, which had just been found there. Johnson's plane was scheduled to have left already, but it had been delayed. We caught him at the air-line office.

Johnson told us that he had been wakened at dawn by a woman screaming in the street outside his bedroom window. He couldn't see very clearly, but two men appeared to be raping her. Several others were standing around, watching. When it was all over, the woman picked herself up and the three of them went off together, seemingly the best of friends. Maybe this was just a manifestation of the Indian holiday spirit—for the carnival season is now beginning.

January 24.

Carnival in La Paz is preceded by the Alacitas Fair, which is held on the Plaza San Pedro. (This square also contains the prison

from which Villaroel's Chief of Police was taken to his death.)
We visited the fair yesterday with Mrs. Wasson, and again with
Osborne today.

It is dedicated to Ekeko, an Indian household god. You can
buy plaster images of him at many of the booths. He is a red-nosed,
cheerfully grinning little personage laden with an assortment of
miniature cooking utensils, coins, balls of wool, tiny sacks of sugar,
coffee, salt, rice and flour; a kind of Bolivian Santa Claus. Ekeko
is said to bring prosperity and grant wishes. If you buy a toy house,
or a cow, or a sheep at the Alacitas, you will get a real one before
the year is out. There are also model automobiles and planes, for
the extreme optimists.

In addition, there are all sorts of full-sized wares for sale:
ponchos and rugs of vicuña wool, filigree silverwork, fruit and
candy, musical instruments, carnival costumes and masks. The
sellers are mostly Indian women, muffled in many shawls and petticoats and wearing extremely smart brown or black derby hats
edged with silk. The chola women are distinguished by their silk
skirts of gorgeous colors.

The fair extends into the back streets around the Plaza. Here
you find the poorest and cheapest native inns; their courtyards
piled high with baggage and surrounded by galleries of stinking
boxlike rooms. On one booth we saw the dried llama-embryos
which the Indians bury under their houses, for good luck. Mrs.
Wasson warned us not to stare at them too closely, lest our evil
foreign eyes should spoil their magic and anger the proprietress.

Osborne takes photographs wherever he goes. If necessary, he
is always ready to pay his sitters. But the authorities frown upon
the candid camera, fearing that it may create a wrong impression
of Bolivia abroad. The other day, Osborne was snapping some
street vendors when a policeman stopped him and told him: "That
is forbidden. You are only allowed to photograph markets."

"But this is a market," Osborne objected. "Look—they're all
selling things."

"It is not a market," said the policeman. "They merely sat
down for a moment, to rest."

January 27.

The day before yesterday, Caskey rode in the skiers' bus up
to Mount Chacaltaya. I didn't go with him, not feeling equal to

the altitude. The top of the ski-run is over 17,000 feet; the highest in the world.

The Chacaltaya run is open throughout the year. Its site was chosen by Raúl Posnansky, the son of a local archaeologist, after much exploration. He founded a club which included several engineers, who gave their services free to construct a road. The club's lodge and ski-tow started to operate in 1943. About two years later, Posnansky himself was killed by an avalanche while climbing in the mountains.

According to Caskey, the last stretch of the road up to the lodge is pretty hair-raising. Mrs. Wasson's brother saw a jeep with several people go over the edge of it, some months ago, and had to spend hours scrambling about the cliff-face, helping look for the broken bodies. At length, he found a decapitated head. . . . The ski-run itself doesn't sound like a good place for beginners; it is very steep and ends in rocks. But a growing number of Bolivians, both boys and girls, have learned on it.

Caskey came back greatly impressed by the magnificence of the view—which extends over Lake Titicaca to the mountains beyond the Chilean frontier—and by the stamina of the skiers; despite their exertions at this tremendous height, they sang all the way home—jazz hits, Bolivian folk-songs, *Oh, Susanna* in English, *Yankee Doodle* in Spanish.

I have been to call on the Rector of the San Andrés University, Dr. Hector Ormachea Zalles, and on Dr. Abel Alarcón, the Professor of Oratory. Dr. Alarcón is a charming old gentleman who looks exactly like the actor, Vladimir Sokoloff. He has taught at the University of Southern California, and has published several novels, including one called *California the Beautiful*. The San Andrés is a real university, not a technical school; it has departments of social science, exact science, political science, biology, law, philosophy and letters. Dr. Zalles showed me a very impressive building plan for a skyscraper campus, which he hopes will be finished within five years. Education is practically free. Only, at present, there aren't nearly enough students.

Through Dr. Alarcón, I met two of them who spoke English; Pedro Valdivia and Freddy Reynolds. (British and Irish ancestors are not uncommon in Latin American families.) Both boys had seen something of the 1946 revolution, but only as onlookers. They said they were sure that the students' rising was carefully organized by grown-up agitators. Its immediate cause was the arrest and torture of several students who had protested against government interference in the affairs of the University. A meeting was held to demand their release. At the end of it, one of the students jumped to his feet, fired a revolver into the air and shouted, "To the Plaza Murillo!" Everybody followed him. When they reached the Plaza, the police fired blanks. The boys attacked them. Soldiers arrived and fired live rounds over their heads. Some of the students—the organized core of the resistance—drew revolvers and shot back. And so the killing began.

Pedro and Freddy were more interested in sports and dancing, however, than in politics. They both belonged to social clubs. There are many such clubs in La Paz, and a few of them have English names: Family, Splendid, Danger, Always Ready, The Strongest, etc. The two boys seemed to be fairly intimate friends, but when Pedro had to leave us they both raised their hats. The students treat each other with the most formal politeness, like elderly men.

Today, the press is beginning to release news of an abortive plot against the Government, organized by elements of Villaroel's old party. The reports are alarming but rather vague; perhaps they are being played up deliberately. It seems that some kind of an unsuccessful attempt was made to seize the Plaza Murillo and the government offices, while most of the population was at the Alacitas Fair. Apparently the Government takes this quite seriously, however, for it has put guards on the tin mines and set up a passport control on the road to the plateau. You now have to have a special permit to leave the city. The chief agitator is said to be a union leader named Lechin, half cholo, half Turk, who has a sort of national-socialist program.

The new Chinese Ambassador has laid an enormous floral tribute—a Chinese flag made of flowers—at the foot of Bolívar's statue on the Prado. For the past two days, a crowd has been standing around and staring at it in wonder.

January 29.

Gave a talk about Hollywood at the American Cultural Institute. When it came to asking questions, the audience seemed much more interested in trick effects, model shots and back-projection than in the private lives of the stars. One man, an astrologer, knew from his horoscope that he could become a famous writer if he could ever get inside a movie studio. And, after all, why not? The process works often enough, the other way around. I have seen Hollywood drive writers to astrology.

January 31.

This morning, we set off for Lake Titicaca. The two other passengers in our hired car were strangers to us, and agreeable surprises. One of them was an Englishman, Alec MacGregor, who lives in Rio. The other was his brother-in-law, an eighteen-year-old Franco-Brazilian boy named Alain Costilhes. They have turned out to be very pleasant traveling-companions.

The weather was splendid. Big white clouds moving over the plateau, and all the snow peaks visible—some shining in sunlight, others dark with storm. As we rattled over the plain, we talked of Gandhi's murder, the Russian crisis and the atomic bomb. MacGregor described the vulgarity and corruption of upper-class life in Rio; Brazilian high society, he said, thought of nothing but money and rich marriages. Nearly every subject we touched on was depressing in the extreme, and yet we were all cheerful. You couldn't help feeling exhilarated in such surroundings, on such a morning.

At length the road climbs into the low hills which surround Titicaca and descends again to the lake shore. Here the lake narrows to a channel, the strait of Tiquina, which connects the main northern part of Titicaca with its much smaller southern end. Big clumsy boats with sails made out of sugar sacks ferry cars and passengers across to the peninsula of Copacabana. It is a very beautiful place, sheltered and fertile, with the village of Tiquina facing you from the green hillside opposite, across the dark blue water. At the mouth of the strait, you can see two small islands. By some optical illusion, they appear to be floating on air, a few feet above the surface.

Tiquina has a fairly comfortable hotel, with good food, run by a German. We had to wait for lunch until an enormous wedding-party had finished eating. The bride is the daughter of the Mayor of La Paz. Now they have driven on to Copacabana for the wedding ceremony, which will take place tomorrow. They will fill the hotel there to capacity, so we are going to spend the night here.

This afternoon we went out sailing; not as far as we should have liked, because our boatmen were anxious to keep well away from the Bolivian and Peruvian customs launches which patrol the lake to prevent smuggling.

Later, I talked to the German manager. He is very disgusted, and says it is impossible for a foreigner to run a hotel here. The authorities discriminate against him all the time. The German manager of the hotel at Copacabana has already been forced to sell out, and a Bolivian has taken his place. And this man thinks he will have to leave soon.

An American journalist named Theodore Arter was here when we arrived, resting in bed. But our driver, with surprising brutality, made him get up and pack, saying that he must drive over to Copacabana at once because there would be no car to take him there tomorrow morning. Where poor Arter would sleep when he got to Copacabana, the driver seemed neither to know nor to care. Arter, who is fat and amiable, took this very philosophically, however. He told us that he had traveled all over the world and was used to discomfort. We felt rather guilty when he left. The only reason that we can't be pushed around like this is that we're a party and have exactly four times his nuisance value.

Stories of Brazil: The man who, in the midst of a passionate and already long-established love affair, one day decided to give his girl friend a pleasant surprise, and bought her some flowers. But she misunderstood this gesture; thinking he was trying to pay her off. So she shot him dead. . . . The drunken bully, brother of a former dictator, who terrorized the night clubs of Rio. It was unwise to disobey his slightest whim. Once, a girl dared to refuse to dance with him. He shot her in the leg. . . . Foreigners say: "A rich Brazilian is a monkey who fell out of a coconut tree into a Cadillac."

February 3.

The distance from Tiquina to Copacabana is about twenty miles. The road winds through the hills, which are small but very steep, giving you wonderful glimpses of the lake. Its color changes constantly, taking on all the tints and shadows of the sky.

And then you come over a ridge and see the town below you, lying out on the flat shore, beside a tall volcanic hill. The whole valley is richly cultivated, with Incaic terraces around its slopes, and the place has a sunny Italian charm—the charm of long peaceful habitation. Copacabana has always been a center of pilgrimage. The Incas used to embark here for the sacred Island of the Sun. And with the coming of Christianity the town acquired a miraculous Virgin which has grown famous throughout South America as the Virgin of the Lake.

The Hotel Copacabana gives itself the airs of luxury; but at the moment it is shabby, almost ruinous. When we arrived there—the morning of the day before yesterday—the wedding-party was still in church. We found Arter somewhat dazed from lack of sleep. They had put him in a small room with seven others, opening into a foul-smelling choked-up toilet which was used continually throughout the night. Added to these disturbances were frequent explosions from the near-by hill, where merrymakers kept letting off charges of dynamite strong enough to make the windows rattle. The explosions went on at irregular intervals all through that day and night, and only stopped yesterday afternoon, presumably because the ammunition had run out.

The Bolivian manager seemed completely demoralized. He ran around shouting at his willing but almost imbecile staff; each of his orders contradicting the last. The wedding-party had obviously been too much for him; and he still had to produce cocktails and the wedding-breakfast. Until this was all over, it was plainly no use asking him for food, much less bedrooms. So we strolled out into the town.

Except for its fine church, Copacabana is a very poor dirty little place. Nothing has been freshly painted. Everywhere there is a line, about four feet high, along the streets, where the adobe walls have been rubbed bare and brown by passing bodies. The gutters were full of garbage, and we had to keep picking our way amidst piles of drying excrement.

The fiesta—the reason for our visit—was already well started. Hundreds of Indians had come into town from villages all over the plateau; and more and more of them were constantly arriving, crammed into ancient groaning trucks. The square in front of the church was lined with booths, and at two of its corners there were strange gaudy bamboo structures hung with paper flowers, silver mugs, and crossed spoons and forks. (The Wassons say that a display of silver is a feature of every fiesta in the Bolivian highlands.) Beneath one of these structures a kind of altar had been set up, with tall gilt candlesticks, a white cloth, and a piece of red material upon which coca leaves were spread. The costumes were even more wonderful than those we saw at the Alacitas. Yellow, scarlet and blue predominated; and, on the church steps, was a group of beggars with stringed instruments who wore ponchos of an exquisitely faded rose-pink which would have delighted any theatrical designer. We saw a woman carrying a life-sized doll on her back, instead of a baby. I suppose this was a charm against sterility.

Presently, the dancing began. Groups of musicians appeared, beating drums and playing pipes. They wore hats with big plumes and spangled coats which were cut like bullfighters' jackets. Behind them, couples formed and moved slowly around the square, taking small birdlike steps, very grave, almost courtly, sometimes joining hands and executing a figure-eight turn. The heavy little women, narrow-shouldered and wide-hipped, in their new derby hats, shawls and many swirling petticoats, seemed half-hypnotized by the rhythm of their own movements. Their broad perspiring faces were vacant and placid. Obviously they could continue doing this for hours.

Much noisier and livelier were the bullfighting groups. The "bulls" are played by masked men in three-cornered hats with long strands of false hair over their shoulders; they move within contraptions of wood and cowhide, which have bull's heads and real horns. The "toreros" booted and spurred, are armed with whips and wooden swords. The play is very rough. The toreros get rolled in the dust and viciously jabbed. Now and then, one of the bulls charges the crowd, knocking down anybody he can catch.

One of·the nicest features of this fiesta was the lack of barriers between sacred and profane. There was a perpetual coming and going between the church and the square. Dancers still sweating from their exertions kept entering the shrine, kneeling for a few moments before the image of the Virgin, then coming out again to dance and drink some more. In front of the church, there is a great stone Calvary, which was decorated for the occasion with paper festoons, and cardboard figures of Christ, Mary and the Two Thieves. At the feet of the crosses, a party of Indians held a non-stop picnic. For some mysterious reason, they had all sprinkled each other with confetti.

Caskey and I rashly decided to climb the volcanic hill. It is steep anyway, and, at this altitude, the effort nearly burst our lungs. I finished the last stretch on my hands and knees—an appropriate posture, for at every turn of the path there is a shrine to mark one of the Stations of the Cross.

During the afternoon, the wedding guests left for La Paz. Their bedrooms looked as though they had been occupied by a hostile barbarian army, complete with horses.

While we were at supper, the lights kept going out; the fiesta had evidently spread to the power-station. Arter, MacGregor and Alain talked about Brazil. Despite all their criticisms, I can't help feeling that it must be much the most interesting and exciting country in South America, and I believe they really love it. I only wish we would have time to go there.

Later, we returned to the square. It was in darkness, except for a row of dim candle-lanterns set along the church wall and a string of colored lights around the Calvary. We had to keep close together to avoid losing each other in the black labyrinth of the crowd. A brass band had joined the pipes and drums, and the noise was terrific. Everybody was drunk. The night sky looked like a planetarium, with each constellation diagramatically distinct. For the first time, we saw the over-publicized Southern Cross, lying low over the rooftops on its side, like a small kite.

Presently there were rockets. The Indians soon got tired of firing them into the air, and started aiming them at their friends on the other side of the square. The friends had rockets, too, and an alarming artillery duel developed. By a miracle, no one was seriously hurt. After this, people began to roll themselves in their blankets and lie down in odd corners to sleep.

Our own rest was disturbed—and not only by the dynamiting. The hotel bedrooms have windows opening onto an outer corridor, enabling every passing guest or houseboy to lean in and look us over. This they did, with interested comments, until Caskey slammed the window shut so suddenly that he nearly cut a man's nose off. Poor MacGregor fared worse, because his room included a toilet. This, apparently, was in the public domain. When he locked his door, indignant strangers hammered on it, demanding to be let through.

Yesterday morning, the dancing began again. There were several new masked figures who didn't belong either to the bands or the bullfighting groups but operated independently, like harlequins. One of them was a demure and sinister cat; another a bright yellow lion. The cat kept putting his paws over his face and squatting down to scare the children. The lion chased and pinched the girls. You noticed that even the grown-ups were a little afraid of them. It was as if they embodied some sort of totemistic magic.

Sometimes the crowd of dancers swallowed us up. In the midst of it, where the pipes squealed and the drums thudded, you were conscious of a weird, very ancient kind of excitement—not in the least like the superficial jazzy stimulation of a modern carnival. Although the rhythm was so compelling, none of the Indian onlookers twitched their shoulders or tapped with their feet. It went much deeper than that. Perhaps they were keeping time with their heartbeats or their peristaltic movements. Their faces, like those of the dancers, were quite impassive. No doubt some faint hint survives here of the atmosphere of Incaic ritual.

The Indians—normally so shy and suspicious—seemed to take our presence for granted, and even to welcome it. We got pushed around, prodded, chased, and occasionally hugged by drunks, just like everybody else.

By late afternoon, the final maudlin repentant phase of the fiesta had begun. Women crouched in corners, sobbing over their last empty bottle, or knelt before the high altar of the church, in tears. A little blind had been drawn down over the shrine of the Virgin; she was no longer At Home. Shrines always have to "rest" like this, after a big religious ceremony. They are like banks on which there has been a heavy draft.

Last night, the square was almost deserted. Nearly everybody had gone home. Only one small group danced on, drunk beyond all sense of time or place, by the light of a single flickering candle.

This morning, we are going to drive back to La Paz.

February 6.

Kenneth Wasson invited Caskey and me to come with him to Oruro, a mining town about 130 miles south of La Paz, where he is going to film the Carnival and the famous Diablada festival. He and Caskey left by train this morning. I decided to stay here. For several days, now, I've been feeling ill; the altitude seems to be taking effect. Chief symptoms: waking, suddenly breathless, at about 3 A.M.—you lean out of the window and gasp for air; palpitations, gas-pains and causeless anxiety, as in Bogotá; an elderly timidity in crossing the street or descending a steep flight of stairs—as if your bones had become very brittle; general pessimism, laziness and misanthropy.

Had tea with Dr. Georg von Terramare, the Austrian drama-tist. He and his wife, the actress Erna Terrel, have been living here since before the war. In fact, there are so many Austrian refugees in La Paz that von Terramare was able to find a cast and an audience for a play he wrote in Viennese dialect and directed himself, about the dancer Fanny Elssler. However, I don't feel that he and his friends are happy here, as the Schneiders are happy in Quito. And I'm not surprised. Despite the often beautiful weather and the permanent splendor of Illimani, there is some-thing unhomely and mournful about this city. I imagine the Indians sitting around the rim of the plateau and looking down at it like condors, waiting for it to die. . . . But no doubt I'm just talking through my altitude, as usual.

Spent the evening at the Anglo-American Club; another haunt of exiles. There is usually a dice-game going on at the bar, between wealthy Paceños and members of the U.S. Air Mission. "I've got that well-known thing. . . . Upside down . . . Don't get ner-vous now . . ." The Paceños laugh politely, understanding about one word in twenty; their excellent school-English doesn't include any slang later than 1914. I talked to a refugee with a thick Central European accent who assured me that he was British—a British engineer, working up at one of the tin mines. "Sometimes, when I'm up there, I think I'll go mad. Nobody to talk to. The Indians are nothing but animals. . . . And then I get back to town and I see a film. That's all we've got—Bette and Ingrid and Rita—and we're grateful. They make life worth living. You tell them that when you get back to Hollywood. You tell them that, old man."

February 8.

Yesterday morning I decided to go and look for the Mary-knoll Fathers who are running a mission up in the Indian suburb of Villa Victoria. Seen from close quarters, it is even worse than I'd imagined. The taxi I'd taken from the hotel had to stop at the edge of it; from there on in, I picked my way through bogs of mud.

Only about half of the houses, I learned later, have electric light, and none of them are heated. There is hardly any sewerage.

A boy guided me to the house of Father James Flaherty. It was no different from the others, except that it was clean inside and adequately furnished. Father Flaherty is a young man, very fresh and husky-looking, probably a football player. I liked and respected him immediately. You feel a reserve of power in him which is impressive. We started straight away on the subject of the Latin American Church. Father Flaherty denied that the Mary-knollers had come down here to "reform" it; under the circumstances, he couldn't very well do otherwise. But he quite admitted the justice of much Protestant criticism. He lent me a book—*Call for Forty Thousand* by Father John J. Considine—which, he said, would discuss the problem much better than he could. I read it last night. Here are some of Father Considine's chief points:

His book is so named because he believes (after a very extensive tour of inspection) that the real trouble in Latin America is a shortage of priests. The continent has a third of the world's Catholics. If you allow one priest for every two thousand people, then at least forty thousand more are needed.

He remarks, several times, that the situation is far worse today than it was during the Colonial period. When the independence movements started in the various Latin American countries, Spanish priests were apt to be thrown out because they were identified with Spanish imperialism. (In actual fact, the Spanish Jesuits repeatedly defended the Indians from the reactionary policy of Madrid.) So the bishops had to ordain whatever native applicants they could get, and these were often men of inferior quality and education. Also, anti-clerical legislation—particularly in Ecuador—restricted priests from doing social work and confined them to their sacramental duties. According to Father Considine, it is now considered socially degrading to become a priest or a nun. All these factors have operated to lower the standards of the priesthood.

He is carefully fair to the Protestants, saying that he doesn't believe that their converts are bought or insincere; and he agrees with the missionary we talked to in Cuzco that Protestantism has helped to keep the Catholics up to the mark. When some nuns complained of the altitude in Puno, their bishop reminded them that the Adventists were running an excellent hospital in Juliaca, which is slightly higher, and added, "Surely the brides of Christ can endure as much as the wives of the Protestant missionaries?"

Father Considine doesn't say definitely where he hopes to find his additional forty thousand priests, but the inference is that many of the first batch will have to come from the United States. This, of course, raises a problem similar to that of the U.S. technicians, doctors, engineers and architects in South America. How will they be received by the local populations? Won't the old cry be raised against Yankee imperialistic penetration? And won't the Communists be able to use this as a new line of attack on the Church? Obviously they will. At present, says Father Considine, the Communist Party tends to leave the Protestants alone and concentrate on the Catholics as the historical enemies of progress. But that situation will alter.

Today I invited Father Flaherty to lunch and we talked about the book. He certainly isn't over-optimistic, but he doesn't seem too depressed, either. In his view, the original conversion of South America to Christianity during the sixteenth and seventeenth centuries is now a rather dubious advantage. Because, when the influence of the Church was later weakened, the Indians lapsed into a highly complicated condition of paganism. Having no priests, they continued to perform the Catholic sacraments, but with an admixture of Incaic rituals and superstitions—so that, today, it is nearly impossible to disentangle the one from the other. It would be easier to have to start from scratch. He can't do much with the older people; they won't come to confession. So he works mostly with the young.

After lunch, Father Flaherty drove me down to Obrajes, and out beyond. In contrast with the plateau, the valley seems almost tropical. It is sheltered by eroded fangs and organ-pipes of rock, brilliantly tinted with iron oxide, blue and green and crimson. You look back and see La Paz, no longer apparently at the bottom of a bowl but quite high on a shelf, with the Obrajes ravine far below. Father Flaherty says that, so far, he hasn't suffered much from the altitude. Most foreign priests do, and there is a rule that they must spend a month out of every year down at Cochabamba, which is four thousand feet lower. He has been in La Paz over five years. I asked him how much longer he would stay here. "Oh," he answered quite casually, "I suppose the rest of my life." When a young man retires into a Trappist monastery, people shudder.

But if they had to choose, I think most of them would prefer Our Lady of Gethsemane to Villa Victoria.

We drove back to the city in time to see the Carnival procession. The Drews had invited me to watch it from the windows of the Cultural Institute. The Prado was crammed with spectators. First came the masked clowns, called *Pepinos,* in their striped costumes, making a white river between the dark banks of crowd. You have to get a police license to wear this costume, and carry its number pinned on your back or chest, so that destroyers of property can be identified. The *Pepinos* are armed with a cardboard baton like a folded fan which is known as a "kill-your-mother-in-law." They use it to slap girls. The girls often slap back, and then there is a fight. In order not to be recognized, *Pepinos* talk in disguised falsetto voices.

Next came parties of Indians, most of them in matching costumes, who danced a kind of endless chain-dance which wove its way slowly forward. They were followed by the floats—Philip Morris pageboys, yachtsmen, bullfighters, horsewomen, Victorian ladies, men dressed as Chola girls. The whole procession moved down to the University and gradually dispersed. But the Indians went on dancing, uphill and down, throughout the rest of the day, and the *Pepinos* roamed the streets. As I was walking with Father Flaherty to his car, one of them squealed something at him. He grinned, evidently understanding, and told me: "I usually keep out of the way at Carnival time. Some of them get so fresh it makes you want to haul off and punch them."

February 9.

The Carnival still continues, but without any special organization. It isn't nearly as hectic as I had expected. Brief outbursts of dancing here and there, and an occasional smack from the *Pepinos.* Perhaps the weather is to blame. It has turned wet and cold.

Across the street from our hotel there is a house with a little window, at which three children sit all day long. A lady who teaches at the American Institute got interested in them and found out that their mother locks them in for safety while she is away at work. So she bought them some toys and Carnival masks to play with.

On the corner, where two streets intersect, there is a traffic policeman mounted, as they all are in this city, on a wooden pulpit. I saw an Indian woman making a great scene with him, and asked what was the matter. It seems that she thought he was there to sell beer, and was very indignant because he couldn't give her any.

Caskey returned this afternoon from Oruro. He greatly enjoyed the trip and thinks he has some good photographs. Thanks to Wasson's influence, they were both allowed to get right into the arena among the dancers and take pictures of them at close quarters.

The Diablada is a symbolic dance representing the victory of Good over Evil, the angels over the devils. The devils wear pink tights, red-and-white boots decorated with dragons and serpents, velvet capes sewn with silver thread, coins and bits of mirror. They have long flaxen wigs spreading over their shoulders. (It is perhaps significant that blonds, being more typical of a foreign race, should play the heavies.) Their masks are terrifying—and curiously Tibetan: great horns, popping eyes, ferocious jagged teeth. The angels have wings, white robes, helmets, curly swords and shields. The shields are hub-caps off cars. Many of the dancers spend all their annual savings on their costumes. To rent them, they will sell their whole crop, or even the family cow. Only men take part in the dance itself. Their women are kept busy supplying them with food and drink during the intervals.

The procession begins on the outskirts of town. Here the parades assemble. At the head of the procession are donkeys laden with silver—plates, bowls, knives, forks, spoons, crosses and coins. Each family displays its wealth in this manner, the richer inhabitants riding in silver-hung American trucks.

First, they go to the church, where angels and devils kneel side by side to be blessed by the priest, then on to the arena. Each angel must now kill seven devils, representing the seven deadly sins. Sloth slouches to meet his fate with dragging feet and dies voluptuously yawning. Anger attacks with a roar. Lust ogles his slayer. Gluttony waves a beer bottle, and empties it before he collapses. When all of them have been conquered, an eighth figure remains—the embodiment of Carnal Womanhood, in scarlet velvet skirts. Just as the angel is about to kill her, she falls on her knees, begs forgiveness and is pardoned.

After the Diablada, the dancers are formally received by the Prefect in his mansion. The reception, as Caskey describes it, must be grotesque and beautiful: the old state chamber, with its pink walls, baroque mirrors and Colonial portraits, and the dancers, still wearing their gorgeous costumes but now unmasked and showing their dark strongly-carved Indian faces. He says that the high moment of the evening was when the Prefect asked Carnal Womanhood for a dance. She was a big man with enormous feet, and the Prefect had a hard time avoiding them.

February 12.

We are leaving La Paz tomorrow, so now is the time for a summary of information and impressions gathered from talks with the Wassons, the Drews, Osborne and several others.

Bolivia is more than twice the size of Spain, with a population of about nine people to the square mile. It could be a very rich country, even without its mines; for its vast lowland area beyond the mountains can produce sugar, coffee, tea, rubber, quinine, rice, timber, cattle and oil. And yet, because the roads are so bad and transportation is so expensive, La Paz eats Argentine meat, runs its cars on foreign gasoline and builds with imported timber. Ninety percent of foreign exchange is earned by the export of minerals, chiefly tin ore. This means that the Indian mine-workers—less than two percent of the population—are keeping Bolivia economically alive.

What will happen when the price of tin falls? A major crisis—unless, in the meanwhile, steps have been taken to develop other resources. Roads will have to be built. The agriculture of the plateau (where the soil is excellent) will have to be radically reorganized. Immigration to the underpopulated lowlands will have to be encouraged. These projects are considerably more ambitious than the labors of Hercules. Can they possibly be carried through while there is still time? It seems extremely doubtful. Nearly everyone agrees that the present Government, under President Enrique Hertzog, is honest and public-spirited. But its position isn't very secure, and its difficulties are enormous.

At the base of everything is the Indian problem; with the cholos, they make up eighty-five percent of the population. At present, the majority of them are contributing nothing whatsoever to the national economy; they merely produce enough for their own needs. Bolivia belongs to them, by right of numbers. But how can they be expected to feel this, how can they be expected to co-operate, until they govern it? How can they govern until they have been educated? And how can they be educated, as long as the present cultural deadlock exists?

Racial hatred, we are told, is intense—even worse than in Colonial times. It explodes, now and then, in risings, riots, or isolated incidents—as when, for example, last year, a party of Indians raided a white farm, killed the men and raped the women. Communists and other extremists who encourage revolution here are like scientists playing around with the atom; they may easily start a chain-reaction which will defeat their own purposes and destroy them. Obviously, the chances of a gradual peaceful change are very slight. Nevertheless, the moderate reformer must work and hope. The alternative is too bad to be accepted.

The big estates of the plateau are now being run on a kind of feudal system. The Indian works three or four days a week for his landlord, in exchange for a small holding. A few are wealthy enough to be able to pay others to do this. But none of them get any share in the profits. The arrangement is unsatisfactory for everybody concerned, including the landlord, for it results in a minimum of production. The more forward-looking farm-owners realize this, and would prefer to give land to the Indians outright. But they can't afford to do so, because the Government would tax them just the same, knowing that it could never collect from the Indians themselves. In addition to the large estates, there are also a number of independent Indian communities which cultivate their land co-operatively, without any surplus for export. Every attempt to alter this situation has so far failed.

As for the roads into the lowlands, these could be built without too much difficulty. Labor is cheap, and the Indians have been successful roadmakers, even over the worst terrain, ever since the Inca period. But the problem of settlement is far more serious. A highland Indian can't live near sea level for any length of time. (The men who attacked the farmhouse I mentioned above weren't executed; that might have shocked public opinion. They were simply deported to the jungle, where they will almost certainly die within a couple of years.) If the lowlands are to be developed, this will have to be done by immigrants brought from abroad.

Four years ago, the Bolivian Government and the Institute of Inter-American Affairs started to work together on a public-health program. At first, the I.I-A.A. paid for everything; later, the Bolivians began to share expenses. Clinics and laboratories have been built, health education has been expanded, scholar-ships have been founded in the States to train doctors and nurses. At present, everything is running very smoothly. One of the I.I-A.A. officials told me: "I've worked for Uncle Sam twenty years, and this is the first program I've struck where the dollars get down to where they're needed, and don't stick to the palms of the politicos."

Needless to say, Washington doesn't back this project out of sheer neighborly love. Quite aside from the medical business in-volved—millions of dollars' worth of U.S. drugs, surgical equip-ment and construction materials—the U.S. needs Bolivia's metals, rubber and oil. Better health-conditions lead to increased produc-tion and make effective counter-propaganda against Communism. Washington wants political stability and is prepared to pay for it—though perhaps not highly enough.

Meanwhile, other foreign governments are greatly interested. The British, necessarily—for nearly all of Bolivia's tin is exported to their smelters. The Argentines—because Perón is waiting for an opportunity to form his South American bloc. The Brazilians —because they fear Perón—don't want an Argentine satellite on their borders, and would anyway like to open up trade routes into the Bolivian lowlands. So it looks as if poor Bolivia's fate may well be settled elsewhere.

On top of it all, this unhappy country is cursed with the most inflamed kind of nationalism. Bolivians seem to hate and fear all their neighbors. They have their reasons, of course; every hater has. There is the unavenged military defeat by Paraguay in the Chaco war. (But who wants the Chaco, anyway?) There is the never-to-be-forgiven-or-forgotten seizure by Chile of Bolivia's out-let to the Pacific. (But the Chileans later had to build a railroad at their own expense from La Paz to Arica; and the harbor dues amount to much less than it would cost the Bolivians to operate the port themselves.) Bolivia at least doesn't have to maintain a navy, now. ("It's a wonder," says Caskey, "that they don't have one on Titicaca.") The Army is burden enough. Far too big for a police force, far too weak to keep out the Argentines, it is a constant drain on Bolivia's finances. And the General Staff is absurdly extravagant. U.S. Air Force advisers actually have to dissuade it from ordering all sorts of costly equipment which could never be used on any of the existing airfields. . . . But one has really no right to criticize, or feel superior. We are all infected by this same filthy and humiliating disease. Bolivia's case is only a little more acute than most.

the city and the plains

February 17.

HERE WE ARE in Buenos Aires. We left La Paz early on Friday afternoon, four days ago. The Wassons came to the station to see us off. Sorry as we were to say good-bye to them—and to the Drews and the Osbornes—we felt almost indecently glad to be going. We had grown weary, weary to the bone, of those inhumanly gigantic mountains, that somber plateau haunted by its Incaic ghosts, that weird rarefied manic-depressive atmosphere. Our nerves and muscles and gastric juices were in open revolt at last against the tensions of this switchback journey, unashamedly demanding a bit of vulgar comfort, home cooking, and solid urban flatness. As the train pulled out, Caskey danced a joyful little jig, singing: "So long, La Paz! Hello, B. A.!" It was like starting for an exciting cocktail party.

Needless to say, we had plenty of time to calm down. Throughout the rest of that day, the train crossed a barren featureless landscape, swept by gusts of rain. The few villages looked dirtier and poorer than any we had seen. Life there seemed to have reached the bottom of its wretchedness. Outside of a madhouse or a prison, I suppose no place of existence could be worse. I was relieved when night shut down, gloomy and cold, on this dismal scene and excused me from thinking guiltily about its inhabitants. To forget them, we invited Olga Orozco, who was traveling in the same coach with us, to share our bottle of whisky. She is a very attractive young Argentine poetess whom we met at the Wassons' house in La Paz. The liquor lasted longer than our Spanish, but we had a pleasant evening, just the same.

By next morning, we were already beginning the slow descent from the plateau. There was a big river, surrounded by pink and golden cliffs. The mesas above them were weathered into massive

183

architectural forms, like fortifications and entire cities. The valleys grew greener, and there were orchards and gardens. The slower the train went, the faster I seemed to be getting through the crime-stories we had bought in La Paz. I realized with dismay that there weren't going to be nearly enough for the whole trip.

We reached Villazón, the frontier town, at sunset. It is a bleak little place, on a bare drab table-land. Squalor stares with forlorn cynicism from all its windows at the comfortable passengers in their well-lighted train, as if to say: "Of course you won't get off here—and why the hell should you? We have nothing to offer. We'd clear out too, if we could." There were a lot of soldiers in the streets, but the frontier itself didn't seem to be guarded at all. La Quiaca, on the Argentine side, is quite as poor but with a noticeable difference: you don't feel the same passive hopelessness. The customs examination, contrary to everything we had been told in advance, was courteous and quick. The official appeared to be chiefly interested in knowing if we had something called "Timay"; finally I guessed that he meant *Time Magazine*. It is not actually banned at present, but it has been viewed with grave disapproval by the authorities since last December, when it reported a rather pointless joke about the parents of General San Martin. (Their bones have just been brought back from Spain to be reburied beside those of the Protector in Buenos Aires cathedral. A spectator at the ceremony is alleged to have said: "Did you hear that next year they're going to bring back his horse?") The Argentines chose to regard this remark—or rather, the publicity *Time* gave to it—as a national insult. They are incredibly touchy —especially where the United States is concerned. You must always remember to say, "I am a North American" and not, "I am an American," lest you should appear to be laying claim to the entire Western Hemisphere.

On Sunday morning, the dust began. We were now descending steadily through semi-desert country, thickly covered with cactus, toward the plains. It grew very hot. We kept opening the windows for air and shutting them again to avoid being smothered. Even when the windows were shut, the dust filtered in, through the framework, through the ventilators, and under the door. It found its way into our baggage and made outlines of our buttocks on the leather seats. The food in the restaurant car was full of it.

It is always like this, we are told, during the summer months. We picked the worst time of year to make this journey.

By evening, we were out on the pampas, the flat boundless grasslands, where Nature is heavy and lazy and rich. Heavy dark men in baggy white trousers and accordion-pleated riding-boots, with knives in silver scabbards and handkerchiefs knotted, Gaucho style, around their throats. Lazy gentle cattle, bred into walking packets of meat. Rich pastures, and fields of monster sunflowers— grown for their oil. Once, we passed through a black cloud of locusts. Several of them flew in through the window and jumped around the compartment like violent clockwork toys.

Throughout yesterday, the last day of the trip, the train became more and more crowded. We talked to a couple of passengers at our table who spoke English. They were full of pride in everything Argentinean, and praised their country with innocent provincial enthusiasm. North Americans must have been like this, thirty or forty years ago, when the States were still a complacent Garden of Eden into which guilt and doubt hadn't entered.

We arrived in Buenos Aires very late, around 10.30 P.M. Berthold Szczesny was at the station to meet us. He had been waiting for hours. He came bursting through the crowd like a delighted sheepdog, thumped our backs, pumped our hands, tried to pick up all our baggage at once, hustled us into a car, and drove us out at top speed to Beccar, the suburb where he lives.

Dear Berthold! In all the years I have known him—nearly twenty, now— he has hardly changed a bit. When we first met, he was a boy of eighteen, in Berlin—footloose, reckless, irresponsible to the point of lunacy, his head full of more romantic nonsense than a pulp magazine. He hadn't a cent. If he earned any money, he spent it at once—on drinks all around, or on some showy thing in a shop-window which took his fancy for the moment. He was going to travel, he told me, all over the earth; he was going to be the lover of beautiful, aristocratic women; he was going to have the most amazing adventures; and, finally, he was going to own a car and a swimming pool and a house, to which he hereby invited me to come and stay for as long as I liked. I laughed at him, of course, and said, Yes, I'd be delighted. And now—here we are.

If I started to write out all Berthold's adventures, I should fill a separate book. And, even then, I couldn't do justice to his style

as a storyteller. He has been a stoker, a boxer, a bartender, a cowboy. He has shipped out to South America as a stowaway. He has
helped smuggle German refugees into England. He has been imprisoned by the Gestapo. And—in retrospect at least—he has
enjoyed every minute of it. His enjoyment of his own experiences
is mingled with a kind of awed detachment, as though he were
reading from a classic masterpiece. The Szczesny Saga is, in fact,
a subtle and quite unconscious blending of the would-be and the
might-have-been with the actually-was. By temperament, Berthold
is an artist.

One story I must record. It belongs, as one might say, to his
later manner, for it happened only last summer while he was in
New York. No longer a penniless stowaway, but romantically im-
pulsive as ever, he had suddenly taken a ticket on a plane up from
Buenos Aires. A fine warm evening found him alone, strolling
along East Fifty-fourth Street. He passed the doorway of El
Morocco. He had often heard the name. He decided to look in.
"I wasn't drunk, you understand. I'd had one Martini—perhaps
two. Well, two at the most. So I walk into this bar and I look
around. Everything very elegant. All the chairs and couches covered with that stuff—striped, you know—like a zebra. Man, I
think, this is all right! So I see a table, and I sit down, and I say
to the waiter, bring me a brandy."

(Berthold's eyes, as he tells this, are shining with admiring
wonder. They are the eyes of the ragged Berlin boy who admiringly watches his elder Doppelgaenger, the well-dressed, sophisticated young man, ordering a drink in a famous New York night
club.)

"There aren't many people at the bar, and presently I start to
notice one of them. He's a young chap, with fair hair. Looks
rather pale, but quite ordinary. Wears a dark-blue suit. Quiet.
Very correct. He keeps looking over at me. I keep looking over at
him. I feel as if I'd seen him somewhere before. Well, sure enough,
after a little while, he gets up and he comes over to my table.

"I say: 'I believe we know each other.'

"And he says: 'Certainly we know each other. You buried me
in Africa.' "

(Berthold pauses, smiling quietly, for about thirty seconds, to
let this really sink in. He has a very good sense of timing.)

"Well, then I recognize him. . . . It was like this. One time,

I was a stoker on a German boat. A real tin can. And there we were, going up the Gambia River. That's Africa—the West Coast. Man, was that a heat! I think to myself, this is the worst you've seen yet. And then the crew start to get the fever, the malaria. One of them has had it before, and he's worse than the rest. I remember where we came to a side-river, and it was narrow. We had to back up it, because we couldn't turn around to come down again. So this chap that had the malaria so badly, he dies. And the Captain says we must bury him at once. So I and two others, we go on shore, and we bury him, and we pile a big heap of stones on the grave. We do that, you understand, because we don't want the natives to come and dig him up again. . . .

"Well, this chap, the one we buried—I wish I could remember his name—there he stood looking at me, in a blue suit, right in the middle of the El Morocco! And he says: 'You buried me in Africa.' Which was true.

"And then he says: 'But don't tell anyone. Because I'm here on leave.' "

(Berthold makes another pause. This time, he is waiting for me to ask: "And what did you say?")

"What did I say? Man, what would you have said? I tell you, Christoph, my tongue was like a lump of lead. And I was cold as ice, all over. I don't know how I got out into that street. It was a good thing I'd paid for my drink already, because if that waiter had come after me, I'd have run. I'd have run away from everybody. I'd have had the whole Police of New York running after me. I wouldn't have cared. . . . Well, I walked around for hours. And I thought I was going crazy. And then I went back to the hotel, and I didn't close my eyes all night.

"Well, in the morning, I think and I say to myself, Man, you have to go to El Morocco again, this evening. And if he's there you'll walk right up to him and you'll hit him, as hard as you can, right in the face. And if he's got a face—if there's anything there, you understand—then you'll pay damages, a hundred dollars, five hundred dollars, a thousand dollars—what does it matter? Only you have to hit him—to be sure. . . .

"So that evening, I go back to El Morocco. And there he is. Just the same as last night, sitting at the bar. And so I come up, all ready to hit him. I think he doesn't see me. But just when I get quite close, he turns around and I see that he's very angry.

"He says: 'I told you already—I'm on leave. I don't wish to be disturbed.'

"He says that very quietly, and he sits there looking at me. I can't do anything. My arms are weak, just like a baby's. I turn around and go out of the bar. . . .

"Other nights, I come back there, several times. But he isn't there. I never see him again."

Whatever anyone may think of this story, one thing is certain: Berthold himself believes it, absolutely. He will even discuss all kinds of rational, but wildly unlikely, explanations. Perhaps the man wasn't dead when they buried him. Perhaps he struggled out from under the stones and ultimately found his way to New York and the El Morocco. But why should he be so displeased to see Berthold? Well, perhaps he'd become a spy of some sort —say, an underground Nazi agent. But why, in that case, did he introduce himself? Well, perhaps . . . No—one just gives it up. . . .

Sitting opposite me, grinning, with a glass of whisky in his hand, Berthold glances complacently around the large attractive living room, at the Great Dane lying beside his chair, at the phonograph with its records, at the paintings by Pedro Figari and Diego Rivera, at the tanned cowhide rugs, at my novels on the bookshelf (pure tokens of friendship, since he doesn't know enough English to be able to read them), at the jeep under the tree in the garden and the swimming pool seen through sliding glass doors. In addition to these, his immediately visible assets, there is a small factory, a stone-mill, in another section of the city, of which he is part-owner. . . . Shaking his head in amused wonder, he supplies the concluding sentence of the latest chapter of the Szczesny Saga, which is also his comment on the whole: "Yes indeed, Christoph —when I think of those old days in Berlin—and now here we are—well—who would ever have thought it?"

February 19.

Berthold has been taking us out sightseeing. Large cities are often spoke of as being "international," but I suppose that Buenos Aires must be the most truly international city in the world. Its population—at any rate in the business sections of town—appears to be a three-part mixture of British, German and

Latin (Italian almost as much as Spanish.) Its banks and offices have a definitely British atmosphere; they recall the solid solvent grandeur of Victorian London. Many of its restaurants are German; they have the well-stocked *Gemuetlichkeit* of pre-1914 Munich and Berlin. Its boulevards and private mansions belong to the Paris of forty years ago.

But this does not mean that Buenos Aires and its inhabitants have no national character. Quite the reverse. For these foreign elements have been blended and transformed into something indigenous, immediately recognizable, unique. Many cities are big in actual acreage, but Buenos Aires, more than any other I have seen, gives you the impression of space. Space for the sake of space. Space easily, casually afforded. Space squandered with a sort of imperial magnificence. You feel here an infinite freedom of elbow-room which corresponds naturally to the expanse of the nearby estuary and the ocean, and to the vastness of the surrounding plains. The other basic characteristic is weight. The public buildings are laden with ponderous statuary; their arches, doorways and staircases are wide and massive. The people, despite their briskness and usually good proportions, seem curiously heavy and earthbound. Their faces—regardless of racial origin— have a placid, somewhat bovine expression. This is hardly surprising, considering the amount of meat they eat. (Last month, over 40,000 tons were consumed by this city alone!) If you go into a restaurant and order a dish of liver or kidneys, the waiter will ask: "And what else?" Two or three steaks are often served on top of each other, like hotcakes. You see slim young girls eating them, as a matter of course.

Buenos Aires seems both very modern and very old-fashioned. Its stores sparkle with newness: clothes, furniture, automobiles and advertisements are self-consciously up-to-date—so much so that you wonder if every object over five years old hasn't been deliberately destroyed to make room for innovations. And yet, as I have said, the mood of its architecture belongs to a much earlier epoch, when luxury was grave, assured and untroubled by anxiety or a bad conscience. The truly contemporary kind of elegance, the European kind, which consists in improvising from cheap materials, in making shabbiness chic, would be shocking and unthinkable here. Also, Berthold tells us that social conventions (as in other South American countries) have remained rigid. There are very few cafés to which a girl of good family can go unchaperoned, and these she may only visit during the prescribed afternoon hours. Any continued show of attention by a male is regarded as compromising, unless it leads quickly to a proposal of marriage. Coupled with this, inevitably, is the time-honored masculine institution of the Double Standard. Every self-respecting boy must have a past, to take with him to the altar. And after the wedding, of course, the real fun begins—because, then, you are in a position to "betray" and be "betrayed". . . . These people are still living inside an old French novel.

The dockyards stretch for miles—all along the dark brown waters of the River Plate. The installations are on the same vast scale as the buildings of the city. There is one particularly huge and magnificent modern grain-elevator which Caskey has spent a lot of time photographing. Since the end of the war, the Government has been buying all kinds of surplus and discarded military machinery from Canada and the United States. Around the dockside streets and in every available parking-space, you see airplanes, tractors, motor-buses, jeeps, amphibious landing-craft, and strange elephantine engines already outmoded and archaic, designed for some forgotten and now inappropriate lethal purpose. They seem to have been acquired quite irresponsibly, without regard for quantity or quality. They are all for sale, to any private individual crazy enough to want them sight unseen; you aren't allowed to examine them before purchase. Most of them are, even outwardly, in very bad shape; and they will probably stand there for years. But who cares, anyway? Certainly not the foreigners who unloaded all this useless junk on Argentina. Certainly not the Argentine politicians who filled their own pockets with commissions on the deals. Probably not even the victims of their dishonesty, the taxpaying citizens; for this country can well afford to be extravagant.

That's the whole point, says Rolf Katz: life is still incredibly easy here. The wonderful soil and pasture make ranching nearly automatic. Nature works for you. Argentineans have never had any real experience of want. And so they are politically apathetic and easily contented.

Rolf Katz is another of my old Berlin friends. He has lived here for about ten years, after a gradual emigration from Europe, via Paris and London. He is an economist by profession; and one of the very few people I have ever met who has really read, studied and digested Marx. Now he is the director of a weekly bulletin called the *Economic Survey*, which appears in Spanish and English versions. It is the only publication of its kind in Argentina, and it has a great reputation in government and stock-exchange circles—even though its conclusions are often unpalatable. Rolf is always scrupulously accurate, critical and frank.

I had supper with him last night. And it was so exactly like the old days in his flat out in the Berlin suburbs that, at moments, I felt quite young again—a woolly-minded boy asking naïve questions and being answered by the great face of the oracle opposite, the soft powerful pipe-smoking figure in the comfortable chair. Set in pale fleshy cheeks, Rolf's dark-blue eyes, small well-formed nose and firm mouth have the beauty of intellectual honesty. He is the truly cogitative man. My ignorance and mental clumsiness amuse him, as always. He smiles indulgently. Gripping his pipe between white even teeth, he begins to speak in his rapid indistinct German, with strange bubbling sounds: "No, Christopher—please excuse me if I say this—but again your question is incorrectly formulated—if we are to come to a basic understanding of this problem, it will be necessary to examine not only its economic and quasi-economic, but also its social-political aspects—and, in order to do this, we must not lose sight of the fact that . . ." The voice goes on and on. I listen very carefully, knowing by experience that, sooner or later, Rolf will say something quite simple and definite, something I can understand.

In one respect, I find that Rolf has changed. His predictions are as positive as ever, and with good reason, since so many of them have come true. But he has lost a great deal of his political dogmatism. He no longer believes in the planned socialist state, or in any state which concentrates power in the hands of the government. He apologizes for quoting Lord Acton's well-worn line, but—"power always corrupts." Capitalism may be a mess, but it is a relatively impotent mess; and at least you can keep its edges tidy by a vigilant cultivation of civil liberties and constitutional rights. "Marginal activity," in other words, is the only sphere within which one can still be of some use. . . . It is strange and rather touching to hear Rolf make this admission, because I know that he must have arrived at it unwillingly and with acute mental pain. It is the measure of an honest man's disenchantment. To end up, after twenty years of dialectics, in the same boat with Aldous Huxley!

February 21.

Yesterday, we drove out with Berthold and Tota Cuevas de Vera to spend the week end at her *estancia*, El Pelado; a four-hour trip from Buenos Aires. It is about 86,000 acres—a big ranch for these parts; down in Patagonia, the sheep farms are even larger.

Tota is an old friend of Maria Rosa Oliver and Victoria Ocampo (whom we shall be seeing in a few days); we first met her last summer in New York and have already become very fond of her. Although she has grown-up children, there is something about her which makes you think of a shy little girl; her pleased but anxious smile seems to be pleading for kindness from her elders. It is utterly ridiculous to think of her as a Countess—"La Señora Condesa"—but she actually is married to a Spanish nobleman and has a name which would take up half a line if I were to write it out in full.

El Pelado means "The Bald One." The ranch is so-called because it used to be bare; but now there are woods around the house and big trees on the lawn—English oaks, mostly, and deodars. The house has high spacious rooms and is quite large, but not at all grand or pretentious. In fact, I'm a little disappointed; I'd expected something much more vulgarly magnificent.

Tota has been driving us around. The ranch is like a small self-contained agricultural republic. There must be hundreds of people living on it—some as employees, some as tenants, some as independent farmers owning their land. (For the Perón Government has ordered many of the big landlords to sell a portion of their estates, to be subdivided into small holdings.) El Pelado breeds cattle, horses, hogs, sheep and chickens. It grows corn and fruit and vegetables. It has a tannery and a perfume factory and a dairy which not only provides milk and butter and cheese but also basic material for plastics. It even has its own railway station, from which an entire trainload of its produce leaves, once a week, for Buenos Aires.

Driving over the ranch is like being far out at sea in a tiny boat. Under that enormous sky, surrounded by that level vastness, you feel almost submerged in the land. Everywhere, there are birds. Wild emus running in flocks, partridges whirring up from cover, plovers circling and calling, gray owls and hawks perched on the fences. Miniature blizzards of papery yellow butterflies close in upon the car, bringing it nearly to a standstill. Tota tells us that the locusts have been here this year, already. Their coming always creates a state of serious emergency. The men have to turn out and fight them with flame-throwers.

This afternoon, she showed us the original ranch-house with its watch-tower, where, in the old days, a lookout was constantly posted to guard against surprise attacks by the Indians. There are hardly any of them left now on the Argentine plains, but they still live in the mountains and on Tierra del Fuego. Argentina, like the United States, has practically liquidated its Indian problem. And in much the same manner.

We stopped to watch some men skinning a freshly killed steer. The sun was just setting, and its rays, striking horizontally across the pastures, transformed the carcass into something wonderful and unearthly—a silver mountainside trickling with streams of dark golden blood. Some great impressionist should have been there to paint it.

The men greeted Tota respectfully, but without the slightest hint of servility. Their manner was easy and friendly. The atmosphere of this place is conservative and traditional, but it isn't feudal. El Pelado is a business establishment, and everybody shares, more or less, in its prosperity. Tota herself knows a great deal about farming, and takes her duties as a manager very conscientiously. She certainly can't be classed as an absentee landlord.

Indeed, on the simplest material level, you can hardly imagine a better life than this. The climate is favorable. The earth is abundant. The men and women here aren't rich or highly educated, but they eat and drink well, work without drudgery, and enjoy their leisure. Their children and animals are sleek and strong. In some happier epoch, these advantages might be regarded as minimal; contrasted with the world's present misery, they seem enormous. There must be hundreds of millions of people alive today who would look on El Pelado as something incredible, a kind of Utopia. Unfortunately, such Utopias aren't independent of their surroundings; they can't survive indefinitely in the midst of chaos. Either world conditions will improve and breed more

El Pelados, or they will get worse, and destroy the few that still remain.

February 28.

Here we are in Mar del Plata, staying with Victoria Ocampo. We arrived the day before yesterday, in Berthold's jeep.

Mar del Plata is Argentina's chief seaside resort. It lies on a bulge of the coast, facing southeast, about 250 miles south of Buenos Aires. I'm always vague about the geography of any area I haven't yet visited, so it surprises me to discover that, here, we're already a little south of Melbourne, Australia.

South—that recurring, highly emotive keynote in European poetry, has quite another significance here in Argentina. Instead of leading into the familiar harmonies of sunshine, palms, wine, warmth, blue sea, blue sky and *das Land, wo die Zitronen bluehn*, it introduces a sinister leitmotif of desolation, wind, storm and ice, the mystery of the Antarctic. Or, if you don't want to get too dramatic, it suggests, at any rate, the peculiar aloneness of this southern end of the continent, pointing into a vast cold sea where there is no other land at all on this side of the world, except the polar regions.

Sur (South) is the name of the literary magazine which Victoria Ocampo owns and edits. It is probably the best of its kind in South America. *Sur* is sometimes criticized because it isn't specifically Argentinean; it contains a large proportion of translations, and occasionally has numbers devoted entirely to the literature of a single country. But Victoria's critics must be nationalistic to the point of idiocy if they seriously imagine that Argentina alone could supply enough worthwhile material to keep such a periodical going. And anyway this is not Victoria's intention as an editor. She is quite as much interested in introducing modern foreign writers to Argentina as in introducing Argentinean writers to the rest of the world.

For better and for worse, Victoria is an aristocrat—fearless, generous, commanding, demanding. Her hospitality is total. If it so pleases her, she will import guests from the corners of the earth, entertain them for months and send them home again. She knows what she wants, and she asks for it. She knows what she likes, and she praises it. She cares nothing for fashions, either in dress or ideas. She will show up at a smart party in a turban, an expensive fur coat, jewels, slacks and beach shoes. If she feels hungry, she eats; never mind if her guests are on time or not. She prefers French to Spanish, and usually writes in that language —so people accuse her of being a xenophile. She replies by staying on in Argentina in these days when she and her kind are becoming increasingly unpopular with the Government. It would be very easy for her to run away.

She is a big strong woman, with decisive gestures. The large white flower which she habitually wears on her coat seems naturally related to her smooth, warmly colored face; like a blossom with its fruit. She is extraordinarily handsome—although, no doubt, like all youthfully celebrated beauties, she imagines that she has grown ugly because she has matured and changed. Beneath the magnificent surface of her assurance, she is touchingly sensitive.

The first afternoon, immediately after our arrival, Victoria announced that she would show us the town. This she did, with a ruthless briskness which, literally, almost swept me off my feet. She has a way of holding your arm, to steer you in the required direction, which makes you feel like a murderer under police escort, being brought back to reconstruct the scene of his crime. Only— in this case, the unfortunate prisoner was quite innocent. I can accept no responsibility for the dullness and boredom of Mar del Plata. It is clean, tidy, respectable, unimaginative, municipal and colorless, without any character whatsoever.

The Casino looks like a government office—as it should, for the Government owns it. Its atmosphere is neither amusingly honky-tonk, as in the cheaper joints of Las Vegas, nor impressively elegant, as at Monte Carlo or Estoril. The players swarm around the tables as though they were bargain-counters. There are no chairs. Most of the time, you reach over somebody's shoulder to place your bet, without being able to see the wheel or the numbers. I find this kind of gambling as uninteresting as betting on horses without going out to the racetrack. But perhaps I am unduly bitter. During the past three days, Berthold, Caskey and I have all lost heavily.

There are three other guests here in addition to ourselves— Tota, Angelica Ocampo, Victoria's sister, who is a poetess, and Maria Rosa Oliver.

I have known Maria Rosa for several years, now. We first met on a visit she paid to Hollywood, during the war. Some of her muscles are paralyzed, so that she can't walk, but it is impossible to think of her as a "cripple." Her wheel-chair has become such an integral part of her personality that she looks incomplete without it. If I were a caricaturist, I should draw only those wonderful dark eyes, the brilliant smile, and the wheels.

Of all the people I have ever met in my life, I think Maria Rosa is the most immediately easy to talk to. Wherever she goes—and she has traveled a great deal in Europe and North America—she seems to inhabit the element of intimacy. You start being friends with her at once, without any preliminaries whatsoever. And the extraordinary thing is that you never regret it. Plenty of women, and some men, know how to extract confidences, how to lure strangers into familiarity; but nearly all of them leave you with a nasty hangover later, a sense of betrayal. This is because they themselves were only flirting; they weren't really interested in you at all. Maria Rosa *is* interested—indeed, she is absolutely fascinated, by the people she meets. Talking to her, you have that strange and rare experience, which I have tried to describe elsewhere in a story, of a contact below the surface of labeled personality. Two anonymous human voyagers (who, for convenience in dealing with the police, customs officials and other bureaucrats, temporarily describe themselves as Maria Rosa Oliver and Christopher Isherwood) pause for a moment, remove their identification-masks, and compare notes on their respective journeys.

Because Maria Rosa's life has these physical limitations, she has thought deeply and compassionately about the less evident but often far greater limitations which condition the lives of others. She has much political and psychological wisdom. And she has learned to live within her means, to accept her human situation—to make a virtue of it, indeed, and an advantage. This acceptance goes so far beyond mere resignation, or even courage, that it is impossible to feel sorry for her and impertinent to admire her. One even envies her. Her existence seems so neat and snug, so well-ordered and interesting, so bright and positive. When her pretty expressive face and animated little figure come gliding into the room, everybody becomes more cheerful.

Victoria disapproves of hard liquor and absolutely refuses to serve it to her guests. We all came down here forearmed with bottles of whisky. Every evening before dinner, we gather in Maria Rosa's bedroom for a couple of drinks. The first time we did this, Victoria walked in. I feared a scene—but I was quite wrong. Victoria smiled, sat down, and began to cross-examine us with the greatest good humor. Why did we drink? What was the pleasure? How did it feel to get drunk? We could only advise her to try it for herself.

Victoria has taken us to visit two of the biggest *estancias* in this neighborhood, La Armonía and Chapadmalal. They are both museum pieces, but in strongly contrasting styles. La Armonía looks like a millionaire's summer villa from the Newport of the Henry James period. You sit on the terrace, being served tea or whisky and soda by uniformed men-servants in white gloves, and look out over faultless lawns at an ornamental lake, where a statue of a girl with a book is visible among the reeds. There is a dummy windmill, as at Versailles. Every afternoon, the lady of the house goes driving around the estate in a miniature victoria drawn by two dappled greys and accompanied by a young groom on a pony, in Gaucho costume, who canters ahead to open the gates. I found the whole place fascinating but slightly uncanny. It has the air of something removed from reality—something described or imagined rather than seen. Can this be Argentina, you ask yourself; can this possibly be 1948? Perhaps not. But, in that case, where am I, when am I? What in the world am I doing here? Maybe it is I who have wandered into somebody else's dream. Maybe it is I who don't altogether exist. . . . Maria Rosa reassures us that La Armonía often has this effect upon its guests. We have no need to feel uneasy.

There is nothing in the least unreal or uncanny about Chapadmalal—though, in its own way, it is just as odd. Driving through stately woods, you come upon an authentic British country home —a Victorian Gothic mansion, surrounded by flower gardens and stables. Chapadmalal is an equine paradise; this is where some of the greatest stallions in the world are bred. They live like prima donnas, in stalls as immaculate as showcases, attended by an English groom.

Our hostess, the Marquesa de Salamanca, seemed far more British than Spanish. A gracious dowager, horsey and hearty, she speaks English without a trace of accent. Her majestic dining room is full of racing and breeding prizes; medals, plaques and huge silver cups in which you could easily bathe a baby. In one of the sitting rooms, there are trophies of another kind; photographs of European nobility with intimate inscriptions. "Isn't that the Queen of Spain?" I asked half-jokingly, pointing to the picture of a lady much embellished with pearls and aigrettes. "No, not that one," said the Marquesa casually. "Let me see—yes, she's over here."

After tea, she showed us the farm. We watched the piggy little bull calves guzzling from the udders of wet-nurse cows, or frisking, clumsy and bollocky, around the paddock. The Marquesa and Caskey talked horses; she was delighted to find that he had been raised on a stud farm in Kentucky. She told us that horses are trained quite differently in Argentina than elsewhere. In consequence, they are much gentler and hardly ever buck or fight. The style of riding is different, too. You don't use the bit. You simply lay your rein across the horse's neck to show it which way you want to turn.

Perhaps the exotic and "transplanted" quality of these two *estancias* is due to the fact that they, and other such places, have been imposed upon a landscape naturally without features—a flat emptiness of sun, grass and wind. It is a blank canvas upon which you have to do all the painting yourself, right up from the basic outlines. Nature provides no background, gives no helpful hints. Darwin expressed the opinion that trees could never be grown here; so it has become a patriotic point of honor to plant them. The woods have been as carefully cultivated as orchids, and their owners are very proud of them.

March 3.

This morning, I drove back with Victoria to Buenos Aires. Caskey and Berthold followed later, in the jeep. We started very early, before dawn, and saw the sun rise, huge and ember-red, over the pampas rim. The whole plain was streaming and heaving with ground mist, and the few clumps of trees stood out black, like islands. The chauffeur drove around ninety, which I hated—for the highway, though straight, is too narrow, and anyway my nerve has been broken by this journey for months to come. Victoria seemed quite unperturbed, however. Trying to hint that she should tell him to slow down, I said: "This is the kind of road which killed Lawrence."

The hint didn't work, but it got us on to one of Victoria's favorite topics. For years, T. E. Lawrence has been her hero. She never met him—his fatal motorcycle accident took place before she had the opportunity—but she knows his family; in fact, one of his brothers is due to arrive here in a day or two to stay with her. Victoria has written a book about Lawrence herself; short and full of quotations, but very perceptive.

While we were at her house, Caskey and I both read her copy of Lawrence's still-unpublished Air Force novel, The Mint. Caskey interested me—and somewhat hurt Victoria's feelings—by finding it boring. As a modern veteran, he doesn't think a training camp is worthy of so much fuss. I don't agree with him—I think that half a dozen descriptive passages alone make the book unique—but I can see that it is unsatisfactory. Lawrence has left so much of himself and his past out of it that most of the drama of the central situation is lacking. I can supply that drama—the drama of the prince in disguise, of the Arab commander in a private's uniform—because Lawrence and his legend are the property of my English generation. Caskey, naturally, can't. I doubt if, nowadays, The Mint can stand alone. You have to know so much about the author before you open it.

Victoria loves Lawrence deeply—loves his unprotected boyish courage, like a mother; loves his austerity and his spiritual insights, like a nun; loves his unhappiness, like a woman. I'm not sure that I even like him—that's irrelevant, anyway. I am much closer to him, in a sense, than she could ever be. He is a part of the mess I am in. What bind me to him are his faults—his instability, his masochism, his insane inverted pride. Like Shelley and Baudelaire before him, he suffered in his own person the neurotic ills of an entire epoch. And I belonged to that epoch. I can never escape him now.

Dashing into Buenos Aires at last, after a dozen near-misses, we had a very slight collision—to my enormous relief. I had known something was going to happen, ever since I mentioned Lawrence's name. And now a fender was dented, and the curse was broken. Victoria, who had had no such premonitions, was pardonably annoyed. She rebuked the chauffeur severely. I caught his eye, and winked.

some thoughts in buenos aires

LOOKING BACK over the past three weeks, I find that my diary-keeping has dwindled to half a dozen words a day—a bare list of the people who invited us to lunch and dinner. So now I shall have to try to sum up my impressions of the whole period under different headings. This is urgent, because on the 27th we are leaving in a French boat for Le Havre. We are scheduled to stop at Montevideo, Rio and Dakar en route, but only for a few hours—so I don't plan to include our adventures there, if any, in this record. From Le Havre, we shall go to Paris; from Paris to England; from England to New York; from New York back to California. In fact, more than half of our journey is ahead of us. It makes me feel quite exhausted to think of all that mileage still uncovered.

Berthold's hospitality puts us both to shame. I have never known such a host. Plenty of people say "make yourself at home" or "the house is yours," but Berthold really means it. We have to guard ourselves from praising his pictures, books, clothes or other possessions, lest he should give them to us. We have to be perpetually on the watch lest he should pay for our laundry, our cigarettes, our bus-tickets, our drinks at bars and the things we buy in shops. Several times we have had to prevent him from fixing our breakfast and serving it to us in bed.

The most charming of all his acts of kindness took place the day we drove out with him to see his factory. One of its employees, named Angel Paviglianitti, spends his spare time composing topical or complimentary verses which he recites at weddings, birthdays and other social gatherings. He has made quite a profession out of this, and his facility, through long practice, has become amazing. A few days before our visit, Berthold commissioned him

200

to write me a poem of welcome—supplying, of course, the necessary personal details. (Berthold's house is on the Calle Rivadavia.
The Nollendorfstrasse is where I used to live in Berlin. The Cosy
Corner was a Berlin bar much frequented by Berthold, Auden and
myself. The Richmond is a fashionable café on the Calle Florída,
one of Buenos Aires' chief shopping streets.)

This poem was presented to me on my arrival at the factory.
Here is a rough translation:

> *From the stream of the River Spree*
> *To the valley of the Plata,*
> *Joining Nollendorfstrasse*
> *With the Calle Rivadavia,*
> *Life that kept us apart*
> *Brings twenty years to an end*
> *And now—so far from my homeland!—*
> *I meet you again, my friend.*
>
> *Remember, Chris, those evenings*
> *In the old Cosy Corner bar?*
> *Today we can repeat them*
> *At the Richmond on Florida,*
> *And, just the same as long ago,*
> *With a whisky and a rye*
> *We'll go back through the years we've lived*
> *And all the times gone by.*
>
> *Down the pathways of boyhood's*
> *Bohemia we'll stray*
> *Homesick for the illusions*
> *And the dreams of yesterday.*
> *Now, when the world applauds you*
> *And fame's in your possession*
> *You've surely not forgotten*
> *How you gave me an English lesson?*
>
> *And all the while we were cut off*
> *From one another's sight*
> *The glory of your name, friend Chris,*
> *Was like a shining light*

Which reached these shores, made radiant
A treasure hid within
The many golden pages
Of your book, Goodbye Berlin.

I wish I could write Berthold something in exchange for this. But my German isn't what it was; and, anyway, the poem ought to be in Spanish, since he has just become engaged to an Argentine girl. (Unfortunately, the wedding won't take place until several weeks after we've left.) However, I feel quite sure that Angel Paviglianitti will do much better, when the time comes, than I ever could.

The other day, Caskey had a rather curious adventure. We had agreed to meet at the British Consulate, where we were to get our visas for England. Caskey, who was alone, decided to come there by the subway, which he had never used before. However, he took the wrong train, and soon realized that he was lost. He got out at one of the stations—this wasn't a rush hour, so it was quite deserted—and was just about to climb the stairs to the street when a young man stopped him. Caskey doesn't know exactly what the young man said, but it had something to do with money. The next moment, he had grabbed Caskey by the jacket and ripped out a big piece of its lining, together with the inside pocket and Caskey's wallet. They had quite a fight, rolling on the ground, punching and kicking, until the young man, who was bigger than Caskey, broke free, scrambled to his feet and ran up the stairs. By the time Caskey reached the street, he had gone.

We both agreed that it would be useless to tell the Police. The wallet didn't have much money in it, anyhow. The real loss was Caskey's papers—his driver's license, social security card, and so forth—and these the young man would almost certainly have thrown away. We decided to be philosophical and forget all about it. "More was lost on Mohács field."

But now comes the unusual part of the story. A day or two later, the Police called us to say that the wallet had been found in the street. They had traced it to us with a good deal of trouble, through a Buenos Aires address on a friend's card. All the money was in it and none of the papers were missing. Shortly after this, Caskey was walking across the park in front of the railway station when the young man came up to him. He was very friendly and apparently wanted to offer some explanation. But Caskey was still angry with him and couldn't understand him anyway, so he refused to listen. And now we shall never know what made the young man change his mind.

I have been twice to visit the Ramakrishna Mission, which is in a town called Bella Vista, about an hour's train ride from Buenos Aires. Swami Vijoyananda, who runs it, is unfortunately away in India at present, but I couldn't have had a warmer welcome. This is the only Ramakrishna center in South America; in the United States there are thirteen of them. When Swami Vijoyananda first came here, he met with a good deal of unpleasantness. He got threatening letters, and his lectures were interrupted by Catholic hecklers. Now things are temporarily much better, though there is no telling when this stupid persecution may not be resumed. And perhaps, from the Catholic point of view, it isn't so stupid, after all. Swami Vijoyananda and the forty or fifty members of his congregation don't look very formidable, certainly, in the midst of a country which is officially and predominantly Catholic—one Hindu monk amongst three thousand priests! But the Vedanta Philosophy which Vijoyananda teaches is, in fact, a direct challenge to any Church or sect which claims a monopoly of the truth. Its challenge is contained in the assertion that spiritual truth can be found in many different places and in many different forms. If the Mission were exclusively dedicated to the cult of Sri Ramakrishna as the Son of God, you could dismiss it as merely pagan. But what are you to do with people who declare that Christ was also a Son of God, and Buddha and Krishna as well? How are you to deal with a philosophy which doesn't attempt to convert you to a new creed, but which tries to give you a better understanding of your own? Every religious monopolist must naturally resent any such attempt to construct a world-wide synthesis. This, surely, is far more disconcerting than ordinary schism? It isn't hard to defeat an avowed opponent like the missionary we met in Cuzco; sooner or later, his own hatred will make him overreach himself. But how can you defeat a man like Vijoyananda, who comes to you as a friend, writes a warmly devotional book about Christ, and yet refuses absolutely to take sides in your dogmatic quarrels?

I suppose the atmosphere of the Mission at Bella Vista would seem very cranky and funny to an outsider. To me, it was like coming home. Sitting cross-legged on the floor, before the shrine with its familiar photographs, and listening to the familiar Sanskrit words, I felt myself back in our temple on Ivar Avenue in Hollywood. There was nothing strange here. When the meditation period was over and we all sat down to lunch, my mood still persisted; even though I was surrounded by people talking Spanish. There was no need for forced amiability and polite smiling. We knew why we were in this house. And we were glad to be together.

Everybody wanted to hear news of Prabhavananda and the other Swamis in the States. What did the Hollywood temple look like? How many students lived in the household? Were they young or old? What were their names? Couldn't we send some photographs? Behind all of these questions there was a certain wistfulness. It isn't easy to belong to such a small minority group, exiled in the climate of an alien and potentially hostile tradition, thousands of miles from your nearest fellow-thinkers. Hate, in such a situation, is very sustaining; so are self-righteousness and missionary zeal. Perhaps they occasionally help some of the weaker members here. But I very much doubt it. Bigotry isn't difficult to detect. You can see it in people's eyes, hear it in the harsh triumphant tones of their voices. I glanced around me and saw only mental openness, eager interest. These men and women looked very ordinary and unpretentious. They might have been family guests at a birthday party. As a matter of fact, this was a birthday— Sri Ramakrishna's.

Eric Linton was with me on both my visits to the Mission. He is a British business man who has spent most of his life in Buenos Aires. None of his associates seem to think any the worse of him for his peculiar beliefs. But he tells me that he never speaks of them unless he sees that someone is really interested. He is devoted to Vijoyananda. From talking to him, I have quite a vivid impression of the Swami's character. He must be extraordinarily cheerful, courageous and energetic. In photographs, he has that serio-comic expression which I have so often seen on the faces of monks of the Ramakrishna Order. Hindus aren't constrained by that unfortunate Western notion that serious subjects must necessarily be taken seriously; they don't confuse laughter with levity. Ramakrishna's own spiritual genius was frequently expressed in humor—not the sly clever kind, but real rampageous clowning, childlike silliness, extravagance worthy of the Marx Brothers. The most most Christians can manage is to be bravely gay. The Hindus roar and dance and roll on the floor. Of course, it is all a matter of taste; such antics aren't for everybody. But fun of this sort, in the Occident, is a much neglected by-product of spirituality. And it can move mountains. It is utterly subversive, outrageous, unself-conscious, improper, infectious. Indeed, it is one of the purest and most beautiful aspects of Love.

The original type of gaucho—the homeless horseman, the knife-fighter, the romantic wanderer of the plains—is as extinct as the cowboy of the Old West. But his legend—like that of the cowboy in our Western movies—is very much alive. It is classically preserved in the epic poem, *Martín Fierro*, Argentina's national *Iliad*, from which most people can quote at least a few passages. And probably the Gaucho legend has something to do with that excessive cult of *Machismo*, Maleness or Virility, which still flourishes here, even among the city-dwellers of Buenos Aires.

Certainly, Argentineans aren't the only ones who overwork this silly word. Anybody who has ever been employed by a Hollywood studio has heard it, ad nauseam. Every screen-writer knows the kind of producer who tells you: "Look, this guy in our story, he's got to be one hell of a guy, see? What I mean—he's got to *have* something. He's got to be *virile*. . . ." If the proposed character happens, unfortunately, to be an artist or an intellectual, then our producer will want to compensate for this sissyish occupation by making him get into a fist fight, ride a spirited horse, defy the police, or, at any rate, climb a house and enter through the balcony window. He must show that he's a Man.

But the Argentinean idea of virility appears to be somewhat different. It includes two concepts, honor and sexual potency, which are not fashionable in the States. The notion that a man has his honor—in the sense that the Chinese talk of their "face"—is something that the U.S. American finds a bit ridiculous. If he is insulted, he may get angry and hit out, or he may pretend to be angry and sue, but he doesn't feel that a sacred part of himself has been violated and must be repaired. He doesn't understand the code which prescribes the formalized antagonism and the ritual purification of the duel. So he doesn't fight duels—and the Argentineans do.

Again, though U.S. Americans admire potency—as who doesn't?—they recoil puritanically from too much of it. The great lover, the professional boudoir-crasher, is—with a few nationally-known and indulged exceptions—a suspect type. In the movies, he is apt to be played by a foreign heavy with slick hair. The Cowboy Hero is shy with all girls and faithful to one of them. His claim to be a man is based on his physical courage and strength. The urban neo-gaucho, on the other hand, equates super-maleness with potency—a rather dubious equation, since, as any physiologist could tell him, the most extreme degrees of sexual capacity are often found in nervous, highly-strung, underdeveloped men. . . . What the women have to say about all this nonsense, I don't know. No doubt, like other women elsewhere, they make the best of what they get, think their own thoughts, and sometimes, privately smile.

Caskey has tried several times to get an introduction to Señora Perón. He thinks she is wonderful-looking and is anxious to photograph her. Now, I'm afraid, he won't have the opportunity. Most of the people he asked affected not to take him seriously. "You want to see Evita? What on earth for? No! You must be joking!"

Behind these evasions and refusals I find an attitude which I think is stupid and wrong. Many opponents of the Perón regime—especially those who belong to the upper class—attack Señora Perón because of her past and her humble social origin. This is not only uncharitable and snobbish; it is politically idiotic. Señora Perón's past is the most sympathetic thing about her; and her critics would do much better to concentrate on her present and her future. What is this famous past, anyway? Evita is said to have been a very bad radio actress, who only kept her position at the studio through the influence of Colonel Perón, to whom she was at that time not yet married. Well—if you want examples of bad actresses who keep their jobs through personal influence, you don't have to look as high as a dictator or as far away as Buenos Aires. Again, it is said that Evita had other previous love affairs, many of them. How dreadful! Just like Sarah Bernhardt.

No—it isn't the obscure little actress who is the sinister figure; it is the beautifully poised, graciously smiling First Lady of Argentina, President Perón's legal wife and all-too-influential adviser. She may have been a bad actress once, but today she is a highly efficient demagogue. She may have been vulgar and noisy and temperamental; now she is coldly vindictive, ruthless and ambitious. It is even believed that she may wish to become President, after Perón's term expires. Under the present Constitution, Perón can't succeed himself—though, of course, he wouldn't have much difficulty in getting this rule amended, if he chose to do so.

Señora Perón is extremely shrewd. She has built up her personality like a great star, and she advertises it daily through the press and the radio, and by frequent personal appearances. Her pictures are plastered all over the city. Her jewels, clothes and furs are lavishly displayed. Every star should have her pets; so she keeps cats. We have been told—I don't know how truly—that each one of them is named for a famous date in Argentine history. I like to think of her calling down the passages of her residence: "July 9th, July 9th, July 9th—where are you? Come and get your milk!"

There is no doubt that she is immensely popular. And her appeal to the masses is psychologically very sound. It is—as I have said above—the appeal of a star, inviting both self-identification and admiration. She is their Evita—just a working-class girl—one of themselves, their mother, their sister, their truest friend. Let the snobs sneer and turn up their noses and attack her reputation; it's only because they're jealous of the great love affair between Argentina and herself. What have *they* ever done for Argentina, anyway? And, besides all this, she is also the First Lady, the dazzling representative of their Party's wealth and power, the shining exemplar of what any one of them might become, the projection of their dearest dreams. Señora Perón knows her public and what it wants. She doesn't make the mistake of seeming to apologize for her exalted position. A friend of ours one day asked his cook if she didn't disapprove of the luxury in which Evita lives. "Why, no . . . !" was the answer, in a shocked voice. "Of course not! Of course she must have her jewels. Isn't she our queen?"

President Perón himself is, of course, equally advertised, but somehow I haven't nearly such a clear picture of his personality. And the people I have talked to actually disagree a good deal in their estimate of him. Some find him cultured and intelligent, others pompous and stupid. Some see him as the States' most dangerous enemy in South America, others believe that he really desires U.S. friendship. Some are inclined to exaggerate the extent of Evita's influence over him, others minimize it. He is a big man, heavy but still handsome. His photographs often show him smiling a large confident all-embracing political smile. "Isn't this great?" it seems to say. "Aren't we doing wonders? Aren't you enjoying this best of all possible regimes? I know I am. I don't mind admitting it—I love my job!"

It is instructive to contrast Perón's smile with Hitler's somber careworn scowl. I remember it on the Berlin election posters of late 1932, above the inscription: "Hitler—our last hope." The Nazis came into power at a time when conditions in Germany were at their worst; and this, in a sense, was an advantage. People expected comparatively little, and were in the mood to welcome any improvement, however temporary or specious. They wanted to believe in somebody or something. They wanted a change. Perón, on the other hand, had to appeal to an electorate which was in quite a different mood. The Argentinean working-class was underprivileged, certainly, but neither desperate nor starving. It had to be wooed and coaxed, not curtly ordered to man the pumps. The Peróns are still in the position of being Argentina's favorite uncle and aunt: they are expected to amuse and entertain, to produce gifts and delightful surprises. If a serious depression comes, all that will alter. They will be subjected to much sharper criticism. They will have to show positive results. So far, they haven't met any real test.

The Nazi and Peronista governments don't, in fact, much resemble each other. Perón is at the head of an oligarchy, a kind of powerful monarchy under republican forms, not a totalitarian regime. He hasn't built a police-state. His party machine isn't highly organized. His repressive measures are indirect and underhanded, not open and brutal. Opposition newspapers are bought out or threatened with curtailment of newsprint. Printers of anti-Peronista literature are apt to be informed by the authorities that their workshops will have to be closed because they are too small, or insanitary, or somehow don't comply with the latest regulations.

When actual terrorism is employed, its methods are usually amateurish and haphazard. There was, for example, the case of a political journalist who dared to attack the economic policy of Miguel Miranda, Perón's most important minister. One night, shortly after the attack was published, two men came to the journalist's house in a suburb of Buenos Aires. They told him that they were plain-clothes detectives and that he must accompany them. They all three got into a car and drove off. What followed was a scene of extraordinary farce. The journalist, who had had some previous experience of such situations, realized at once that the men had no particular relish for their job. They had been told to beat him up, and they wanted to do this with the minimum of effort and unpleasantness. So, when one of them gave him a half-hearted poke in the ribs, the journalist slumped theatrically on the floor of the car, as if he had received a knock-out blow. The other man kicked him gingerly. The journalist, well-padded by nature, felt nothing, but uttered agonized groans. Much encouraged, his tormentors dealt him a few light smacks. He roared with pain and howled for mercy. After this, they left him alone, evidently feeling that their brutality had gone far enough. But a final punishment was in store. The journalist was driven several miles into the country, put out of the car and told that he would have to walk home. Within a few minutes, he had stopped a passing motorist and been given a ride. He was probably back at his house even before his attackers had had time to make their report. . . . The affair created some scandal in the press. The Government, needless to say, denied all knowledge and responsibility. And the journalist, quite undaunted, continued to criticize. Goering—had he been alive and in power—would certainly have chuckled fatly and said: "We understand these things better in Germany."

Talking of Nazis reminds me that there are persistent rumors that some of their leaders are hiding here. Hitler himself, and Martin Bormann, are the two most often mentioned. It is said that they escaped from besieged Berlin, reached the coast and made the voyage to Argentina in a U-boat. Their secret landing was witnessed by certain unfortunate people, who were later murdered lest they should betray it. And now the fugitives are supposed to be living on a sheep farm in Patagonia. One hesitates to believe this story, if only because it is a variant of the basic immortality legend which is so often attached as a postscript to the apparent death of great or notorious men. (It used to be said, for example, that T. E. Lawrence's motorcycle accident was a fake, designed to cover up his disappearance from public life in order to enter the British Secret Service!) But, if Hitler and the others really are alive, they are certainly getting punished. Their existence, on a cold windswept sheep farm, hundreds of miles from any-where, must be one of a positively Dantesque boredom. I doubt if men of their temperament could survive it for very long.

One thing is certain: there must still be plenty of people in this country who would be ready to assist such an escape. Argentina's wartime policy proved that—but Washington is anxious, at present, to let bygones be bygones. One foreign observer said to me bitterly: "The moral is—for all South American countries—that you should always side against the United States in a war. If their enemies win, you'll be sitting pretty. If the United States wins, you'll be forgiven anyway, and she'll lend you all the money you want, just to make you feel ashamed of yourself. In fact, you'll get a lot more than their allies."

This same severe critic also blames Washington for treating South America as an entity, for encouraging the idea of the Latin American Good Neighbor bloc—thereby preparing the ground for the formation of a bloc against the United States. He believes that Perón designs to accomplish this, just as soon as the U.S. is occupied elsewhere, with Russia. First, he will gain control over Chile, Uruguay, Paraguay and Bolivia; then he will work for the encirclement of Brazil, and so, by degrees, become the leader of the Continent.

If these are really Perón's ambitions—and he has certainly made some progress, already, toward the first-mentioned group of objectives—what are his chances of success? Probably not very great. Bolívar discovered how difficult it is to bind South American countries together in any sort of federation. Most of them seem to have a deep constitutional dislike for each other. Nor does Perón's experience in handling a working-class of almost purely European origin equip him to grasp and solve the Indian problem of the mountain states. And besides, these countries don't form a natural economic bloc. Their economies are not complementary. Bolivian tin, for example, can only be smelted if it is mixed with ore from Malaya, which means that it must go to England. Smelters, anyway, are very difficult to build—and, supposing that Argentina did manufacture sheet tin, what would it be used for? Argentina doesn't deal in canned goods. Inside the country, they are not needed to any great extent. Outside the country, they are not needed at all. Argentina exports its meat whole and frozen.

Perón has two weapons he can employ: loans and anti-U.S.

propaganda. I'm not qualified to judge the political effectiveness of loans, but I can well imagine that certain South American governments might welcome them as the start of a profitable game, in which Argentina and the States were played off against each other, with both sides being blackmailed to raise the stakes and neither of them being finally favored. As for anti-U.S. propaganda, that should be very effective up to a point—the point at which Argentina gets so powerful that its neighbors begin to fear and hate it even more than its opponent.

Actually, at the moment, Perón's chief propaganda drive is directed against Great Britain, not the U.S.A. It centers on the Antarctic—or, at any rate, that segment of it which is directly south of Cape Horn—and also includes the Falklands and their dependent islands. The British occupation of the Falkland Islands is, of course, an Argentinean grudge of more than a hundred years' standing. Every year, the Government presents a protest against it to the British Ambassador. In this country, you must never forget to call the islands The Malvinas; to use the other name is a national insult.

Recently, the Peronista press has been full of demands that the Malvinas and a part of Antarctica shall be recognized as Argentinean territory. In this demand, Argentina has allied itself with Chile, which is also to get its slice. There are even reports that uranium ore has been discovered down there—in which case, of course, the dispute would become serious; provided that the uranium could ever be mined. At present, however, it seems very doubtful that Perón really wants the Malvinas, much less the Antarctic. He is simply whipping up nationalistic sentiment and making an inexpensive bid for Chilean friendship. I don't think the British are much alarmed by all this. They probably know that Washington wants them to stay in the Falklands and would support them if necessary. They have sent a cruiser into the area to "show the flag," but its visit, so far from producing any unpleasant incidents, has actually caused a little mild fraternization. At one of the smaller islands, on which three Argentinean whalemen were living in a hut, the British commander solemnly went ashore, made a formal protest against their presence, and invited them to dinner. On another island, British and Argentinean sailors had a game of football. It is only here, on the mainland, that feeling runs high. The other day, in a Buenos Aires beauty parlor, an English lady complained about the way they had fixed her hair. "*I don't care if you don't like it!*" cried the barber angrily. "What about the Malvinas?"

Many of Argentina's railroads were built and, until recently, owned by British companies. Then the Argentine Government bought them. This was a normal business deal in which there is no reason to suppose that the British were by any means the losers. But Perón's propaganda bureau has been presenting the transaction as a great national victory over foreign economic infiltration. Every railway station, and many a building, displays triumphant posters: "Perón does it!" "Now they're ours!" On the day when the railways were actually handed over to the State, an Englishman we know met one of his Argentinean friends, who said to him, quite seriously and with genuine sympathy: "You must be feeling very sad this morning."

And now, looking back over this journey, I ask myself: what are the deepest impressions that remain? How shall I answer when people ask me, "What is South America like?"

I shall have to begin, of course, by pointing out that we haven't seen South America—even superficially—as a whole. Except for a few hours' sightseeing, we are going to miss Uruguay— which many people consider the most civilized and genuinely democratic republic on the continent—and Brazil—which must be an entire amazing world in itself, differing from all other Latin countries in this hemisphere because of its Portuguese traditions and its large socially-accepted Negro minority. We haven't been in Chile or Paraguay or the three Guianas. And we can scarcely be said to have visited Venezuela. Nevertheless—since travelers are expected to generalize—I won't be too cautious. I must be always understood to refer chiefly to the countries we did visit, and to exclude Argentina, unless I mention it specifically.

My deepest impression is that we have been traveling through an empire in the final stage of its dissolution. True, its provinces have all revolted long since and established their independence. Even the last outward forms of Madrid's domination have disappeared. But the new republics aren't yet really free, really integrated. They haven't yet become nations.

If they felt truly free and integrated, they surely wouldn't be so suspicious of each other. It would be natural for them to enter into a close federation. All of them have the same cultural background. All of them, except Brazil, speak the same language. I believe that their mutual suspicions are founded on their memories of the Spanish empire. They are terribly afraid of finding themselves, once again, under some central authority. They daren't surrender any of their sovereign power.

In order to become nations, they must cease to be colonies. Nature is at work on this project, gradually interbreeding Indians with Latins. But Nature works very slowly. And meanwhile, a great tide of social revolution is sweeping the world—a tide which the Communists and others are trying to direct and control. In colonial countries, this social uprising of the underprivileged must also take the form of a racial uprising, and so there is a real danger that the ruling minority may be not only overthrown but persecuted and liquidated, because they are Spanish.

The immediate prospects are appalling. Decades of upheaval. Military rule. Mob rule. Endless violence, relieved only by periods of sheer exhaustion. Foreign intervention, perhaps, imposing for a while an unpopular discipline. Then more revolts, more bloodshed . . . Or am I being too pessimistic? There are forces on the other side, driving toward peaceful development and change. They may be much stronger than they look. This is especially true of those strange beings, the men and women of genuinely disinterested goodwill—doctors, nurses, engineers, architects, teachers, priests and ministers, professional people of all sorts, and even an occasional politician—who are to be found doing their jobs in their various departments. They are scattered, usually obscure, and comparatively few, but their influence is incalculable.

Perhaps it is the lack of national cohesion which makes much South American art and literature so obviously derivative. Foreign influences—Mexican and European—are too strong to be healthy. I think this is true even of Argentina, but probably not of Brazil, where the racial and cultural elements have been so well fused that an indigenous style is already possible. On the other hand, this excessive preoccupation with alien cultures has produced some extraordinary scholars. Jorge Luis Borges, whom we have met here in Buenos Aires, is an example. He knows classical and modern English literature as few Englishmen or Americans know it, and can quote entire paragraphs from the most unexpected authors, with very amusing and subtle comments.

The upper-class code of morals and manners is strictly old-world Latin: extreme surface politeness, exaggerated care for one's public reputation (you can do anything you like as long as people can still *pretend* that they don't know about it), and an approach to women which is either exquisitely chivalrous or enormously insulting, according to the way you look at it. All this, needless to say, I detest. And I am sure that the day will come when South Americans themselves will get tired of it and grow much more spontaneous. Already—if one of them sees that you really *mean* a compliment or an act of courtesy—he will respond with an enthusiasm which is none the less touching because it shows how insincere his everyday protestations are. His sensitivity is acute, both to praise and criticism. (Argentineans, being more self-confident, react a little differently from the others; but they mind just as much.) Albert Franklin—whose book, *Ecuador; Portrait of a People*, is not only a standard work but particularly popular in that country—tells us that once, when he was passing through Quito for a few hours, the newspapers ran headlines: "Our Friend is in the Capital!"

The bane of nearly every South American state is its Army—or rather, its General Staff. Armies are supposed to defend the countries which support them, and to stay out of internal politics. Down here, it is usually the other way around. The officers of the General Staff seldom distinguish themselves in the field, but they exercise a decisive and quite irresponsible political power. They make and unmake presidents, crush popular demonstrations, split into factions and fight each other like feudal barons. At best, they are parasites, and an expensive nuisance. It will be very difficult to get rid of them. Once established, they are like the Secret Police; they survive revolutions and regimes. And the majority of them are unfitted for any useful occupation.

In the background, there is always the Catholic Church—sometimes unpopular and politically hamstrung, but still wealthy and enormously powerful. Its past record is dubious and its present condition is deplorable—and yet, in default of any better institution, it must be supported. It does at least represent an aspiration toward higher values. It prevents the bad from becoming even worse, and holds things together in its loose ethical bag. Also, it contains within itself, by its very nature, the perpetual possibility of regeneration. One day, it may emerge from its reactionary obscurity and show some really progressive leadership.

Visiting journalists have devoted a lot of paper to assessing the influence of Communist or Fascist elements in South American countries. I think these terms are often used very loosely and misleadingly. Here, as elsewhere in the world, a social revolution is taking place. This revolution is a natural readjustment of balance, and it is being made by masses of human beings, not political parties. Certain political parties—the Communist Party among them —step into this picture and claim to represent the revolution. If two or more of them do this in the same place, they will ultimately clash and fight for its sole leadership. (This situation has arisen in Peru, for example, between the Communists and the Apristas.) But the revolution is larger than all the parties put together, and it will go on with or without them. They may help it for a while and later obstruct it. They may encourage it to commit unnecessary acts of violence, or they may restrain it from such acts. Any intervention in excess of this is merely due to the personal ambition of men who hope to find themselves in power when the dust and smoke have cleared away.

Again, there are those who, quite as naturally, oppose this revolution because they fear that it will take away from them what they at present possess. These people form a minority—otherwise no readjustment of social balance would be necessary. But even this minority is larger than all the parties which claim to represent it. And it will lose, with or without their help. The only question is, will the defeat be accepted in a civilized manner—as it is gradually being accepted in England—or will it be postponed, though not averted, by atrocities and repressive measures?

What I am trying to say is this—and it is really very obvious— let us not waste time tying on labels, investigating party affiliations and counting party memberships. Such classifications and statistics prove very little. Take the Apristas. Are they Socialists, as they say, or are they Fascists, as the Communist Party claims? Probably, potentially, a bit of both—given the circumstances and the occasion. And what about the Peruvian Communist Party itself—allied, at this very moment, with the Army and the Right Wing? Fascist is as Fascist does.

The question of a party's influence only becomes important

when it concerns the relation of that party to the imperialistic designs of a foreign government. The Nazis, for example, favored certain parties in South America because they hoped to gain control of the continent. They had no interest in the parties or their programs, as such. They saw them simply as vehicles of their will to power. Today, the Russian Government is accused of similar designs. If these accusations are true and the Russians are, in fact, working through local Communist parties, then it would be far simpler and more accurate to describe such parties as "Pro-Russian," since they will inevitably be forced to betray communism, capitalism, the workers, the landowners, the entire country, in their efforts to obey the changing dictates of Russia's foreign policy.

Actually, I believe—though on admittedly insufficient evidence—that Russian influence in South America is at present very slight. Overt Nazi influence obviously doesn't exist at all; its directive center has been destroyed. Nevertheless, there must still be a lot of ex-Nazis on the continent, especially among the great German settlements of Argentina and Southern Chile. Probably many of these cherish their old loyalties and nourish new ambitions, awaiting a more favorable political situation in which to declare themselves.

But I had better drop these amateur speculations and get back to what I know at first hand—the sample of South America which I actually saw, touched, tasted, heard and smelled. How should I describe it?

Best, perhaps, by contrasts—the strongest I can find. For this is a land of opposites, startlingly opposed. Snow-mountains towering sheer up out of jungle and tropical plain. Glaciers overhanging banana plantations. Condors circling over cows. Airline passengers looking down on pack-trains of llamas. Brand-new Cadillacs honking at mules. Coca-Cola cuties on mud-huts. A girl in a Parisian hat buying eggs from a market-woman in a blanket. A blond Negro talking Spanish to a red-headed Chinese. A filthy barefoot little boy stridently selling lottery-tickets in a luxurious fake-Tudor bar, where a commercial pilot from Texas is drinking pisco sours with a Dutch oil-driller. An ex-officer of the R.A.F. flying a party of head-hunting Indians and a cargo of live pigs down a tributary of the Amazon. A marble church with altars of gold and silver in the midst of a crumbling adobe slum. A thousand-year-old ruin scrawled with political slogans. A murderer sneaking out with his prison guard to visit a brothel and a movie. A professor of history, just home from lecturing at Harvard, appointed a cabinet minister, jailed during a military putsch, exiled to Argentina, recalled and made Ambassador to Venezuela—all within six months. The descendants of the Incas learning about Marx, or the doctrine of the Trinity, or the mechanism of a jeep. The descendants of the Conquistadores laboriously restoring an Incaic temple under the direction of an American archaeologist.

It is a land of violence. Thunder and avalanches in the mountains, huge floods and storms on the plains. Volcanoes exploding. The earth shaking and splitting. The woods full of savage beasts and poisonous insects and deadly snakes. Knives are whipped out at a word. Whole families are murdered without any reason. Riots are sudden and bloody and often meaningless. Cars and trucks are driven into each other or over cliffs with an indifference which is half-suicidal. Such an energy in destruction. Such an apathy when something has to be mended or built. So much humor in despair. So much weary fatalism toward poverty and disease. The shrug of the shoulders, and the faint smile of cynicism. No good. Too late. It's gone. Finished. Broken. They're all dead. Ignore it. Use the other door. Sleep in another room. Throw it in the gutter. Tie the ends together with string. Put up a memorial cross.

The young mother rotten with syphilis, the cattle magnate glutting himself in a French restaurant, the Indian mine-worker ruining his tubercular body with coca, the seedy pimp plucking the sleeve of the moon-faced tourist, Atahuallpa baptized and strangled, Alfaro torn to pieces, Valencia translating Wilde above a courtyard of violets—are these significant emblems of South America? No. They are only aspects of the present and the past. They are only bubbles on the water of the pot. What is cooking in there, with such ominous sounds, nobody now alive will ever know. A new race and a new culture, certainly. Perhaps an entirely different kind of sensibility, an original approach to life, expressed in other terms, another language. But, whatever it may be, it is cooking. And it will go on doing so, mysteriously, noisily, furiously, through all the bad times that are coming.

A major figure in both twentieth-century fiction and the gay rights movement, **Christopher Isherwood** (1904–1986) was born in England and later lived in Berlin and California. He is best known for his classic work *The Berlin Stories*, the basis for the movie and stage successes *I Am a Camera* and *Cabaret*. He is also the author of *The Memorial, Lions and Shadows, Prater Violet, The World in the Evening, Down There on a Visit, A Single Man, A Meeting by the River, Christopher and His Kind, My Guru and His Disciple*, and *Where Joy Resides: A Christopher Isherwood Reader*, all published by the University of Minnesota Press.

William Caskey (1921–1981) was born and raised in Lexington, Kentucky. A photographer and artist, he was Christopher Isherwood's companion from 1945 to 1951.

Jeffrey Meyers has published forty-three books and more than five hundred articles on modern American, English, and European literature. His most recent books include the father-son biography *Inherited Risk: Errol and Sean Flynn in Hollywood and Vietnam* and a biography of Somerset Maugham. He is one of twelve Americans who are Fellows of the Royal Society of Literature. He lives in Berkeley, California.